ACCELERATED GERMAN

BY

LISA SCHLOTMANN, RLS (German)

Former Lecturer in Adult Education

INGE R VEECOCK, RSA Cert in TFL

Lecturer in Adult Education

INGRID K.J. WILLIAMS, M.A.

Senior Lecturer at Ealing College of Higher Education

Front Cover by Philip Giggle
Memory Maps by Mahesh Raval
Line Illustrations by Kathy Ward
Recorded by Post Sounds Studios Ltd.,
2/7 Springbridge Mews, London W1

Origination by Print Origination Southern Ltd.,
MM House, Sebastopol Road,
Aldershot, Hants.

Printed in Great Britain at The Bath Press, Avon

First Published in Great Britain 1986
Second Edition April 1989

Reprinted September 1989

ISBN 0 905553 21 7

ACCELERATED GERMAN

Welcome to your Accelerated Learning German Course. You will find it a very different and, we are sure, more enjoyable way to learn.

Accelerated German is unique because it has been developed by a team consisting not only of professional language instructors, but also psychologists.

No learning can take place without memory, so our start point was to study memory and how to make the new facts memorable. Presenting a new language in ways that make it memorable automatically makes it much easier and quicker to learn. The whole background to, and rationale for, these new techniques are explored in the paperback book ACCELERATED LEARNING.

Here is how to get the maximum out of your course.

1.   Read through the Step by Step Guide. It is really important to follow each step in turn. Keep this Step by Step Guide in front of you as you progress through each Act. This way you will not miss any steps out.

2.   Before you start the Course do practise the breathing and relaxation exercises described in the ACCELERATED LEARNING book. We know that a relaxed frame of mind does make learning very much easier and quicker. It is all too easy to miss this step out, but you will be well rewarded if you follow it through faithfully.

3.   Start by reading through the 'German Name Game'. You will find it an exciting insight into how the German language has evolved and how similar it is to English.

4.   Then commence the Accelerated Learning Course proper. Remember the key to learning is to build up mental associations and to involve all your senses. You will then be able to recall the language in your mind's eye, or 'your mind's ear' when you need it. That is why we use music, pictures, rhymes and games. Do play the games and do fully act out the story, (which is why we call each lesson an 'Act'.) These are vital elements that make the vocabulary memorable.

The style of the Memory Maps is deliberately simple, something you could reproduce yourself, because we want to encourage you to add to them and personalise them to your own learning requirements.

So now you are ready to begin. You can be sure you will enjoy the experience of Accelerated Learning and you can be equally confident of the results you will achieve.

'Gives at least a 300% speed up in learning is the verdict of Dr. Don Schuster, Professor of Psychology at Iowa University.

'Incorporates all the latest and important discoveries in learning in a unique way.' is the verdict of Dr. Noel Entwistle, Professor of Education at Edinburgh University.

'Highly imaginative and soundly based' is the comment of Dr. Jan van Ek, Professor of Languages at Gronigen University, Holland, and language consultant to the Council of Europe.

Accelerated Learning then has the support of these and many other experts. But the most important verdict is your own. Our final and most important piece of advice is........enjoy yourself! Then the learning will follow automatically.

Colin Rose
Course Designer

P.S. Your success is our success, so please do not hesitate to write to us with any comments or questions. We have an Advisory Service at your disposal.

INTRODUCTION

Hello. Let me tell you something about your *German* course. It has been prepared on the principles of Accelerated Learning to enable you to gain a rapid and enjoyable introduction to German. When you have finished the twelve units, you will be able to understand and use German well enough for everyday situations.

Each unit contains a *story* and an *exploitation section.* We call the story "Acts" because the course is constructed like a drama — with the characters using practical language in practical situations, just as you might have to do. You will hear each act read in several different ways. The different readings have been planned so that you will become completely involved in the learning process — and also so that learning will be easy and enjoyable. The *exploitation* material will help you practise and activate the language contained in each act. It is best to read the English text of the acts first. You will subconsciously begin to pick up some of the German while you read.

Then switch on the tape until you are familiar with the English text. You can relax and follow either German or English in your book and listen for the intonation and rhythm of the German language.

The story begins with our main character, *Peter Wilson*, arriving in Hanover. *Hanover* is situated on the southern edge of the North German Plain, surrounded by delightful scenery. It is the regional capital of Lower Saxony and has a population of about ½ million. It is a busy and beautiful city, where past and present, nature and art, trade and commerce all contribute to its attractions. Situated at the crossroads of major European roads and railway connections, it is known throughout the world for the Hanover fair. A visit to Hanover is rewarding at any time of the year. You might know that it was the former royal residence of the Guelph dynasty.

In Hanover you can visit theatres, concerts, museums, art exhibitions and of course the zoo. You might walk down to the flea market held every Saturday by the river *Leine*, a meeting point for young and old.

Imagine now you are with Peter Wilson in Hanover, who has been asked to deliver a package to a certain Fräulein *Hilde* who lives at Blütenweg number 8. When he calls at her house he discovers that the package is not for her but for her uncle, Mr. *Wilhelm Holz*. Hilde asks Peter to come back to meet her uncle the following day and Peter goes off to spend the night in a nearby hotel where Hilde has booked a room for him. So off you go now. Viel Spaß! Have fun!

Act 1	Akt 1
Scene 1	Szene 1
Arrival in Hanover.	Ankunft in Hannover.
Narrator:	**Erzähler**
Peter stands in front of the house.	Peter steht vor dem Haus.
That is the address:	Das ist die Adresse:
Blütenweg number eight.	Blütenweg Nummer acht.
The house is large and white.	Das Haus ist groß und weiß.
A block of flats!	Ein Hochhaus!
Peter walks slowly to the door.	Peter geht langsam zur Haustür.
There are the names:	Da stehen die Namen:
He reads: 1 H. Büttner	Er liest: 1 H. Büttner
2 H. Wunderlich	2 H. Wunderlich
3 H. Holz	3 H. Holz
4 W. Vogelsang	4 W. Vogelsang
5 E. Becker	5 E. Becker
Five names.	Fünf Namen.
Four floors and the groundfloor.	Vier Stockwerke und das Erdgeschoß.
Five flats.	Fünf Wohnungen.
Where does Hilde live?	Wo wohnt Hilde?
What is Hilde . . . called?	Wie heißt Hilde . . . ?
He has not got the note with her name!	Er hat den Zettel mit Hildes Namen nicht!
Peter presses the first bell button.	Peter drückt den ersten Klingelknopf.
He waits.	Er wartet.
A voice says:	Eine Stimme sagt:
"Hello".	„Hallo".
"Hello. I am Peter Wilson	„Guten Tag. Ich bin Peter Wilson.
Are you Miss Hilde?	Sind sie Fräulein Hilde?
"No, I am Mrs. Meyer."	„Nein, ich bin Frau Meyer."
"I am looking for Miss Hilde.	„Ich suche Fräulein Hilde.
Do you know a Miss Hilde?	Kennen Sie ein Fräulein Hilde?
Do you know where she lives?"	Wissen Sie, wo sie wohnt?"
"Unfortunately not.	„Leider nicht.
I don't live here.	Ich wohne nicht hier.
I am on a visit."	Ich bin zu Besuch."
"Thanks."	„Danke."
Peter presses the second bell button.	Peter drückt den zweiten Klingelknopf.
Perhaps Hilde is called - H. Wunderlich?	Vielleicht heißt Hilde - H. Wunderlich?
He waits.	Er wartet.
Nothing.	Nichts.
Nobody answers.	Niemand antwortet.
Bad luck!	Er hat Pech.
Peter looks up.	Peter sieht hoch.
On the third balcony are	Auf dem dritten Balkon sind
red geraniums.	rote Geranien.
He presses the third bell button.	Er drückt den dritten Klingelknopf.
He waits.	Er wartet.
"Yes please?"	„Ja bitte?"
"Hello, I am Peter Wilson,	„Guten Tag, ich bin Peter Wilson,
are you Hilde Holz?	sind Sie Hilde Holz?
"Yes, I am Hilde Holz.	„Ja, ich bin Hilde Holz.
Just a moment."	Augenblick."
Peter waits. He is lucky!	Peter wartet. Er hat Glück!
SSSUUUMMM. The door opens.	SSSUUUMMM. Die Tür springt auf.

2

Act 1	Akt 1
Scene 2	**Szene 2**
Peter Wilson and	**Peter Wilson und**
Hilde Holz.	**Hilde Holz.**
Peter goes into the house.	**Peter geht ins Haus.**
He waits in the hall.	**Er wartet im Treppenhaus.**
A beautiful house, he thinks.	**Ein schönes Haus, denkt er.**
A girl comes down the stairs.	**Ein Mädchen kommt die Treppe herunter.**
She is tall and has long, blonde hair.	**Sie ist groß und hat langes, blondes Haar.**
She has a pretty face.	**Sie hat ein hübsches Gesicht.**
She has blue eyes.	**Sie hat blaue Augen.**
She smiles.	**Sie lächelt.**
"Hello. I am Hilde Holz."	**„Guten Tag. Ich bin Hilde Holz."**
They shake hands.	**Sie gibt ihm die Hand.**
"Who are you please?"	**„Wer sind Sie bitte?"**
"I am Peter Wilson.	**„Ich bin Peter Wilson.**
I am from England.	**Ich komme aus England.**
I have a parcel for you."	**Ich habe ein Paket für Sie."**
"Can you identify yourself?	**„Können Sie sich ausweisen?**
It is important."	**Es ist wichtig."**
"I have my passport on me."	**„Ich habe meinen Reisepaß."**
He gives her the passport.	**Er gibt ihr den Paß.**
"You are Peter Wilson from London.	**„Sie sind Peter Wilson aus London.**
You are a student.	**Sie sind Student.**
You are twenty-three years old.	**Sie sind dreiundzwanzig Jahre alt.**
You are English.	**Sie sind Engländer.**
Yes, that's right;	**Ja, richtig;**
you are the man I'm expecting.	**Sie sind der Mann, den ich erwarte.**
Welcome to Hanover."	**Willkommen in Hannover."**
"Thanks. Is that all?"	**„Danke. Ist das alles?"**
"No, the parcel is for my uncle.	**„Nein, das Paket ist für meinen Onkel.**
He is called Wilhelm Holz.	**Er heißt Wilhelm Holz.**
He'd like you to stay in Hanover tonight.	**Er möchte, daß Sie heute nacht in Hannover bleiben.**
A hotel room is reserved for you.	**Ein Hotelzimmer ist für Sie reserviert.**
The hotel is called "Hotel Sun."	**Das Hotel heißt „Hotel Sonne."**
It is in King's Street.	**Es ist in der Königsstraße.**
The hotel is not large.	**Das Hotel ist nicht groß.**
It is small but comfortable.	**Es ist klein aber bequem.**
Please stay there tonight."	**Bitte bleiben Sie heute nacht dort."**
"Where is the hotel?"	**„Wo ist das Hotel?"**
"It is easy to find and not far."	**„Es ist leicht zu finden und nicht weit von hier."**
Go left into the King's Street and it is one hundred metres on the right."	**Gehen Sie links in die Königsstraße und es ist hundert Meter rechts."**
They agree to meet at ten in the morning.	**Sie verabreden sich für zehn Uhr morgens.**
"Good night. Till tomorrow."	**„Gute Nacht. Bis morgen."**
"Good night."	**„Gute Nacht."**

Act 1

Scene 3

In the Hotel.

Peter walks to the hotel.

He goes into the hotel.

The receptionist welcomes him.

"I am expecting you already.

Have you got your passport?

Your room number is number seven.

It's on the first floor."

"Thanks."

He takes the key.

The room is very nice.

Peter goes to bed.

The bed is comfortable.

He is tired but happy!

What a day!

He soon falls asleep.

Akt 1

Szene 3

Im Hotel.

Peter geht zum Hotel.

Er geht ins Hotel.

Die Empfangsdame heißt ihn willkommen.

„Ich erwarte Sie schon.

Haben Sie Ihren Reisepaß?

Sie haben Zimmer Nummer sieben.

Es ist im ersten Stock."

„Danke."

Er nimmt den Schlüssel.

Das Zimmer ist sehr nett.

Peter geht zu Bett.

Das Bett ist bequem.

Er ist müde aber glücklich.

Was für ein Tag!

Er schläft bald ein.

If you have time to sit down have a look at the memory map. It tells the story in pictures. Choose your favourite of the different readings and follow the story on the memory map in your book. Involve yourself by highlighting or underlining any words that you particularly need to fix in your memory.

Pronunciation/Intonation

Now that you have recalled the story with the memory map, you will hear some German words and phrases. Try to imitate the speakers as closely as possible, and repeat each little part.

- ei -

(a) **eins?**
nein! zwei.
drei?
nein, eins!
klein.
Sie ist klein.
weiß.
weiß?
Das weiß ich nicht.

- ch -

(b) **ich.**
nicht.
Ich nicht!
leider nicht.
weiß ich nicht.
leicht.
leicht?
vielleicht. Pech!
Er hat Pech. Wer hat Pech?
Herr Wunderlich.

- ach, och, uch -

(c) **acht, Nacht.**
nach Hannover!
hoch, Hochhaus
er sucht.
Besuch. Ich bin zu Besuch.
Gute Nacht.

Akt 1, 1

Part Two: Functional Dialogues
Teil zwei: Dialoge

You will now hear a few dialogues using the same vocabulary as in the story, but in different everyday situations. You know all the situations already, but the narrator has gone and Peter has to cope on his own in German.

Dialogue 1	**Peter is trying to find Hilde.**	**Dialog 1**	**Peter sucht Hilde.**
	He is standing in front of the house and tries several bell buttons.		**Er steht vor dem Haus und drückt die Klingelknöpfe eins, zwei.**
Voice:	Hello.	**Stimme:**	**Hallo.**
Peter:	Hello. I am Peter Wilson. Are you Miss Hilde?	**Peter:**	**Guten Tag. Ich bin Peter Wilson. Sind Sie Fräulein Hilde?**
Voice:	No, I am Mrs Meyer.	**Stimme:**	**Nein, ich bin Frau Meyer.**
Peter:	I am looking for Miss Hilde. Do you know where she lives?	**Peter:**	**Ich suche Fräulein Hilde. Wissen Sie, wo sie wohnt?**
Voice:	Unfortunately not. I do not live here. I am on a visit. Peter rings the third bell.	**Stimme:**	**Leider nicht. Ich wohne nicht hier. Ich bin zu Besuch. Peter drückt den dritten Klingelknopf.**
2. Voice:	Yes, please?	**2. Stimme:**	**Ja, bitte?**
Peter:	I am Peter Wilson. Are you Hilde Holz?	**Peter:**	**Ich bin Peter Wilson. Sind Sie Hilde Holz?**
2. Voice:	Yes, I am Hilde Holz. Just a second. Good afternoon. I am Hilde Holz. Who are you please?	**2. Stimme:**	**Ja, ich bin Hilde Holz. Augenblick. Guten Tag. Ich bin Hilde Holz. Wer sind Sie, bitte?**

Dialogue 2	**In the Post Office** (Peter is asked by the official to prove his identity. P.O.O. - Post Office Official)	**Dialog 2**	**In der Post** (Peter zeigt den Reisepaß Pb - Postbeamter)
Peter:	My name is Peter Wilson. You've got a packet for me.	**Peter:**	**Mein Name ist Peter Wilson. Sie haben ein Paket für mich.**
P.O.O.:	Can you identify yourself?	**Pb:**	**Können Sie sich bitte ausweisen?**
Peter:	I have my passport.	**Peter:**	**Ich habe meinen Reisepaß.**
P.O.O.: reads:	You are Peter Wilson from London. You are a student. You are 23 years old. You are English. O.K. Here you are.	**Pb liest:**	**Sie sind Peter Wilson aus London. Sie sind Student. Sie sind dreiundzwanzig Jahre alt. Sie sind Engländer. Ja, gut. Bitte schön.**
Peter:	Is that all?	**Peter:**	**Ist das alles?**
P.O.O.:	Yes, here is the package. Good-bye.	**Pb:**	**Ja, hier ist das Paket. Auf Wiedersehen.**
Peter:	Good-bye.	**Peter:**	**Auf Wiedersehen.**

Dialogue 3	Where is the hotel?	Dialog 3	Wo ist das Hotel?
Peter:	Where is the hotel "The Sun" please?	**Peter:**	**Bitte, wo ist das Hotel "Sonne"?**
Passer-by:	It is in King's Street. That's not far from here.	**Passant:**	**Es ist in der Königsstraße. Das ist nicht weit von hier.**
Peter:	How do I get there, please?	**Peter:**	**Bitte, wie komme ich dorthin?**
Passer-by:	Turn left here into King's Street, and the hotel is hundred yards on your right.	**Passant:**	**Gehen Sie hier links in die Königsstraße, und das Hotel ist hundert Meter rechts.**
Peter:	Thank you. Good-bye.	**Peter:**	**Vielen Dank. Auf Wiedersehen.**
Passer-by:	Good-bye.	**Passant:**	**Auf Wiedersehen.**

Dialogue 4	In the hotel At the reception desk	Dialog 4	Im Hotel An der Rezeption
Peter:	Good evening. I am Peter Wilson. Mr. Holz booked a room for me.	**Peter:**	**Guten Tag. Ich bin Peter Wilson.** **Herr Holz hat ein Zimmer für mich reserviert.**
Receptionist:	Good evening. Yes, I am expecting you already. Have you got your passport? You have room number seven, that's on the first floor.	**Empfangsdame:**	**Guten Abend. Ja, ich erwarte Sie schon. Haben Sie Ihren Reisepaß? Sie haben Zimmer Nummer sieben, das ist im ersten Stock.**
Peter:	Thank you. Good night.	**Peter:**	**Danke. Gute Nacht.**
Receptionist:	You are welcome. Good night.	**Empfangsdame:**	**Bitte schön. Gute Nacht.**

Er schläft bald ein

Sie haben

Zimmer Nummer sieben

HOTEL SONNE NO 7

Part Three: Personalised Dialogues
Teil drei: Dialoge

Now it's your turn to take part. Read the dialogues first, visualise the scene, think what you would say, switch on the tape and join in.

Dialog 1

Wie heißen Sie?	(say who you are)
Wo wohnen Sie?	(say where you live)
Wo wohnt Hilde?	(say where Hilde lives)
Und wo wohnt Peter Wilson?	(say where he lives)

Dialog 2

Wohnen Sie hier?	(say yes I live here or No, I don't live here.)
Sind Sie aus England?	(say yes I am from England or No I am not from England.)
Wo ist das Paket?	(say here is the parcel.)
Ist das alles?	(say yes, that's all.)

Dialog 3

Ist das Hotel "Sonne" in der Königsstraße?	(say yes it is in King's Street)
Ist das weit?	(say no, that is not far.)
Ist es rechts oder links?	(say it is on the right hand side, hundred metres on your right)

Dialog 4

Hat Herr Holz ein Zimmer reserviert?	(say yes, he has booked a room.)
Hat Peter einen Reisepaß?	(say yes, he has a passport.)
Hat er Zimmer Nummer acht?	(say no, he has room number seven.)

(The correct answers are at the back of the book)

Part Four: Exercises
Teil vier: Übungen

Übung 1 - Exercise 1
Read the questions and answers aloud, and repeat.

Suchen Sie etwas?   **Ja, ich suche Fräulein Holz.**
Sind Sie Fräulein Holz?   **Nein, ich bin nicht Fräulein Holz.**
Wohnen Sie hier?   **Ja, ich wohne hier.**

Übung 2 - Exercise 2
Read the following question aloud and find the correct answer.

Suchen Sie etwas?   a) **Tut mir leid, ich bin Hans Büttner.**
                                  b) **Ja, Fräulein Hilde.**
                                  c) **Ich wohne im ersten Stock.**

Übung 3 - Exercise 3
Read the questions and answers aloud. Repeat.

Wo wohnen Sie?   a) **Im Erdgeschoß. Ich bin Hans Büttner.**
                                  b) **Im ersten Stock. Ich bin Heinrich Wunderlich.**
                                  c) **Im zweiten Stock. Ich bin Hilde Holz.**
                                  d) **Im dritten Stock. Ich bin Walter Vogelsang.**
                                  e) **Im vierten Stock. Ich bin Erika Becker.**

Übung 4 - Exercise 4
Read the questions and find the right answers. Then say them aloud and write them down.

Example: **Wer wohnt im zweiten Stock?**
Answer: **Hilde Holz.**

1) **Wer wohnt im zweiten Stock?**   1) ....
2) **Wer wohnt im vierten Stock?**   2) ....
3) **Wer wohnt im dritten Stock?**   3) ....
4) **Wer wohnt im Erdgeschoß**   4) ....
5) **Wer wohnt im ersten Stock?**   5) ....

(The correct answers are at the back of the book.)

11

Part five: Games, Puzzles and Rhymes
Teil fünf: Spiele, Rätsel und Reime

1. **Ein Würfelspiel**   A game: throw a dice
    Eine Wohnung zu gewinnen   To win a flat

We will now give you the opportunity to win a flat in a German **"Hochhaus."** However, some flats are already taken. (Look at the picture, the ones with "X"). Take a dice and throw for luck:

Haben Sie Glück? (Are you lucky?)

Ja, Nummer eins, zwei, drei, vier, fünf. (Yes, numbers 1,2,3,4,5)

Sie haben Pech! (You are unlucky.)

Nummer sechs. (Number 6)

Now read the first question:

„Wo wollen Sie wohnen?"

Then throw the dice and answer:

„Im . . . . Stock." [Im ersten, zweiten, dritten, vierten, fünften Stock.]
„Links oder rechts?"

Make a choice wherever a flat is still available.

Whenever you throw a number six you say:

„Ich habe Pech."

But don't be discouraged, try again until all the flats have been taken.

Whenever you are lucky and throw the numbers 1 - 5 say: **„Ich habe Glück.**
Ich habe eine Wohnung im . . . . Stock. Rechts oder links.

Viel Glück

2. Look at the map. It contains the countries where German is spoken.

1) Take a piece of paper and write out the underlined letters.
By putting them into the right order and forming two words, you will find a phrase, which is used in all the countries on the map.

(The correct answer is at the back of the book)

2) Imagine that you are in a TV studio in Berlin. (Berlin was named after some Bärlin, bear cubs, which were found there by a duke. Note: Pronounce it „**Bearlean**".)

All towns on this map are represented by their teams in their various TV studios. They are taking part in a show of which you are the quizmaster. You have to call on each team in turn.

a) Start with: **Hier ist Berlin. Guten Tag Bonn.**

b) Now answer for each team: **Hallo Berlin. Hier ist . . . Bonn. Guten Tag Berlin, hier ist . . . .**

3. Rhymes

Rules are easier learnt in rhymes, e.g. 'i' before 'e' except after 'c'.

Therefore we have put some German language explanations into rhymes. Most people find learning easier this way and it is also more fun. We like to call the verb "action word" because this word expresses the action taking place in a sentence.

In English, only "s" or "es" needs to be remembered when he, she, it or "one" is involved with the action, e.g. he brings, she goes.

In German, however, the verb can end in **e,** or **t** or **en.**

Now listen and repeat.

Wer hat "e"? - ich - only one
Wer hat "t"? - er, es, sie - but neither you nor me.
Wer hat "en"? - wir, Sie und sie.

1 .... **ich stehe** ....
2 .... **er kommt** ....
3 .... **wir möchten** ....

1. **Ich stehe und gehe,**
   ich bleibe und wohne,
   ich komme und warte,
   ich suche und finde.

2. **Wer kommt und wer geht?**
   Wer fragt und wer sagt? } **- er, sie, es.**
   Wer denkt und wer lächelt?

3. **Wir möchten Sie fragen,**
   Sie lächeln und sagen,
   wir drücken, sie springen.

Activities:	Now try to make up your own little verse. **stehen, gehen, heißen, wohnen, drücken, sagen, antworten, suchen, springen, denken, kommen, lächeln, warten, erwarten, möchten, bleiben, finden.**

You can check with the help of the text of Act 1 whether you've put in the endings correctly, as all these words appear in the story in one form or another.

e.g.:

Zum Beispiel: **Er lächelt, sie sagt:**
ich möchte, daß er fragt.
Wir kommen und bleiben,
sie warten und schreiben. (To write).

4. Complete the sentences below. One dash for each letter. Only the first letter of each word is a capital letter, except the one in the second line.

Peter geht langsam zur H ═ — — — — —

Ich bin — ═ — London.

Die E — — — — — ═ — d — — —e heißt ihn willkommen.

Rote G — — — — — ═ —

Er drückt den K — — ═ — — — — — — —

Er geht zu ═ — — —

Auf dem — — ═ — — — sind rote Geranien.

ilde hat ein hübsches — — — ═ — — —

Das Haus hat vier — — — ═ — — — — — —

Er hat ein — — ═ — —

If you read the letters on the double dashes downwards, you will find a word which will keep a waiting person happy for a little while.

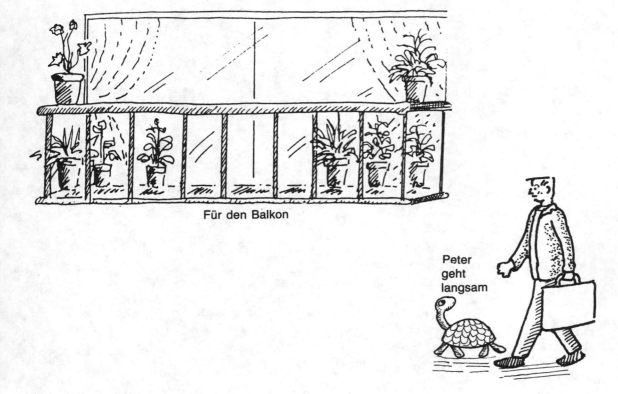

Für den Balkon

Peter geht langsam

15

Word cards - why and how to use them.

Nouns or words which are the 'name of a thing' or an 'abstract', e.g. the house=**das Haus,** or the love=**die Liebe,** have 'the' in English in front, but there are 3 different words for 'the' in German, **der, die, das.**

In order to get familiar with the use of **der, die, das,** each new word or noun will be found together with these words right from the beginning. For easier learning and quicker progress we have printed these words in the following colour code:

> **der**-(red backwards) are in red
> **die**-are in green (same sound)
> **das**-blue

We have grouped and divided the words into subject areas e.g. 'the house' and everything that belongs to this area; the person and some parts of the body; plus a few odd ones which have no specific subject area.

In German we write words together which in English are kept separately:

> **der Knopf**-the button
> **die Klingel**-the doorbell
> **der Klingelknopf**-the bell button

We have included these words from Act 1 in our word cards so that you can get used to them from the very start. Also included are some useful phrases which occur in Act 1.

In order to learn the words most effectively we recommend the following steps:

1. Cut them up, say each word aloud.
2. Find the illustration for each in the text or on the memory maps.
3. Put the card face down and look at the illustration only.
4. Take a piece of paper, write out the words with the **der, die, das** according to the illustration.
5. Check on the word card how many **der, die, das** you get right. Correct spelling is not necessary at this stage; it is mainly an exercise for the use of **der, die, das.**
6. Try to repeat this 'game' until you get all **der, die, das** words correct.

Act 2   Akt 2

<table>
<tr><td></td><td>Scene 1
The Hotel Room</td><td>Szene 1
Das Hotelzimmer</td></tr>
<tr><td>**Erzähler**</td><td>Peter wakes up.
He looks around the room.
The bed is comfortable.
The duvet and sheets are warm.
He hears the street noises
and gets up.</td><td>**Peter wacht auf.
Er sieht sich im Zimmer um.
Das Bett ist mollig.
Die Bettdecke und das Laken sind warm.
Er hört den Straßenlärm
und steht auf.**</td></tr>
<tr><td></td><td>He goes to the large windows.
He pulls back the curtains
and opens the window.
Down there is the street.
It is still wet.
During the night it has rained,
but now the rain has stopped.</td><td>**Er geht zu den großen Fenstern.
Er zieht die Vorhänge auf
und öffnet das Fenster.
Unten ist die Straße.
Sie ist noch naß.
In der Nacht hat es geregnet,
aber jetzt regnet es nicht mehr.**</td></tr>
<tr><td></td><td>Peter goes back to bed.
The pillow lies on the floor.
He puts it back onto the bed.
The room has nice furniture.
The carpet is light brown.
Peter opens his suitcase and
takes out toothbrush, toothpaste,
soap and shaver.</td><td>**Peter geht zum Bett zurück.
Das Kopfkissen liegt auf dem Boden.
Er legt es wieder auf das Bett.
Das Zimmer hat nette Möbel.
Der Teppich ist hellbraun.
Peter öffnet seinen Koffer
und nimmt Zahnbürste, Zahnpaste,
Seife und Rasierapparat heraus.**</td></tr>
<tr><td></td><td>He goes into the bathroom
and switches on the light.
Everything is spick and span.
There is a bath, a shower and
a toilet.
The bathtowel is large and soft.
Peter shaves himself and has a shower.</td><td>**Er geht ins Badezimmer
und macht das Licht an.
Alles ist blitzsauber!
Da ist ein Bad, eine Dusche und
eine Toilette.
Das Badetuch ist groß und weich.
Peter rasiert sich und duscht sich.**</td></tr>
<tr><td></td><td>He thinks about the parcel.
Why would Mr. Holz want him to stay
in Hanover?
It is an adventure!
Herr Holz pays and the holiday
is free.
Peter dresses quickly.
He looks at his watch.
Already half past nine!
He goes down the stairs to the
dining room. He wants to have
breakfast.</td><td>**Er denkt an das Paket.
Warum möchte Herr Holz, daß
er in Hannover bleibt?
Das ist ein Abenteuer!
Herr Holz bezahlt und der Urlaub
ist umsonst.
Peter zieht sich schnell an.
Er sieht auf die Uhr.
Schon halb zehn!
Er geht die Treppe hinunter
zum Speisesaal. Er möchte
frühstücken.**</td></tr>
</table>

	Scene 2 The Breakfast	Szene 2 Das Frühstück
Kellnerin	Good morning, how are you?	**Guten Morgen, wie geht's?**
Erzähler	The waitress has dark hair and large brown eyes. She is wearing a short, black dress.	**Die Kellnerin hat dunkles Haar und große braune Augen. Sie trägt ein kurzes, schwarzes Kleid.**
Peter	Good morning, what's there for breakfast?	**Guten Morgen, was gibt's zum Frühstück?**
Kellnerin	We have fresh rolls: rolls with seeds or soft rolls with butter, honey or jam. Would you like an egg?	**Wir haben frische Brötchen: Mohnbrötchen oder weiche Brötchen mit Butter, Honig oder Marmelade. Möchten Sie ein Ei?**
Erzähler	Peter smells the fresh coffee and the fresh rolls. Yumm, that smells good.	**Peter riecht den frischen Kaffee und die frischen Brötchen. Mm, das riecht gut.**
Peter	I'd like two rolls. One roll with seeds and a soft roll with butter and honey. I would also like a glass of orange juice and a cup of coffee please.	**Ich möchte zwei Brötchen. Ein Mohnbrötchen und ein weiches Brötchen mit Butter und Honig. Dann möchte ich ein Glas Orangensaft und eine Tasse Kaffee bitte.**
Erzähler	The waitress brings the breakfast. She brings milk and sugar, but Peter would like black coffee. The rolls taste really good.	**Die Kellnerin bringt das Frühstück. Sie bringt Milch und Zucker, aber Peter möchte schwarzen Kaffee. Die Brötchen schmecken wirklich gut.**
Kellnerin	Another coffee?	**Noch einen Kaffee?**
Peter	Yes, please.	**Ja bitte.**
Erzähler	The waitress smiles. She is friendly.	**Die Kellnerin lächelt. Sie ist freundlich.**
Kellnerin	Where do you live then?	**Wo wohnen Sie denn?**
Peter	I live in Hampstead. That's in London. I am a student.	**Ich wohne in Hampstead. Das ist in London. Ich bin Student.**
Kellnerin	Is this your first visit to Hanover?	**Sind Sie zum ersten Mal in Hannover?**
Peter	Yes, I like Hanover. Do you understand my German?	**Ja, Hannover gefällt mir gut. Verstehen Sie mein Deutsch?**
Kellnerin	Yes, your German is good.	**Ja, Sie sprechen gut Deutsch.**
Peter	I can understand a lot, but please speak slowly.	**Ich kann viel verstehen, aber bitte sprechen Sie langsam.**
Erzähler	Peter has his breakfast. He enjoys it. The rolls are fresh. Especially the seed roll tastes good.	**Peter ißt sein Frühstück. Es schmeckt gut. Die Brötchen sind frisch. Das Mohnbrötchen schmeckt besonders gut.**

Act 2   Akt 2

	Scene 3 What's the weather like?	Szene 3 **Wie ist das Wetter?**
Erzähler	Peter sees the receptionist at the door.	**Peter sieht die Empfangsdame an der Tür.**
Empfangsdame	Good morning, did you sleep well?	**Guten Morgen, haben Sie gut geschlafen?**
Peter	Yes thank you.	**Ja danke.**
Empfangsdame	The weather is fine now, isn't it? The rain has stopped.	**Das Wetter ist jetzt schön, nicht wahr? Es regnet nicht mehr.**
Peter	Yes, it's a fine day. It's quite hot already. What's the time, please?	**Ja, ein schöner Tag. Es ist schon ziemlich heiß. Wie spät ist es bitte?**
Empfangsdame	Just a moment. 'Helga', what's the time?	**Augenblick. 'Helga', wieviel Uhr ist es?**
Stimme	Nearly ten o'clock! What's the matter?	**Gleich zehn Uhr! Was ist denn los?**
Peter	Nearly ten o'clock! Perhaps Hilde is waiting already? He hands the key to the receptionist and leaves the hotel.	**Gleich zehn Uhr! Vielleicht wartet Hilde schon? Er gibt der Empfangsdame den Schlüssel und verläßt das Hotel.**

Pronunciation/Intonation

You have already listened to quite a lot of German and tried to practise some specific sounds such as **"ei"**, **"ach"** and **"ich"**. You have heard how Germans tend to stress certain parts of a word or sentence much stronger than others without much of a sing-song. In fact Germans don't raise their voice as much or as often as English speakers do. Listen to the following sounds and intonation patterns and try to imitate the native speaker as closely as you can.

First we'll compare long **"ie"** and short **"i"**.

1. **Im Zimmer liegen vier Kissen. . . . Er rasiert sich und zieht sich an. Bitte bringen Sie mir Milch . . . . Viel Milch bitte! . . .**

Let's now combine some "i" and "ei" sounds and practise them together with a few soft and hard sounds like **"s"** and **"ss"**.

2. **Sie sieht ein Ei . . . . Es ist weich . . . . Sie ißt das Ei. . . . Er riecht seine Seife . . . Sie riecht ziemlich gut, aber er ißt sie nicht . . . . Sie bleiben zwei Stunden im Speisesaal . . . . Es ist heiß hier . . . .**

There is no **"ü"** sound in English. To produce this sound, purse your lips, make them round and push them forward. Do this quite tightly, as if you prepare to whistle. Through your tight, round lips say **"ü"**.

3. **Er ißt sein Frühstück. . . . Fünf frische Brötchen. . . . Hier liegen vier Badetücher. . . . Wo ist meine Zahnbürste? . . . Ich bin müde aber glücklich! . . .**

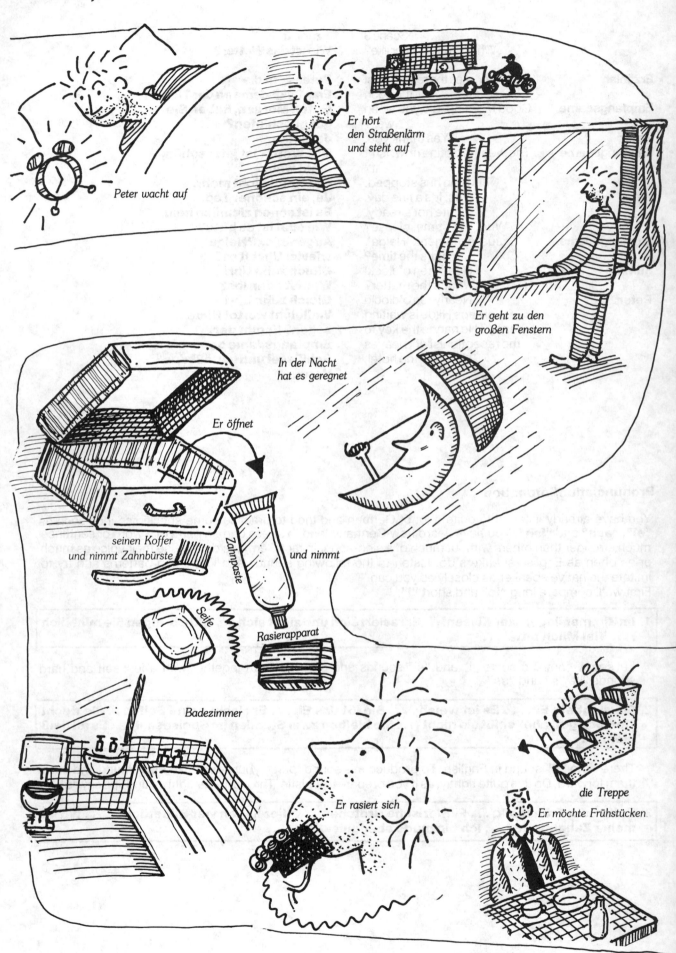

Peter wacht auf

Er hört den Straßenlärm und steht auf

Er geht zu den großen Fenstern

In der Nacht hat es geregnet

Er öffnet

seinen Koffer und nimmt Zahnbürste

Zahnpaste

Seife

und nimmt

Rasierapparat

Badezimmer

Er rasiert sich

hinunter

die Treppe

Er möchte Frühstücken.

Dialogue 1
A student on a Visit

Mrs B:	Here is your room.
Student:	The room is very nice.
Mrs B:	On the bed is only one pillow. Would you like two?
Student:	No thank you. Only one please.
Mrs B:	The bathroom is next door. Would you like to take a shower?
Student:	Yes please.
Mrs B:	Here is the soap and a bath towel.
Student:	Thank you. The bath towel is large and soft. Terrific!

Dialog 1
Ein Student ist zu Besuch

Frau B:	**Hier ist Ihr Zimmer.**
Student:	**Das Zimmer ist sehr hübsch.**
Frau B:	**Auf dem Bett ist nur ein Kopfkissen. Möchten Sie zwei?**
Student:	**Nein danke. Nur eins bitte.**
Frau B:	**Das Badezimmer ist nebenan. Möchten Sie sich duschen?**
Student:	**Ja bitte.**
Frau B:	**Hier ist die Seife und ein Badetuch.**
Student:	**Danke. Das Badetuch ist groß und weich. Prima!**

Dialogue 2
In the Hotel at Reception

Guest:	I do not like my room.
Receptionist:	What is the matter then?
Guest:	I cannot sleep. I hear the street noise.
Receptionist:	Where is your room?
Guest:	On the first floor. My room number is seven
Receptionist:	Would you like a room on the fifth floor?
Guest:	Yes please.

Dialog 2
Im Hotel an der Rezeption

Gast:	**Mein Zimmer gefällt mir nicht.**
Empfangsdame:	**Was ist denn los?**
Gast:	**Ich kann nicht schlafen. Ich höre den Straßenlärm.**
Empfangsdame:	**Wo ist Ihr Zimmer?**
Gast:	**Im ersten Stock. Meine Zimmernummer ist sieben.**
Empfangsdame:	**Möchten Sie ein Zimmer im fünften Stock?**
Gast:	**Ja bitte.**

Dialogue 3
In the Hotel Room

Anna:	I am tired. I go to bed now.
Bernd:	Is the bed comfortable?
Anna:	Very comfortable.
Bernd:	The windows are large. I draw the curtains.
Anna:	Brr! The bed is cold.
Bernd:	Is the duvet not warm?
Anna:	The duvet is terrific, the sheet is terrific, but the bed is not warm.
Bernd:	Just a moment. I switch the light out. I am just coming.

Dialog 3
Im Hotelzimmer

Anna:	**Ich bin müde. Ich gehe jetzt zu Bett.**
Bernd:	**Ist das Bett bequem?**
Anna:	**Sehr bequem.**
Bernd:	**Die Fenster sind groß. Ich ziehe die Vorhänge zu.**
Anna:	**Brr! Das Bett ist kalt.**
Bernd:	**Ist die Bettdecke nicht warm?**
Anna:	**Die Bettdecke ist prima, das Laken ist prima, aber das Bett ist nicht warm.**
Bernd:	**Augenblick. Ich mache das Licht aus. Ich komme gleich.**

Dialogue 4
In the Hotel Room

Christa:	What shall I put on? What is the weather like?
Dieter:	Just a moment. I draw the curtains back and open the window. The street is still wet but it doesn't rain any more.
Christa:	Then I'll put on my short black dress.
Dieter:	No, not the black dress. It is a beautiful day and already fairly hot. The black dress is too warm.
Christa:	Then I'll put on the red dress.

Dialogue 5
In the Hotel

Anette:	Where is the dining room please?
Bernd:	Go down the stairs. The dining-room is on the ground floor.

Dialogue 6
Breakfast

Guest:	Waiter!
Waiter:	Yes please?
Guest:	Two poppyseed rolls please and a soft boiled egg.
Waiter:	What would you like to drink? Coffee, tea, milk or orange juice?
Guest:	A small glass of orange juice and a cup of coffee please.

Dialogue 7
In the Hotel Dining-Room

Guest:	Waiter!
Waiter:	Yes please?
Guest:	The rolls taste really good. What are they called?
Waiter:	They are called milk rolls.
Guest:	Many thanks.
Waiter:	That's all right.

Dialog 4
Im Hotelzimmer

Christa:	**Was ziehe ich an?** **Wie ist das Wetter?**
Dieter:	**Augenblick. Ich ziehe** **die Vorhänge zurück und** **mache das Fenster auf.** **Die Straße ist noch naß,** **aber es regnet nicht mehr.**
Christa:	**Dann ziehe ich mein kurzes,** **schwarzes Kleid an.**
Dieter:	**Nein, nicht das schwarze** **Kleid. Es ist ein schöner Tag** **und schon ziemlich heiß.** **Das schwarze Kleid ist** **zu warm.**
Christa:	**Dann ziehe ich das rote** **Kleid an.**

Dialog 5
Im Hotel

Anette:	**Wo ist der Speisesaal** **bitte?**
Bernd:	**Gehen Sie die Treppe** **hinunter. Der Speisesaal ist** **im Erdgeschoß.**

Dialog 6
Frühstück

Gast:	**Herr Ober!**
Ober:	**Bitte schön?**
Gast:	**Zwei Mohnbrötchen bitte** **und ein weichgekochtes Ei.**
Ober:	**Was möchten Sie trinken?** **Kaffee, Tee, Milch oder** **Orangensaft?**
Gast:	**Ein kleines Glas Orangensaft** **und eine Tasse Kaffee** **bitte.**

Dialog 7
Im Speisesaal

Gast:	**Herr Ober!**
Ober:	**Bitte schön?**
Gast:	**Die Brötchen schmecken** **wirklich gut. Wie heißen die?**
Ober:	**Die heißen „Milchbrötchen."**
Gast:	**Vielen Dank.**
Ober:	**Bitte schön.**

Part three: Personalised Dialogues
Teil drei: Dialoge

Dialog 1
You are sitting in the bar of your hotel, when another guest comes up to you.

Guest:	**Guten Morgen.**
You:	(Greet your fellow guest.)
Guest:	**Schmidt, Thomas Schmidt. Ich komme aus Hamburg.**
You:	(Say your name and where you come from.)
Guest:	**Ach! Aus X! X kenne ich nicht.**
You:	(Say: I do not know Hamburg either.)
Guest:	**Wie ist Ihr Zimmer?**
You:	(Say: I do not like it.)
Guest:	**Was ist denn los? Haben Sie nicht gut geschlafen?**
You:	(Say: no, I have not slept well. I can hear the street noise.)
Guest:	**Das tut mir leid. Sie haben Pech. Wo ist denn Ihr Zimmer?**
You:	(Say: my room is on the first floor.)

Dialog 2
You are with your German friend, discussing the weather and what clothes to wear today.

Friend:	**Wie ist das Wetter?**
You:	(Say: I open the curtains. It does not rain. It is warm.)
Friend:	**Was ziehen wir an?**
You:	(Say: I will put on my short red dress.)
Friend:	**Das gefällt mir gut. Ich ziehe mein hellbraunes Kleid an. Wo ist es?**
You:	(Say: I like the light brown dress. It is in the bathroom. It is wet!)

Dialog 3
You are having breakfast with a friend.

Friend:	**Wie schmecken die Brötchen?**
You:	(Say: the rolls taste good.)
Friend:	**Noch einen Kaffee?**
You:	(Say: yes please.)
Friend:	**Mit Zucker und Milch?**
You:	(Say: no thank you.)

Dialog 4
You are in Peter's hotel room. The telephone rings for Peter, but he is in the bathroom!
Can you help?

Voice:	**Guten Morgen. Ist das Zimmer Nummer sieben? Ist Peter Wilson da?**
You:	(Good morning. Yes this is room number 7. A moment please. He is in the bathroom. He is taking a shower.)
Voice:	**Oh Entschuldigung, dann telefoniere ich in fünf Minuten noch einmal.**

Dialog 5
The phone rings again. Peter is shaving, getting dressed and combing his hair. He asks you to help once more. To keep the caller friendly, say „bitte warten Sie" (Please wait) and call Peter.

Voice:	**Guten Morgen, ich bin's wieder. Ist Peter jetzt da?**
You:	(Yes, he is there. He is shaving. Please wait.)
Voice:	**Vielen Dank.**
You:	That's all right.

(The correct answers are at the back of the book.)

Part four: Exercises and Activities
Teil vier: Übungen

Übung 1
Can you fill in the missing word? One dash for each letter.

Schläft Peter? Nein, Peter — — — — — — — — . **Er** — — — — — **sich im Zimmer** — —.
                               wakes   up   looks   around

Er hört den Straßenlärm und — — — — — — — — . **Er** — — — — — **die Vorhänge** — — —.
                                    gets   up   pulls   open

Er geht ins Badezimmer und — — — — — **das Licht** — —. **Peter** — — — — —
sich schnell — —.
                                switches   on   gets dressed

Übung 2
Can you order breakfast?

You are a family of four consisting of:
a) yourself
b) your spouse
c) your 18 month old baby
d) your 70-year-old grandad whose false
   teeth don't fit.

As you are the only German speaker you will help
the others choosing their breakfast, in explaining
the various items on the menu-card first, and then
advise them on their choice.

a) You make your first choice first, by saying
   out loud:
   „Ich möchte ... "
b) Then choose for your spouse - three items -
   again by saying:
   „Er/Sie möchte ... "
c) Baby and granddad will possibly choose the
   same things, say aloud:
   „Sie möchten ... "

Unsere kulinarischen Spezialitäten

Frühstücks-Karte
Getränke: Frühstück:
Kaffee   weiche Brötchen
Tee   frische Brötchen
Schokolade   Mohnbrötchen
Milch —   gekochte Eier
heiß oder kalt
Butter
Honig

Mat.-Nr. 02120 LR

FRÜHSTÜCKSKARTE

Getränke	Frühstück
Kaffee	- weiche Brötchen
Tee	- frische Brötchen
Schokolade	- Mohnbrötchen
Milch - heiß oder kalt	- gekochte Eier
	Butter
	Honig

Übung 3:

You are in the tiny principality of Liechtenstein on business. All went well for you today and you want to tell your friend in Berlin about it. Ring her/him up and say:

a) a greeting. . . . . .Say your name. . . . .

   Ask the person answering the phone for her/his name . . . .

   Say that you have good luck . . . . .Say where you are . . . .

   Till tomorrow . . . .

b) You are delayed and could not go to see your friend in Berlin. Instead you had to go to Luxemburg. *Write a short picture postcard, saying:*

   "Luxemburg is small. It is important. I have good luck. Till tomorrow."

c) Your trip to Liechtenstein and Luxemburg went really well for you. Therefore you decided to go to Zürich to see a banking friend. There you try to ring your German friend in Berlin to explain the delayed return.

   Sie haben Pech! What bad luck! Your friend is out and his "Ansaphone" is switched on!
   Look at your watch and time your answer. How fast can you say in German:

   "Your name. I am in Zürich. The weather is nice.
   Tomorrow I will be in Berlin. Till tomorrow. Good-bye."

Übung 4

These are the countries where German is spoken. If you take the underlined letters you will find something most people there like for breakfast - **zum Frühstück.** One long word. . . . .

(The answers are at the back of the book.)

Part five: Games, Puzzles and Rhymes
Teil fünf: Spiele, Rätsel und Reime

You want to meet your friend in **Blütenweg** at ten o'clock. It is now three o'clock and you are in a hurry. How fast can you get to your date? Throw a dice and see where you land. If you land on any of the squares marked in bold you have to obey the following instructions.

(1) You have not taken a shower yet. Say that you are taking one.

(4) Where is the soap? Ask for it.

(7) You need to get dressed. Say that you are getting dressed.

(10) Do you want to have breakfast? Refuse politely.

(12) Your watch has stopped. Ask someone what the time is.

(14) Now you have left the hotel but do not know where to go. Ask someone where the above address is.

(16) **„Nur hundert Meter rechts"** the person said. Is that left, right or straight ahead?
You are almost there. Blütenweg 8 is next to the clock. You only need to throw a 3. Was your first throw a 3? **Prima! Glück gehabt!** (been lucky). If not, say the number shown on the dice each time. **Eins, zwei, drei, vier, fünf, sechs? Leider, leider, Pech gehabt.** (Unfortunately been unlucky!). If you liked this game, say **„das gefällt mir."** If you did not enjoy it, say **„das gefällt mir nicht!"**.

Why not play again and follow the instructions for the bold squares whether you actually land on them or not?

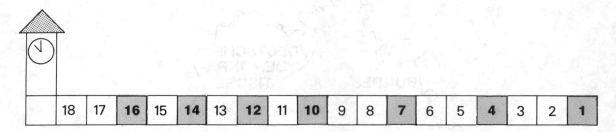

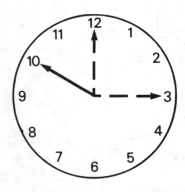

Zehn Uhr
und
viertel nach zehn

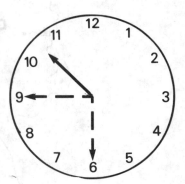

Halb elf
und
viertel vor elf

Die Uhr	The Clock
Es ist zehn Uhr.	It is ten o'clock.
Es ist zehn Uhr fünfzehn	It is ten fifteen or
oder viertel nach zehn.	quarter past ten.
Es ist zehn Uhr dreißig	It is ten thirty or
oder <u>halb elf.</u>	<u>half past ten.</u>
Es ist zehn Uhr fünfundvierzig	It is ten forty-five or
oder viertel vor elf.	quarter to eleven.

Saying the time in German is the same as in English, except for expressing the half hour. In German, we think ahead and say: It's half to the next full hour, whereas in English you say: It's half past the (passed) hour. So half past ten becomes half to eleven in German. Once you know this, it is easy to learn and use the time in German.

Part five: Jingles
Teil fünf: Reime

wissen und kennen
wissen — to know the what? why? who? or when?
kennen — to know if the thing's in your „ken".

I know (=weiß) where the Town hall is,
because I know (=kenne) Hannover very well.

Examples:
Ich weiß, was ich weiß.
Er weiß nicht, wer ich bin,
wie ich heiße, wo ich wohne.
Er kennt mich nicht
und ich kenne ihn auch nicht.

How to ask a question

Wo wohnt Hilde?
Is a question.

Wohnt sie hier?
that is one too.

Hier wohnt Hilde?
is another,
if your voice does make it so.

myself, yourself, himself, herself, themselves, ourselves
Example:
ich wasche mich,
und du wäschst dich,
er will sich auch jetzt waschen.
Wir waschen uns,
Sie (sie) waschen sich,
mit Wasser aus zwei Flaschen!
(Don't be put off by the amount of water used! Water from two bottles!)

I wash (myself),
and you wash (yourself),
he now wants to wash (himself), too.
We wash (ourselves),
you (they) wash (yourself, themselves),
with water from two bottles!

REMINDER

This is a gentle, yet important reminder.

Have you got the Steps in front of you? You should *always* follow each one through faithfully. Always include the visualisation exercise — the step where you close your eyes and visualise the Acts and speak as many words out loud as you can remember. This is a powerful memory device.

Don't forget your activities as you go through this course. By activities we mean not only playing as many of the games and solving as many of the puzzles as possible, but also that you should physically 'work with' the text and/or illustrations. Underlining, highlighting, jotting down any words, phrases, expressions that you particularly want to fix in your memory (or which for some reason have specific significance for you), is important.

Always remember that active involvement is the best method to store new material in your long-term memory.

You should ideally always have writing material ready while you are learning and/or listening to the cassettes.

We recommend you to have a look at these Steps as you progress through this course from time to time.

Viel Erfolg! Much success!

Act 3   Akt 3

Scene 1
Peter visits Hilde

Erzähler	Peter walks along King's Street.
	Only one hundred metres straight ahead
	and there on the right is Blütenweg.
	Peter looks at his watch.
	It's ten on the dot and
	he rings the bell.
	SUUMMM. The door opens.
	Hilde is waiting.
Hilde	Hello!
Peter	Good morning.
Erzähler	He walks up the stairs.
	They shake hands.
Peter	How are you?
Hilde	Fine thanks, I have to go shopping.
	Do you want to come with me?
	Uncle William has rung this morning.
	He would like you to stay another day.
	Is that possible?
Peter	Yes. That'll be all right.
	I have nothing planned for this week.
Erzähler	He is delighted.
	He likes Hilde.
	He likes Hanover.
	He likes the adventure.
	He enjoys the day.
Peter	I'll gladly come with you.

Szene 1
Peter besucht Hilde

Peter geht die Königsstraße entlang.
Nur hundert Meter geradeaus
und da ist rechts der Blütenweg.
Peter sieht auf die Uhr.
Es ist Punkt zehn und er klingelt
an der Tür.
SUUMMM. Die Tür springt auf.
Hilde wartet schon.
Hallo!
Guten Morgen.
Er geht die Treppe hoch.
Sie geben sich die Hand.
Wie geht's?
Gut, Danke. Ich muß einkaufen
gehen. Wollen Sie mitkommen?
Onkel Wilhelm hat heute morgen
angerufen. Er möchte, daß Sie
noch einen Tag hier bleiben.
Geht das?
Ja. Das geht.
Ich habe diese Woche nichts vor.
Er freut sich.
Hilde gefällt ihm.
Hannover gefällt ihm.
Das Abenteuer gefällt ihm.
Der Tag gefällt ihm.
Ich komme gern mit.

Es ist Punkt zehn

Onkel Wilhelm nat
angerufen

Peter
freut
sich

Hannover
gefällt
ihm

	Scene 2 Shopping	**Szene 2 Einkaufen gehen**
Hilde	Now we are going to the bakery, to the butcher's and then to the market. Today is market day.	**Wir gehen jetzt zur Bäckerei, zur Metzgerei und dann zum Markt. Heute ist Markttag.**
Erzähler	The bakery is next to number eight, the big white block of flats. The fresh bread smells good.	**Die Bäckerei ist gleich neben dem großen, weißen Hochhaus Nummer acht. Das frische Brot riecht gut.**
Hilde	Do you know what Pumpernickel is?	**Kennen Sie Pumpernickel?**
Peter	No. What is it?	**Nein, was ist denn das?**
Hilde	That's a speciality.	**Das ist eine Spezialität.**
Erzähler	She buys a packet and shows Peter the dark bread.	**Sie kauft eine Packung und zeigt Peter das dunkle Brot.**
Hilde	That goes well with Tilsit cheese or with ham.	**Das schmeckt gut mit Tilsiter Käse oder mit Schinken.**
Peter	I know ham, but I don't know Tilsit cheese.	**Schinken kenne ich, aber Tilsiter Käse kenne ich nicht.**
Hilde	That's also a speciality.	**Das ist auch eine Spezialität.**
Erzähler	The butcher's shop is opposite. There are many sausages and smoked hams in the window. They enter the shop.	**Die Metzgerei ist gegenüber. Im Schaufenster hängen viele Würste und Rauchschinken. Sie gehen in das Geschäft.**
	Scene 3 At the Butcher's	**Szene 3 Beim Metzger**
	The shop is very clean. The butcher wears a white apron.	**Im Geschäft ist alles sehr sauber. Der Metzger trägt eine weiße Schürze.**
Metzger	What can I do for you?	**Bitte schön. Was darf es sein?**
Hilde	Do you like ham?	**Mögen Sie Schinken?**
Peter	Yes, I like ham.	**Ja gern, Schinken mag ich.**
Hilde	Two slices of ham please. Do you like Salami?	**Zwei Scheiben Schinken bitte. Mögen Sie Salami?**
Peter	Yes, I like Salami.	**Ja. Salami esse ich auch.**
Hilde	A hundred grams of Salami please. Do you also like Leberkäs?	**Hundert Gramm Salami bitte. Mögen Sie auch Leberkäs?**
Peter	Leberkäs I don't know, but I'd like to try it.	**Leberkäs kenne ich nicht, aber ich will es gern probieren.**
Hilde	One hundred and fifty grams of Leberkäs please.	**Hundert fünfzig Gramm Leberkäs bitte.**
Metzger	Anything else?	**Sonst noch etwas?**
Hilde	No, thank you. That's all.	**Nein, danke. Das ist alles.**
Erzähler	She pays. She gives him a twenty Mark note. The butcher gives her a ten Mark note and a few coins change, two Marks and ten Pfennigs.	**Sie bezahlt. Sie gibt ihm einen Zwanzigmarkschein. Der Metzger gibt ihr einen Zehnmarkschein und ein paar Münzen zurück, zwei Mark und zehn Pfennig.**
Hilde	Now to the market.	**Jetzt zum Markt.**

	Scene 4 At the market	Szene 4 **Auf dem Markt**
Hilde	The market is nearby. We can walk.	**Der Marktplatz ist nicht weit.** **Wir können zu Fuß gehen.**
Erzähler	The sun is shining and they walk together along the street. They can hear the noise coming from the market. A lot is going on there. "Fresh strawberries, fresh strawberries." There is the market with colourful sunshades everywhere. Red, blue, yellow, green, large sunshades. Under the umbrella a market woman is sitting. She is selling fruit, vegetables and flowers. Hilde wants to buy some fruit.	**Die Sonne scheint und sie gehen** **zusammen die Straße entlang.** **Sie hören den Lärm. Auf dem** **Markt ist viel los.** **„Frische Erdbeeren, frische** **Erdbeeren!" Da ist der Markt;** **bunte Sonnenschirme sind überall.** **Rote, blaue, gelbe, grüne,** **große Sonnenschirme.** **Unter dem Schirm sitzt eine** **Marktfrau. Sie verkauft Obst,** **Gemüse und Blumen. Hilde will** **Obst kaufen.**
Hilde Peter	Do you like strawberries? Strawberries are my favourite.	**Mögen Sie Erdbeeren?** **Erdbeeren mag ich besonders gern.**
Erzähler	Hilde buys a pound of strawberries. Everything looks so appetising.	**Hilde kauft ein Pfund Erdbeeren.** **Alles sieht so appetitlich aus.**
Hilde Peter Hilde	What kind of apples do you like? I know Cox Orange Pippins and Golden Delicious, but I do not know any German apples. Well then, we'll take 2 kilos of Jonathan	**Was für Äpfel mögen Sie?** **Ich kenne Cox Orange und** **Goldene Delicious, aber deutsche** **Äpfel kenne ich nicht.** **Na gut, wir nehmen zwei Kilo** **Jonathan.**
Erzähler	She takes a red and yellow apple into her hand. 'Eve with the apple' thinks Peter. There are also ripe pears, large black cherries and blue plums. Hilde buys a fresh, green head of lettuce and a long cucumber at the vegetable stand. Peter sees the red tomatoes and has an idea. At the next stand there are pot plants. Peter buys a red geranium plant.	**Sie nimmt einen rot-gelben Apfel** **in die Hand. 'Eva mit dem Apfel',** **denkt Peter. Da sind auch reife** **Birnen, große schwarze** **Kirschen und blaue Zwetschgen.** **Am Gemüsestand kauft Hilde** **einen frischen, grünen Kopfsalat** **und eine lange Gurke.** **Peter sieht die roten Tomaten** **und hat eine Idee. Am nächsten** **Stand gibt es Topfpflanzen.** **Peter kauft eine rote Geranie.**
Peter	For the balcony.	**Für den Balkon.**
Erzähler	Hilde is pleased.	**Hilde freut sich.**
Hilde	Many thanks. That's very kind of you. I like red geraniums. Red geraniums really shine.	**Vielen Dank. Das ist sehr nett von** **Ihnen. Rote Geranien mag ich gern.** **Rote Geranien leuchten!**
Erzähler	They walk on.	**Sie gehen weiter.**
Hilde	I still need some parsley.	**Ich brauche noch Petersilie.**
Erzähler	She buys a little bunch. Now Peter and Hilde are feeling hungry. At the cheese stall, Hilde buys 125 grams of Tilsit cheese.	**Sie kauft ein Bund.** **Jetzt haben Peter und Hilde** **Hunger.** **Am Käsestand kauft Hilde hundert-** **fundfundzwanzig Gramm Tilsiter** **Käse.**

Act 3   Akt 3

	Scene 5 Home again	Szene 5 **Wieder zu Hause**
Erzähler	At home Hilde lays the table. Then she prepares the green salad. Sausage, ham, meat pate she puts on a platter. She puts the pumpernickel on a plate. She opens a bottle of cool Mosel wine.	**Zu Hause deckt Hilde den Tisch.** **Dann macht sie den grünen Salat.** **Wurst, Schinken, Leberkäs legt sie** **auf eine Platte.** **Den Pumpernickel legt sie auf** **einen Teller.** **Sie öffnet eine Flasche kühlen** **Moselwein.**
Hilde	Peter, shall we say - "du" - to one another? "Sie", that's too formal, isn't it?	**Peter, sollen wir "du" zueinander** **sagen? "Sie", das ist zu förmlich,** **nicht wahr?**
Peter	"Du" - I'd like that very much.	**"Du", das möchte ich gern sagen.**
Erzähler	Hilde fills two glasses with wine.	**Hilde gießt den Wein in zwei Gläser.**
Hilde	Would you like to try the wine?	**Möchtest du den Wein probieren?**
Peter	Yes please; cheers.	**Ja bitte; prost.**
Hilde	Cheers.	**Prost.**

Möchtest du den
Wein probieren?

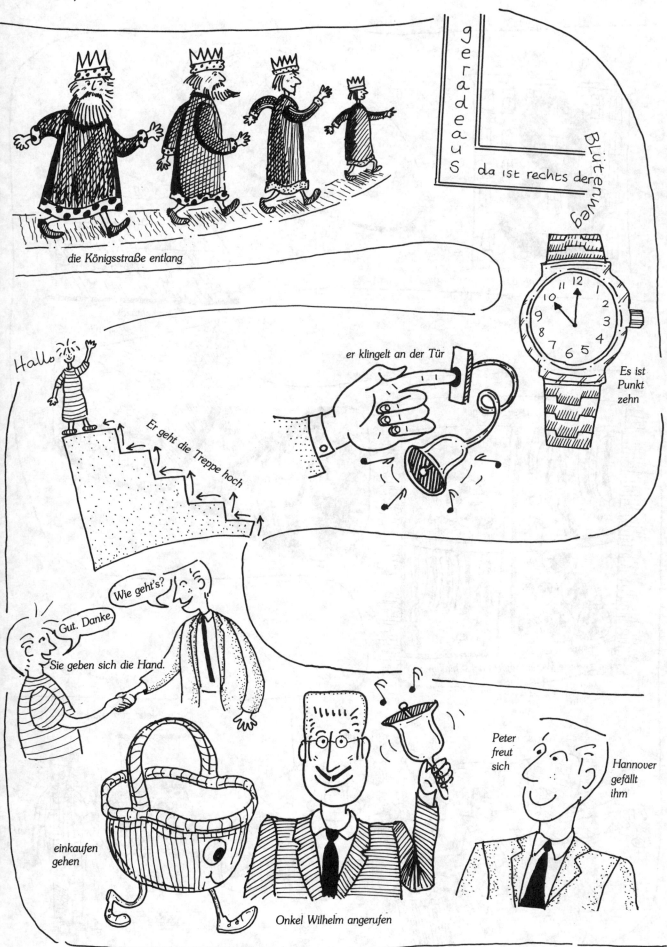

die Königsstraße entlang

geradeaus da ist rechts der Blütenweg

er klingelt an der Tür

Es ist Punkt zehn

Hallo

Er geht die Treppe hoch

Wie geht's?

Gut. Danke.

Sie geben sich die Hand.

einkaufen gehen

Onkel Wilhelm angerufen

Peter freut sich

Hannover gefällt ihm

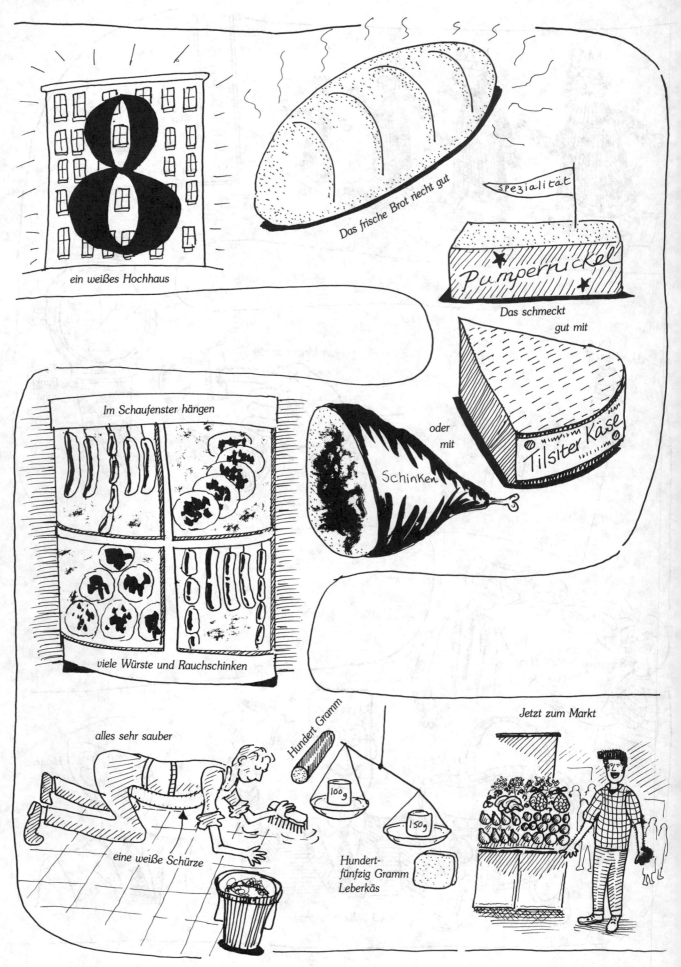

ein weißes Hochhaus

Das frische Brot riecht gut

Spezialität

Pumpernickel

Das schmeckt gut mit

oder mit

Schinken

Tilsiter Käse

Im Schaufenster hängen

viele Würste und Rauchschinken

alles sehr sauber

eine weiße Schürze

Hundert Gramm

100 g

150 g

Hundertfünfzig Gramm Leberkäs

Jetzt zum Markt

Die Sonne scheint

Sie gehen zusammen

Sie hören den Lärm

Unter dem sitzt eine

Schirm Marktfrau

appetitlich

schwarze Kirschen

Birnen

Äpfel

rote Tomaten

Sie verkauft Obst und Gemüse

Blumen

eine rote Geranie

Für den Balkon

37

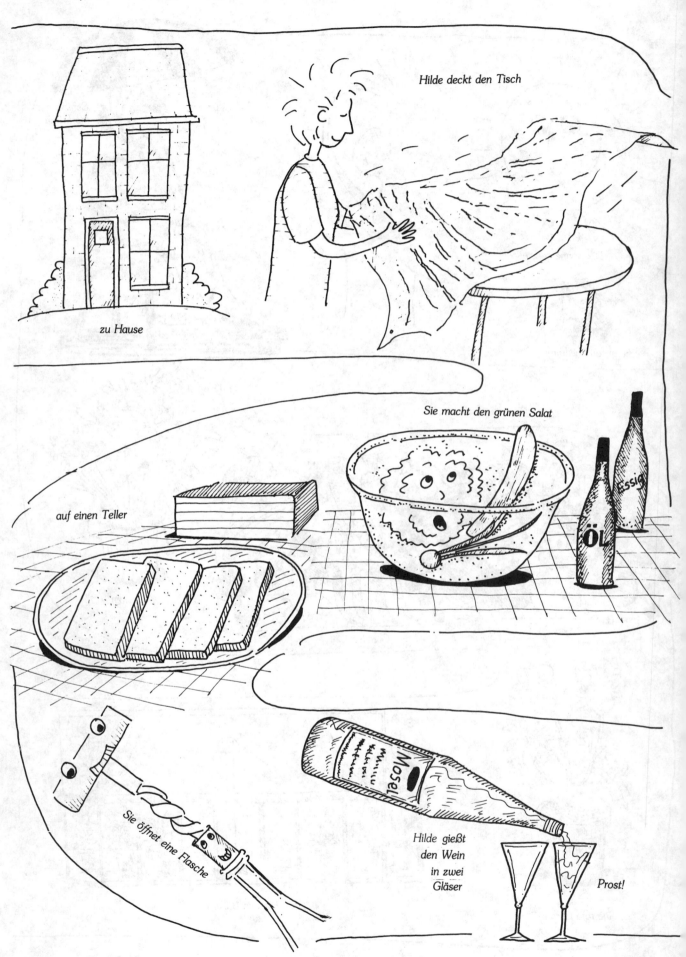

zu Hause

Hilde deckt den Tisch

Sie macht den grünen Salat

ÖL

Essig

auf einen Teller

Sie öffnet eine Flasche

Mosel

Hilde gießt den Wein in zwei Gläser

Prost!

Pronunciation/Intonation — Aussprache/Intonation

We'd like to draw your attention to **three sounds** today: **"w", "v"** and **"z".** First the **"w"** (sound); written as "w" and pronounced like the English letter "v" (vee). This may sound complicated but it is quite easy when you see the letter **written.**
Whenever you see the letter **"w"** in a German word, think of 'velvet'.

---

1. **Now listen and repeat:**
   Wo wollen Sie wohnen? . . . Wir wollen eine schöne Wohnung . . .Wollen Sie Wein aus Wien?
   . . . Auf Wiedersehen! . . .

Now the German **"v".** This is quite easy as it is like the English "f" and the German **"f"** when you **hear** it. When you **see it printed** it is, however, the letter **"v"** and not **"f"** . Think of the English word "fun".

---

2. **Now listen and repeat:**
   Von vier bis fünf . . . Ich habe noch viel Zeit . . . Wir verabreden uns um vier Uhr vor dem Haus
   . . .

Our German **"z"** needs your close attention too. It is **not** a soft sound, as in the English "zero" but like this: **/ts/ts/ts.** Do you hear the little "t" that goes in front of a very sharp "s"?
We produce our **"z"** just behind the teeth with a hard push that makes your stomach muscles work!

---

3. **Now listen and repeat:**
   Haben Sie einen Zwanzigmarkschein? . . . Hier sind zwei Zehnmarkscheine . . . Zwei
   Zahnbürsten sind im Zimmer . . . Meine Zimmernummer ist zweiundzwanzig . . .

Wo wollen Sie wohnen?
Wir wollen eine schöne Wohnung
Wollen Sie Wein aus Wien?
Auf Wiedersehen!

Von vier bis fünf
Ich habe noch viel Zeit
Wir verabreden uns um vier Uhr vor dem Haus

Haben Sie einen Zwanzigmarkschein?
Hier sind zwei Zehnmarkscheine
Zwei Zahnbürsten sind im Zimmer
Meine Zimmernummer ist zweiundzwanzig

	Part 2 Functional Dialogues		Teil 2 Dialoge
1.	On the telephone	**1.**	**Am Telefon**
Erika:	Hello, Irmela, here is Erika.	**Erika**	**Hallo, Irmela, hier ist Erika.**
Irmela:	Hello, how are things?	**Irmela:**	**Hallo, wie geht's?**
Erika:	Fine, thank you. I'm going shopping in a minute.	**Erika:**	**Gut, danke.** **Ich gehe gleich einkaufen.**
Irmela:	So am I. I'm going to the market.	**Irmela:**	**Ich auch. Ich gehe zum Markt.**
Erika:	Oh yes, today is market day. Then I'll go to the market as well.	**Erika:**	**Ach ja, heute ist ja Markttag.** **Dann gehe ich auch zum Markt.**
Irmela:	Shall we meet? Is that possible?	**Irmela:**	**Treffen wir uns?** **Geht das?**
Erika:	Yes, that's possible. Where shall we meet then?	**Erika:**	**Ja, das geht. Wo treffen wir uns denn?**
Irmela:	At the first stall.	**Irmela:**	**Am ersten Marktstand.**
Erika:	When shall we meet?	**Erika:**	**Wann treffen wir uns?**
Irmela:	At 10 o'clock sharp. Is that all right?	**Irmela:**	**Punkt zehn. Geht das?**
Erika:	What's the time now?	**Erika:**	**Wie spät ist es jetzt?**
Irmela:	Nearly ten.	**Irmela:**	**Gleich zehn.**
Erika:	Nearly ten!	**Erika:**	**Gleich zehn!**
Irmela:	Good-bye; see you in a minute then.	**Irmela:**	**Auf Wiedersehen; bis gleich!**

2.	Mrs Meyer and an au pair girl.	**2.**	**Frau Meyer und Au pair Mädchen.**
Mrs Meyer:	I'm going shopping now. Do you want to come with me?	**Fr Meyer:**	**Ich gehe jetzt einkaufen.** **Wollen Sie mitkommen?**
au pair:	Yes, I'd love to. Are we walking?	**Au pair:**	**Ich komme gern mit.** **Gehen wir zu Fuß?**
Mrs Meyer:	Yes. It's not far. We are going to the baker's.	**Fr Meyer:**	**Ja. Es ist nicht weit.** **Wir gehen zur Bäckerei.**
au pair:	I know the baker's. The fresh bread smells good.	**Au pair:**	**Die Bäckerei kenne ich.** **Das frische Brot riecht gut.**
Mrs Meyer:	Then we'll go to the butcher's. I'd like to get some ham.	**Fr Meyer:**	**Dann gehen wir noch zur Metzgerei.** **Ich möchte Schinken.**
au pair:	Oh, the butcher's I know as well. There are a lot of sausages in the window.	**Au pair:**	**Oh, die Metzgerei kenne ich auch.** **Im Schaufenster hängen viele Würste.**

3.	In the dining room	**3.**	**Im Speisesaal**
Guest:	What on earth is that?	**Gast:**	**Was ist denn das?**
Waiter:	That's meat pâté. Don't you like it?	**Ober:**	**Das ist Leberkäs.** **Mögen Sie das nicht?**
Guest:	No, I don't. Have you got ham? I don't like meat pâté.	**Gast:**	**Nein danke. Haben Sie Schinken? Leberkäs mag ich nicht.**
Waiter:	Yes, we've got ham. We also have a lot of sausages. Would you like Salami perhaps?	**Ober:**	**Ja, Schinken haben wir. Wir haben auch viele Würste.** **Mögen Sie vielleicht Salami?**
Guest:	Yes, please. Salami is fine.	**Gast:**	**Ja bitte. Salami schmeckt gut.**

4.	On the market		4.	**Auf dem Markt**

4.   On the market

Anna: Yum, the strawberries smell lovely.
Bernd: Yes, strawberries are my favourite.
             But Anna. The strawberries are not
             fresh.
Anna: Not fresh? What a pity.

5.   At the vegetable stand

Christoph: A long cucumber please.
Doris: Anything else?
Christoph: Yes. A nice lettuce
             please.
Doris: Three Marks please.
Christoph: Here is a twenty Mark note.
Doris: Thanks. And here's a ten Mark note
             and one, two, three, four, five, six,
             seven marks back.

Christoph: Thank you.

6.   At Helga's

Helga: I am hungry; you as well?
Bernd: Yes. When is lunch then?
Helga: Any minute now. The sun is shining.
             We could have lunch on the
             balcony.
Bernd: Terrific. I lay the table.
             What are we having then?
Helga: Tilsit cheese, eggs and salad.
             Would you like some Pumpernickel?
Bernd: Pumpernickel? Yuck, I don't like
             that.
Helga: I've got some rolls as well.
Bernd: Yes, some rolls please.

7.   In the Hotel Bar

Anna: Are you in Cologne for the first time?
Bernd: Yes I am. I don't know it at all yet.
Anna: Tomorrow is market day. Are you
             coming with me?
Bernd: Yes, fine. I have nothing planned
             for tomorrow.

4.   **Auf dem Markt**

Anna: **Mm, die Erdbeeren riechen gut.**
Bernd: **Ja, Erdbeeren esse ich
             besonders gern. Aber Anna. Die
             Erdbeeren sind nicht frisch.**
Anna: **Nicht frisch? Oh! Schade.**

5.   **Am Gemüsestand**

Christoph: **Eine lange Gurke bitte.**
Doris: **Sonst noch etwas?**
Christoph: **Ja. Einen frischen Kopfsalat
             bitte.**
Doris: **Drei Mark bitte.**
Christoph: **Hier ist ein Zwanzigmarkschein.**
Doris: **Danke. Und hier sind ein
             Zehnmarkschein und eins, zwei
             drei, vier, fünf, sechs, sieben
             Mark zurück.**

Christoph: **Danke.**

6.   **Bei Helga**

Helga: **Ich habe Hunger. Du auch?**
Bernd: **Ja. Wann essen wir denn?**
Helga: **Gleich. Die Sonne scheint.
             Wir können auf dem Balkon
             essen.**
Bernd: **Prima. Ich decke den Tisch.
             Was gibt's denn?**
Helga: **Tilsiter Käse, Eier und Salat.
             Möchtest du Pumpernickel?**
Bernd: **Pumpernickel? Uch, das mag
             ich nicht.**
Helga: **Ich habe auch Brötchen.**
Bernd: **Ja, Brötchen bitte.**

7.   **An der Hotelbar**

Anna: **Sind Sie zum ersten Mal in Köln?**
Bernd: **Ja; ich kenne Köln noch nicht.**
Anna: **Morgen ist Markttag. Kommen
             Sie mit?**
Bernd: **Ja gern. Morgen habe ich nichts
             vor.**

Part three: Personalised Dialogues
Teil drei: Dialoge

Dialog 1:
You have concluded your business in Germany and have some spare time before flying home again. Your business contact asks you:

B.c.:	**Kennen Sie Hannover?**
You:	Say: No, I am here for the first time.
B.c.:	**Wie gefällt es Ihnen hier?**
You:	Say: Terrific!
B.c.:	**Möchten Sie Hannover sehen?**
You:	Say: Yes please. I have nothing planned this morning.
B.c.:	**Können wir gleich gehen?**
You:	Say: Yes, that is all right.

Dialog 2:
You have an invitation to lunch. Your host asks you:

Host:	**Heute gibt es eine Spezialität! Mögen Sie das?**
You ask:	What is that?
Host;	**Die Spezialität heißt Leberkäs.**
You say:	I would like to try it.
Host:	**Mögen Sie Obst?**
You say:	Yes, strawberries are my favourite.

Dialog 3:
You want to buy a pot plant for your host but cannot see what you want in the shop. The assistant asks you:

Assist:	**Was darf es sein?**
You ask:	Have you any Geraniums?
Assist:	**Ja. Weiße Geranien habe ich.**
You:	I would like red Geraniums.
Assist:	**Rote Geranien. Nein, leider nicht.**
You:	That's a pity. Good-bye then.

Dialog 4:
You want to buy some vegetables. The assistant asks you:

Assist:	**Bitte schön?**
You say:	One kilo of tomatoes please.
Assist:	**Sonst noch etwas?**
You say:	One lettuce and a cucumber please.
Assist:	**Sonst noch etwas?**
You say:	No, thank you.
Assist:	**Vier Mark zwanzig bitte.**
You:	Here is a ten mark note.
	(How much change do you expect?)

Dialog 5:
You are walking in the street, when a passer-by comes up to you and asks for help.

Lady:	**Entschuldigen Sie bitte, wo ist der Markt?**
You:	I am sorry, I don't live here. Do you speak English?
Lady:	**Leider nicht, ich bin auch zu Besuch hier, aber ich möchte Blumen kaufen.**
You:	Please speak slowly. What do you want to know?
Lady:	**Wo ist der Markt bitte?**

You have now understood what she wants and say:

	100 metres straight ahead.
Lady:	**Vielen Dank.**
You:	Don't mention it.

(The answers are at the back of the book.)

Teil vier: Übungen

Übung 1: Can you fill in the missing word? One dash for each letter.

1.   **Wir —————— jetzt zur Bäckerei.**
2.   **Das frische Brot —————— gut.**
3.   **Pumpernickel —————————— mit Tilsiter Käse.**
4.   **Die Metzgerei ——— gegenüber.**
5.   **Im Schaufenster —————— viele Würste.**

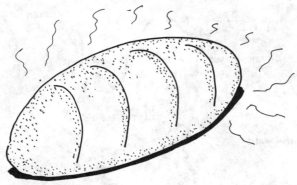

Das frische Brot

Übung 2: Can you find a suitable conclusion to each sentence?

1.	**Sie öffnet eine Flasche**	a.	**frischen, grünen Kopfsalat**
2.	**Rote Geranien**	b.	**ist eine Spezialität**
3.	**Pumpernickel**	c.	**nicht weit**
4.	**Wir nehmen zwei Kilo**	d.	**angerufen**
5.	**Sie kauft einen**	e.	**auf die Uhr**
6.	**Der Markt ist**	f.	**eine weiße Schürze**
7.	**Onkel Wilhelm hat**	g.	**einen Zwanzigmarkschein**
8.	**Peter sieht**	h.	**kühlen Moselwein**
9.	**Der Metzger trägt**	i.	**leuchten**
10.	**Sie gibt ihm**	j.	**Äpfel**

Hilde gießt den
Wein in zwei Gläser

Prost!

Teil fünf: Spiele, Rätsel und Reime

Here are the eleven areas, where wine is grown in Germany. Look on the shelves of your supermarket for German wines and try to read the labels. Now you can see where the wines come from.

On your map you find some letters underlined. Put them together, raise your glass and say - - - - - !

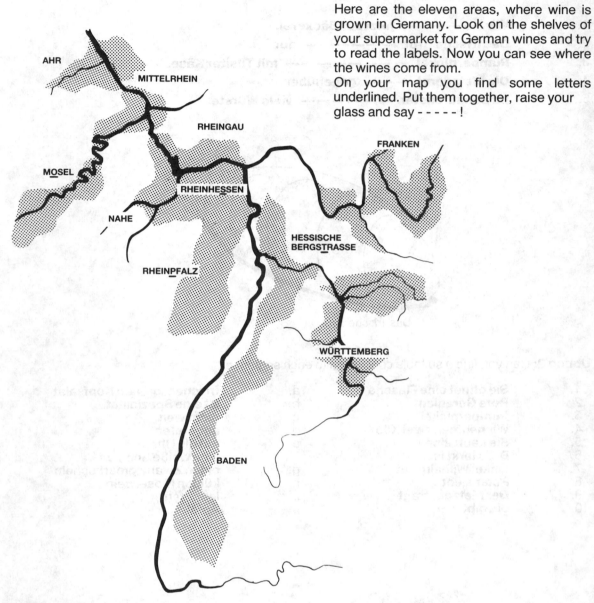

AHR

MITTELRHEIN

RHEINGAU

FRANKEN

MOSEL

RHEINHESSEN

NAHE

HESSISCHE BERGSTRASSE

RHEINPFALZ

WÜRTTEMBERG

BADEN

Guests are coming.

You need a dice and a button for this **„Würfelspiel"**. After each throw, say aloud the number shown on the dice.

The board below represents your dining table.

There are six place settings shown in grey. You must land on each setting in order to fulfil all the tasks.

(6) Go to the delicatessen counter of the butcher's shop and buy three items for your planned luncheon party. Name each item.

(12) You need some salad. Name three kinds of salad vegetables.

(18) It's summer. Choose some fruit.

(24) Now you start to lay the table. Say: six plates and six glasses.

(30) Arrange the cheese and the meat on a platter. Say what you are doing.

(36) Say what you plan to give your guests to go with the meal. When we wish each other an enjoyable meal, we say: **Guten Appetit!**

20	21	22	23	24	25	26	27	28	29	30	31	32	33	34	35	36	37	38
19	18	17	16	15	14	13	12	11	10	9	8	7	6	5	4	3	2	1

The Heavenly Games

Please look out the separate sheet marked Heavenly Game (Akt 3). Cut it up into individual cards. You can now play various games with these cards.

Game 1.

In this first game you are just trying to match up cards by colour, i.e. blue words or phrases with other cards containing blue words or phrases. Red words should be paired with red, green with green.

You will find that you are automatically matching up nouns and adjectives, i.e. objects and the words that describe them.

But you will be doing more than this. In English we only have one word for "the", i.e. we say the man, or the woman, or the child. In German there are three words for "the". So we can say **der Mann, die Frau** or **das Kind.**

The word cards are colour coded so that **der** words are printed in red, **die** words are printed in green and **das** words are printed in blue.

By matching up the cards you also automatically match up the correct "gender", i.e. **der, die** or **das.**

By the way, when a word is in the plural, i.e. there is more than one thing, you always say **die.** So it is **der Mann,** but **die Männer, der Balkon,** but **die Balkone.**

So play Game 1 by spreading the Heavenly Game cards face up on the table and matching the red words together so they make a sensible phrase or sentence. Then pair up the green words and lastly pair up the blue words.

Game 2.

In the first game you ignored the Heavenly Symbols in the top left corner of the cards. Now you must look for them.

You will find:

The sun =**die Sonne**

The moon = **der Mond**

The star =**der Stern**

For the new game you should put all the cards face up on the table.

Now pair up cards by colour and Heavenly symbol. Read aloud the introduction words (printed in black) and then the describing words (adjectives) and nouns.

Take a piece of paper and write out the whole phrase you have made. Read it out loud and check from the text of Akt 3 if you have constructed the sentences correctly.

What will matching the Heavenly Symbols (**Sonne, Mond** and **Stern**) teach you? You will indirectly learn that certain words, like **auf, zu** and **neben** have an effect on the way the following words in the sentences are spoken or written. DON'T make any particular attempt to learn these effects just now — all will become clearer as we progress!!

Picture the Ballerina

A sentence is made up of words, or groups or words that are designed
to impart information. A simple sentence will usually have:

the main idea or subject   — i.e. noun
plus an action word   — i.e. verb
plus a descriptive word(s)   — i.e. adjective

In German the word order in a sentence follows a very specific rule.

If you think of a sentence as a line of dancers, then you can think of the verb - the word that describes the
action - as a ballerina on a star and our ballerina's star is ALWAYS second in the line.

Sie gießt den Wein in zwei Gläser.

Am Gemüsestand kauft Hilde einen frischen Kopfsalat.

Wurst, Schinken, Leberkäs und Tilsiter Käse legt sie auf einen Teller.

Did you notice that in front of the action word there can be one, two or even several words?
However many, they always convey one idea only, e.g.:—

Sie gießt den Wein in zwei Gläser.

Am Gemüsestand kauft Hilde einen frischen Kopfsalat.

Wurst, Schinken, Leberkäs und Tilsiter Käse legt sie auf einen Teller.

See how steady the action word invariably remains in its place, while the other words "dance" around it.

In the excerpts below, taken from Scenes 4 and 5, you see the first idea in a sentence is shaded in grey,
and the action word is marked by the ballerina's star. Compare the English, sentence by sentence with
the German, and read aloud in English how the English would be constructed if it were a German one.
The position of the main subject can vary. It is reversed out - white on black.

Hilde buys a fresh, green head of lettuce and a

cucumber at the vegetable stand.

At the next stand there are pot plants.

Now Peter and Hilde are feeling hungry.

At home she lays the table.

Then she prepares the green salad.

Sausage, ham, meat pate and Tilsit cheese she

puts on a platter.

The Pumpernickel she lays on to a plate.

Am Gemüsestand kauft Hilde einen

frischen, grünen Kopfsalat und eine Gurke.

Am nächsten Stand gibt es Topfpflanzen.

Jetzt haben Peter und Hilde Hunger.

Zu Hause deckt sie den Tisch.

Dann macht sie den grünen Salat.

Wurst, Schinken, Leberkäs und Tilsiter

Käse legt sie auf eine Platte.

Den Pumpernickel legt sie auf einen Teller.

Akt 4

	Scene 1	**Szene 1**
	Peter has to make a phone call	**Peter muß telefonieren**

Peter

That was excellent! I was really hungry. I must say, you are a good hostess.

Das hat prima geschmeckt! Ich war richtig hungrig. Du bist wirklich eine gute Gastgeberin.

Hilde

And I'm also a good cook! I have learnt it from my mother. In Germany, food is important as well.

Ja, ich kann auch gut kochen! Ich habe es von meiner Mutter gelernt. Auch in Deutschland ist das Essen wichtig.

Erzähler

Now Peter wants to make a phone call to England. He has to ring home to say that he is staying for another couple of days in Germany.

Jetzt will Peter nach England telefonieren. Er muß nach Hause anrufen und sagen, daß er noch ein paar Tage in Deutschland bleibt.

Peter

Can I dial direct?

Kann ich direkt durchwählen?

Hilde

Yes, first dial 0044 for England, then the area code for the town, then the private number.

Ja, wähle zuerst 0044 für England, dann die Vorwahlnummer für die Stadt, dann die Privatnummer.

Peter

I have to change some money and I would also like to buy a jacket and a shirt. This jacket is actually a winter jacket and now much too warm.

Zuerst muß ich Geld wechseln, und ich möchte auch eine Jacke und ein Hemd kaufen. Diese Jacke ist eigentlich eine Winterjacke und jetzt viel zu warm.

Erz

Peter telephones and speaks to his mother.

Peter telefoniert und spricht mit seiner Mutter.

Kann ich direkt
durchwählen?

Akt 4

<table>
<tr><td></td><td>Scene 2</td><td>**Szene 2**</td></tr>
<tr><td></td><td>In the Bank</td><td>**In der Bank**</td></tr>
</table>

Hilde	Let's go together, Peter. I know where the nearest bank is.	**Laß uns zusammen gehen Peter. Ich weiß, wo die nächste Bank ist.**
Erzähler	They walk along King's Street and then enter the Volksbank, a big, modern building. Peter asks where the foreign business counter is. There he has to wait. In front of him stands an old gentleman with blue traveller's cheques in his hands. He hands the cheques to the lady behind the counter.	**Sie gehen die Königsstraße entlang und dann in die Volksbank, ein großes, modernes Gebäude. Peter fragt, wo der Sortenschalter ist. Dort muß er warten. Vor ihm steht ein alter Herr mit blauen Reiseschecks in der Hand. Er gibt die Schecks der Dame am Schalter.**
Alter Herr	I would like to change these traveller's cheques. What is today's rate of exchange?	**Ich möchte diese Reiseschecks einlösen. Wie steht heute der Kurs?**
Bank-beamtin	One moment please; today it's 3 Marks and 71 Pfennigs. First you'll have to sign the cheques please.	**Einen Moment bitte; heute drei Mark und einundsiebzig Pfennig. Sie müssen die Schecks zuerst unterschreiben bitte.**
Alter Herr	All right. Could you change 200 pounds please?	**Gut. Bitte wechseln Sie zweihundert Pfund.**
Erzähler	Peter has no traveller's cheques. He has only £40 in cash. He changes his pound notes and receives 148 Marks and a 50 Pfennig piece. Peter and Hilde leave the bank. The sky is blue and the sun is shining.	**Peter hat keine Reiseschecks. Er hat nur vierzig Pfund in Bargeld. Er wechselt seine Pfundscheine und bekommt hundertachtundvierzig D-Mark und ein Fünfzigpfennigstück. Peter und Hilde verlassen die Bank. Der Himmel ist blau und die Sonne scheint.**

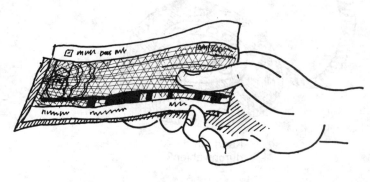

Ich möchte diese
Reiseschecks
einlösen

Akt 4

	Scene 3 Peter buys Shirts	Szene 3 Peter kauft Hemden
Hilde	At the corner there is a men's wear shop. Shall we go in?	An der Ecke ist ein Geschäft für Herrenbekleidung. Laß uns hingehen.
Erzähler	They go across the street and enter the shop. A short, fat gentleman between 40 and 50 comes towards them. He greets them. He has a rosy bald head and is very elegantly dressed.	Sie gehen über die Straße und betreten das Geschäft. Ein kleiner, dicker Herr zwischen vierzig und fünfzig kommt ihnen entgegen. Er begrüßt sie. Er hat eine rosige Glatze und ist sehr elegant gekleidet.
Peter	Can I pay by credit card?	Kann ich mit meiner Kreditkarte bezahlen?
Verkäufer	Yes, that will be fine. How can I help you?	Ja, das geht. Was darf es sein?
Peter	I would like two shirts. One, which I can wear with a tie and a more casual one. Can you show me some?	Ich hätte gern zwei Hemden. Eins, das ich mit Schlips tragen kann und ein Freizeithemd. Können Sie mir ein paar Hemden zeigen?
Verkäufer	Yes, certainly. What colour would you like?	Ja gern. Welche Farbe möchten Sie?
Peter	A blue one please.	Blau, bitte.
Verkäufer	What size are you?	Welche Größe haben Sie?
Peter	I think it is 41.	Einundvierzig, glaube ich.
Verkäufer	I'm sure we have something suitable in your size.	Wir haben bestimmt etwas Passendes in Ihrer Größe.
Peter	I'd like the casual shirt in white please. By the way, I have long arms. Often the sleeves are not long enough. Have you got shirts with extra long sleeves?	Das Freizeithemd in weiß bitte. Übrigens habe ich lange Arme. Oft sind die Ärmel nicht lang genug. Haben Sie Hemden mit extra langen Ärmeln?
Erzähler	The salesman brings three blue shirts and a white casual shirt. Peter looks at the shirts.	Der Verkäufer bringt drei blaue Hemden und ein weißes Freizeithemd. Peter sieht sich die Hemden an.
Peter	I like the light blue one. Ugh, the dark blue one I don't like! I'll take the first shirt please. And the white one as well. That will do fine.	Das hellblaue gefällt mir. Uch, das dunkelblaue gefällt mir nicht! Geben Sie mir bitte das erste Hemd. Das weiße nehme ich auch. Das ist genau das richtige.
Hilde	Peter, this tie would go well with your new shirt. Take it as a present from me.	Peter, dieser Schlips paßt zu dem neuen Hemd. Den möchte ich dir schenken.
Erzähler	Peter is surprised. He is pleased.	Peter ist überrascht. Er freut sich.
Peter	Many thanks! That is really nice of you.	Vielen Dank! Das ist wirklich nett von dir.

mit Schlips

Den möchte ich dir schenken

Akt 4

	Scene 4	Szene 4
Erzähler	Peter buys a jacket	**Peter kauft eine Jacke**
Hilde	Hilde shows him a very	**Hilde zeigt ihm eine sehr**
Peter	smart jacket.	**schicke Jacke.**
	What do you think of that?	**Was hälst du davon?**
Verkäufer	That really looks nice.	**Die sieht wirklich gut aus.**
Peter	Have you got it in my size?	**Haben Sie die in meiner Größe?**
Verkäufer	Yes, certainly sir.	**Ja natürlich.**
	How about this one?	**Probieren Sie die hier doch mal.**
	The jacket is warm and light.	**Die Jacke ist warm und leicht.**
	You can wear it in the autumn	**Die können Sie im Herbst und**
	and in the spring.	**im Frühling tragen.**
	But even in summer there are	**Aber auch jetzt im Sommer gibt**
	cool days.	**es kühle Tage.**
	It's a practical and	**Das ist eine praktische und**
	smart jacket.	**schicke Jacke.**
Peter	What do you think Hilde?	**Was denkst du Hilde?**
	Shall I buy it?	**Soll ich sie kaufen?**
Hilde	It suits you well. Go on, take it!	**Sie steht dir gut. Nimm sie doch!**
Peter	All right then.	**Na gut.**
	How much does that cost altogether?	**Was kostet das alles zusammen?**
Verkäufer	The shirts cost 30 and 40 marks.	**Die Hemden kosten dreißig und vierzig Mark.**
	The jacket is only 99	**Die Jacke kostet nur neunundneunzig**
	marks 50.	**Mark fünfzig.**
	That will be 169	**Zusammen also hundertneunundsechzig**
	marks 50 pfennigs altogether.	**Mark fünfzig.**
	The lady is paying for the tie,	**Die Dame bezahlt den Schlips,**
	isn't she?	**nicht wahr?**
	Do you need anything else?	**Brauchen Sie sonst noch etwas?**
	Socks perhaps or underwear?	**Socken vielleicht oder Unterwäsche?**
	We also sell shoes, coats and	**Wir haben auch Schuhe, Mäntel**
	trousers.	**und Hosen.**
Peter	No thank you.	**Nein danke.**
	Unfortunately, I haven't that	**Soviel Geld habe ich leider**
	much money.	**nicht.**
Erzähler	Peter and Hilde pay and	**Peter und Hilde bezahlen und**
	leave the shop.	**verlassen das Geschäft.**
Peter	I have an idea.	**Darf ich etwas vorschlagen?**
	Let's have a cup of coffee and	**Laß uns eine Tasse Kaffee**
	discuss what we could do this	**trinken und sehen, was wir heute**
	evening.	**abend machen wollen.**
Hilde	That's a great idea!	**Das ist eine prima Idee!**

soviel Geld habe
ich leider nicht

Akt 4, 1

von meiner Mutter gelernt

noch ein paar
Tage bleibt

nach England telefonieren

MONTAG

DIENSTAG

MITTWOCH

wähle
zuerst
0044

nach Hause anrufen

Ich
muß
Geld
wechseln

Winterjacke
zu warm

VOLKSBANK

SORTENSCHALTER

modernes Gebäude

Vor ihm steht

ein alter Herr

Ich möchte diese Reiseschecks einlösen

BANK OF ENGLAND
ONE HUNDRED POUNDS
£100

Wie steht heute der Kurs?

zuerst unterschreiben bitte

Peter und Hilde verlassen die Bank

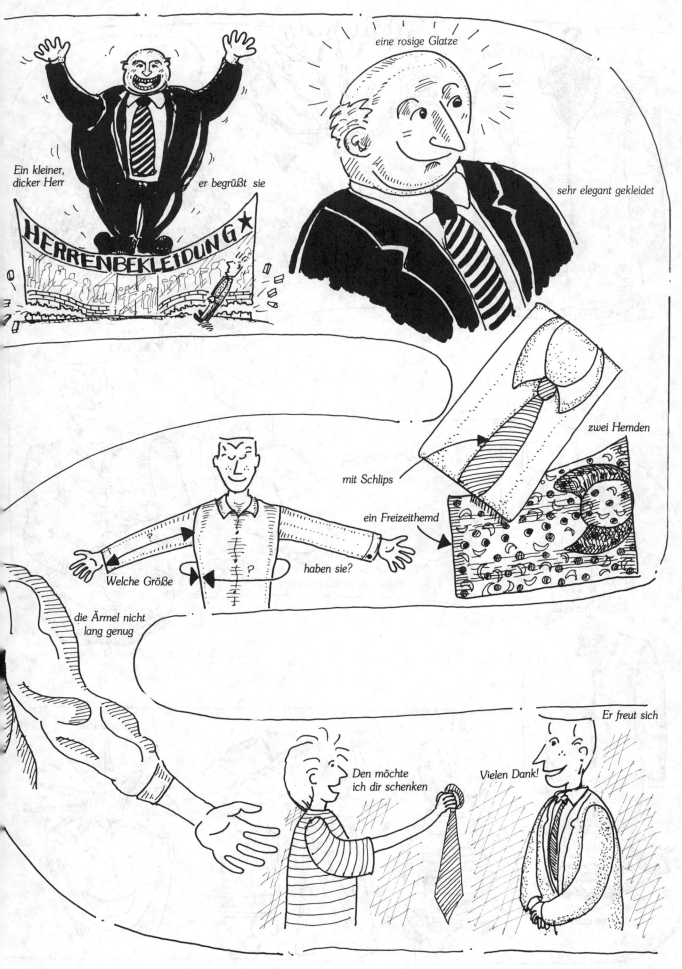

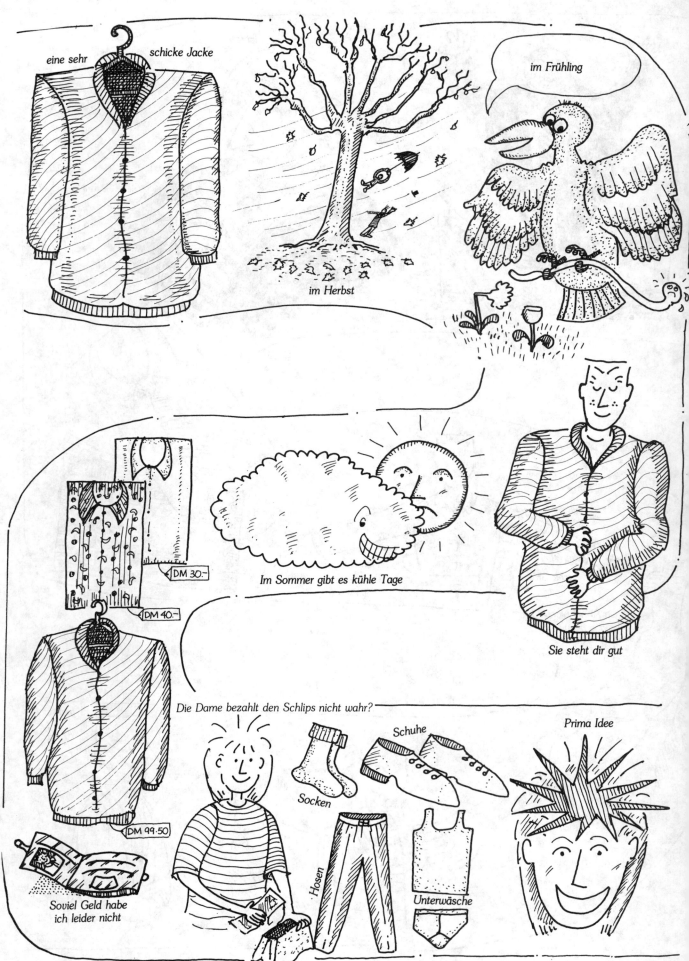

eine sehr schicke Jacke

im Herbst

im Frühling

Im Sommer gibt es kühle Tage

Sie steht dir gut

Die Dame bezahlt den Schlips nicht wahr?

DM 30.-

DM 40.-

DM 99.50

Socken

Schuhe

Hosen

Unterwäsche

Prima Idee

Soviel Geld habe ich leider nicht

Akt 4

Aussprache/Intonation

The German sounds we'll practice today are various **'s'**-- sounds.
First the soft **'s'** /z/. This is like the English **'z'** /zed/ as in **'zoo'** or **'zebra'**.

Listen and imitate the native speaker:

> **Sonne -- Sommer -- saubere -- Socken --**
>
> **Gemüse und Salate sind jetzt sehr billig. --**
>
> **Lösen Sie den Reisescheck hier ein! --**

There are, however, far more German words where no buzzing sounds occur. If you want to check any difference in spelling you can read these up in your book later. It's easier to listen and repeat them first!

> **Wissen Sie was? -- Ich muß etwas essen. -- Ist das alles? --**
>
> **Ich weiß, daß mir Größe achtunddreißig nicht paßt. --**
>
> **Sie müssen mehr Obst essen. -- Im Herbst ist das Obst besonders billig. --**

Notice that the hard **'s'**-- sound which you have just heard on the tape may have to be spelt differently: with a simple **'s'** or **'ss'** or with a letter unknown in English. It looks like this: **'ß'** and is called, 'sharp s' or **'eszet'**.
The following rules may help you to remember how to spell this sound:

> 1. write **'ss'** only if it appears between two vowels and if the first of these vowels is short, e.g. **wissen, müssen, essen, Adresse, Schlüssel.**
>
> 2. always write **'ß'** if it appears
>   a)   at the end of a word instead of an **'ss'**, e.g. **ich weiß, ich muß, groß, Erdgeschoß**
>
>   b)   between two vowels and if the first of these vowels is long, e.g. **Größe, dreißig**
>
>   c)   before a consonant, e.g. **du mußt, ihr wißt, es paßt**

> Another easy German sound for you is the **'shooshing'** sound. Try it:
>
> **Kirschen schmecken gut.**
>
> **Der Schlips ist hübsch.**
>
> **Wo ist der Speisesaal? -- Im ersten Stock bitte!**
>
> **Gibt es eine Spezialität in dieser Stadt? -- Nur Fisch, aber immer frisch!**

Words beginning with **'sp'** or **'st'** are pronounced with the 'shooshing' sound, e.g. **Spezialität, sprechen; Stadt, Straße**. Whenever **'sp'** and **'st'** appear in the middle or at the end of a word, however, they are pronounced as in English, e.g. **Kaspar, Wespe; Gast, Fenster**.

Watch out for German words with 'shooshing' sounds, especially for those that are spelt with **'sch'**. Try to say the following tongue twister:

> **Fischers Fritz fischt frische Fische,**
>
> **frische Fische fischt Fischers Fritz.**

Teil zwei: Dialoge

	Dialogue 1	**Dialog 1**
	Two friends on holiday	**Zwei Freunde im Urlaub**
Gabi	I have to go to the bank	**Ich muß zur Bank gehen**
	and change money.	**und Geld wechseln.**
Heike	Let's go together.	**Laß uns zusammen gehen.**
	I need money as well.	**Ich brauche auch Geld.**
	What's the exchange rate today?	**Wie steht der Kurs heute?**
Gabi	Not so favourable, but I haven't	**Nicht so günstig, aber ich habe kein**
	any more cash.	**Bargeld mehr.**
	Only traveller's cheques.	**Nur noch Reiseschecks.**
	In the restaurant opposite I've	**Im Restaurant gegenüber habe**
	paid with my credit card.	**ich mit meiner Kreditkarte bezahlt.**
Heike	That's possible?	**Ach das geht?**
	What is the food like there?	**Wie ist denn das Essen da?**
Gabi	I found it very good.	**Mir hat es sehr gut geschmeckt.**
	The chef knows how to cook well.	**Der Chef kann prima kochen.**

	Dialogue 2	**Dialog 2**
	At a party	**Auf einer Party**
Herr	Here is the wine.	**Hier ist der Wein.**
	Would you like some?	**Darf ich Ihnen ein Glas geben?**
Heike	Yes please.	**Ja, bitte.**
Herr	Here comes our hostess.	**Hier kommt unsere Gastgeberin,**
	Good afternoon, Mrs Becker.	**guten Tag, Frau Becker.**
Frau Becker	I'm glad to see you.	**Nett, daß Sie da sind.**
	It is very warm today,	**Es ist heute sehr warm,**
	don't you think so?	**nicht wahr?**
Heike	Yes very warm indeed.	**Ja, sehr warm, aber ich habe warmes**
	I don't mind warm weather.	**Wetter gern.**
Frau Becker	You are wearing a jacket and tie.	**Sie tragen Jacken und Schlipse.**
	You may take your jacket off,	**Sie dürfen die Jacken ausziehen,**
	if you want to.	**wenn Sie wollen.**
	It is really hot today.	**Heute ist es wirklich heiß.**

Es ist heute sehr
warm

	Dialogue 3	**Dialog 3**
	In the men's outfitter's	**Im Geschäft für Herrenbekleidung**

Verkäuferin	Good afternoon, what can I do for you?	**Guten Tag; was darf es sein?**
Herr	I'd like a pair of socks. Cotton please.	**Ich hätte gern ein Paar Socken. Aus Baumwolle bitte.**
Verkäuferin	What size do you take?	**Welche Größe brauchen Sie?**
Herr	I take shoe size 9-9½.	**Ich trage Schuhgröße 43.**
Verkäuferin	These here are all 70% cotton and 30% nylon. We don't have any in pure cotton. They are not very practical either. I am sorry.	**Die hier haben alle 70% Baumwolle und 30% Nylon. Reine Baumwolle haben wir nicht. Das ist auch gar nicht sehr praktisch. Tut mir leid.**
Herr	Yes, that's a pity! Good-bye.	**Ja, schade! Auf Wiedersehen.**
Verkäuferin	Good-bye, sir.	**Wiedersehen.**

Socken

	Dialogue 4	**Dialog 4**
	At the bank	**In der Bank**

Dame	Would you please change this 500 mark note into Swiss franks for me?	**Wechseln Sie mir bitte diesen Fünfhundertmarkschein in Schweizer Franken.**
Bankbeamter	Please go to the foreign exchange counter.	**Gehen Sie bitte zum Sortenschalter.**
Dame	Thank you.	**Vielen Dank.**

	Dialogue 5	**Dialog 5**
	At the foreign exchange counter	**Am Sortenschalter**

Dame	I'd like Swiss franks, for 500 marks please.	**Ich möchte Schweizer Franken für 500 Mark bitte.**
Bankbeamter	Certainly. Here is your money and your receipt.	**Ja bitte. Hier ist das Geld und hier die Abrechnung.**
Dame	Could you also give me Austrian shillings for 1000 marks please.	**Geben Sie mir bitte auch österreichische Schilling für tausend Mark.**
Bankbeamter	Cash or traveller's cheques?	**In bar oder in Reiseschecks?**
Dame	Cash please.	**Bargeld bitte.**

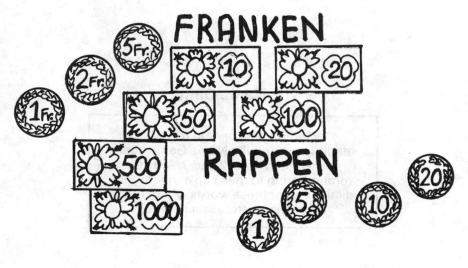

	Dialogue 6 In the department store	**Dialog 6** **Im Kaufhaus**
Dame	How much is this tie please?	**Was kostet dieser Schlips bitte?**
Verkäuferin	10 marks fifty.	**Zehn Mark fünfzig.**
Dame	Here are 20 marks.	**Hier sind 20 Mark, bitte schön.**
Verkäuferin	Thank you; and here are 9 marks 50 back.	**Danke; und hier sind neun Mark fünfzig zurück.**
Dame	Oh sorry, I need some small change. Could you please give me the 50 pfennigs in ten pfennig pieces? Is that possible?	**Oh Entschuldigung, ich brauche Kleingeld. Bitte geben Sie mir die 50 Pfennig in Zehnpfennigstücken. Geht das?**
Verkäuferin	Yes, that's possible. Here you are: 1, 2, 3, 4, 5.	**Ja, das geht. Hier sind eins, zwei, drei, vier, fünf.**
Dame	Thank you.	**Ich danke Ihnen.**
Verkäuferin	You're welcome.	**Bitte schön.**

ich brauche
Kleingeld

The Name Game

You would now benefit a lot from reading through the Name Game again — including Parts 2 and 3. Are you remembering to make up a mnemonic dictionary for these words where there are no linguistic associations?

Teil 3: Dialoge

Dialog 1   In the Federal Republic of Germany public telephones take 10 Pfennig, 50 Pfennig, 1 Mark and 5 Mark coins. Your friend has a 5 Mark coin and wants to change it to make a local call.

Dame	**Entschuldigen Sie bitte. Können Sie ein Fünfmarkstück wechseln?**
You	Just a moment. Yes, that is possible.
	Here are 1, 2, 3, 4, 5 mark pieces.
Dame	**Danke. Ich möchte nur kurz telefonieren. Haben Sie zwei Zehnpfennigstücke?**
You	Oh, you need small change? Just a moment please. Yes, I have five ten pfennig pieces and one fifty pfennig piece.
Dame	**Wunderbar! Hier ist eine Mark. Vielen Dank.**

Dialog 2   The same situation as above but now it is you who wants to change five marks in order to make a phone call.

You	Excuse me please. Can you change a five mark piece?
Passant	**Einen Moment. Ja, das geht. Hier sind ein, zwei, drei, vier, fünf Markstücke.**
You	Thank you. I want to make a telephone call. Do you have two ten pfennig pieces?
Passant	**Ach so, Sie brauchen Kleingeld? Augenblick. Lassen Sie mich mal sehen.** (looks in her purse) **Ja, ich habe zehn, zwanzig, dreißig, vierzig, fünfzig, sechzig, siebzig, achtzig, neunzig, hundert Pfennig in Zehnpfennigstücken!**
You	Great! Here is one Mark. Many thanks.

Dialog 3   You are in your hotel room. You are speaking to the receptionist.

You	I'd like to make a telephone call to Berlin.
Rezeption	**Sie können direkt durchwählen.**
You	Do you know the code number for Berlin?
Rezeption	**Wählen Sie 030, das ist die Vorwahlnummer für Berlin.**
You	Many thanks.

Dialog 4   You want to change traveller's cheques in the bank.

You	I want to change traveller's cheques.
Bank clerk	**Wieviel möchten Sie?**
You	For 200 pounds please.
Bank clerk	**Bitte unterschreiben Sie.**
You	Here you are. Where do I get the money?
Bank clerk	**Hier rechts bitte.**

Dialog 5 You have been swimming with your friend; coming out of the water you realise that somebody has stolen your friend's clothes! He doesn't speak any German. Take him to a man's outfitter's and buy him what he needs. (You see him in the picture.)

Verkäuferin	**Was darf es sein?**
You	This gentleman needs trousers. Have you also got shirts, jackets and shoes?
Verkäuferin	**Ja natürlich. Braucht der Herr auch Unterwäsche? Unterhemden und Unterhosen haben wir auch. Hier bitte schön.** (Shows them some underwear)
You	All right. One vest and one pair of underpants, please.
Verkäuferin	**Und jetzt das Hemd. Hier sind unsere Hemden. Welche Größe hat der Herr?**
You	Size 40. He wants a casual shirt, a white one please.
Verkäuferin	**Hier bitte schön.** (Shows them the casual shirts)
You	This one. How much is it please?
Verkäuferin	**Es kostet fünfundzwanzig Mark. Hosen und Jacken bekommen Sie dahinten und Schuhe auch.**
You	Thank you very much.

(The correct answers are at the back of the book.)

Dieser Herr braucht
Hosen

Teil vier: Übungen

Geldstücke und Geldscheine

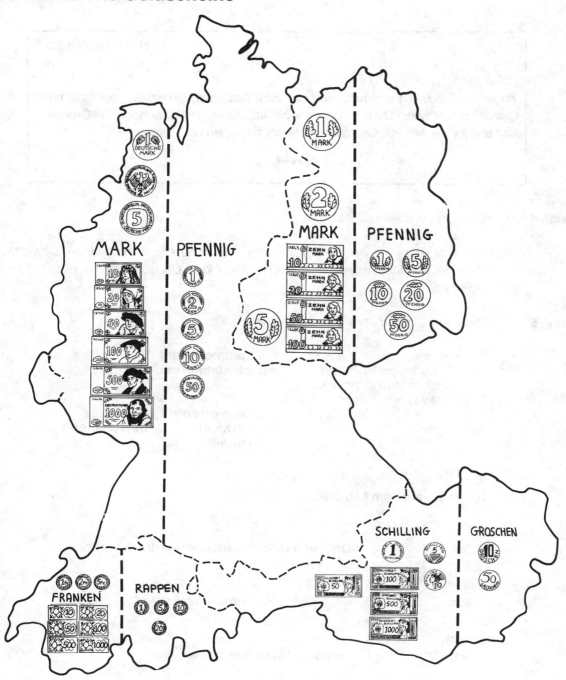

Übung 1 Wie heißen die Geldstücke und die Geldscheine:
a) In der Bundesrepublik Deutschland?
b) In der Deutschen Demokratischen Republik?
c) In der Schweiz?
d) In Österreich?

Übung 2 **Richtig** (right) **oder falsch** (wrong)?
a) In der DDR gibt es Fünfhundertmarkscheine.
b) In der BRD gibt es Zehnmarkstücke.
c) In der Schweiz gibt es Fünfrappenstücke.
d) In Österreich gibt es Zwanziggroschenstücke.
e) In der BRD gibt es Zehnpfennigstücke.
f) In der Schweiz gibt es Fünffrankenscheine.

Say aloud whatever is correct according to the illustration

Übung 3   You are in Hannover but have planned a visit to Austria. Your German friend has dropped a letter into you letter box. As you open it, some coins fall out and you read:

Hannover, den 3.Juli

Lieber Peter!
Ich war in Österreich und habe noch ein paar Groschen. Sie wollen doch bald nach Österreich,nicht wahr? Die Bank nimmt keine Geldstücke, nur Geldscheine. Die Groschen sind also für Sie. Nur 200 Groschen. Nicht viel, nur für ein Glas Wein.

Fritz

Übung 4   Write a short answer to Fritz:

Dear Fritz, True! I do want (to go) to Austria. (It is not necessary to translate go, fly, drive, etc.) Many thanks for the money. That is an excellent idea. Cheers. (Don't forget to put your own signature!)

Übung 5   This is about action words, which have a close friend.

Action words which have a friend,	e.g. **kommen + mit**
leave him at the sentence end,	e.g. **ich komme mit**
they go to him and hold his hand,	
whenever you want to express	

wish	e.g. **ich möchte**	
ability	**ich kann**	**mitkommen**
intent	**ich will**	

Can you unite the friends?
Ich kaufe auf dem Markt ein.

(wish)
1. Er _ _ _ _ _ _   **Obst und Gemüse auf dem Markt einkaufen.**
        would like
(ability)
2. Ich _ _ _ _ _ _ _ _   **Obst und Gemüse einkaufen.**
        am able to
(intent)
3. Wir _ _ _ _ _ _   **auf dem Markt einkaufen.**
        want to

(The answers are at the back of the book)

Übung 6   Other action words with friends, which have occurred so far are:

sich ausweisen, sich umsehen, aufziehen, aufmachen, anmachen, anrufen, durchwählen, einlösen, ansehen und vorschlagen.

Can you separate these words? Keep the action word in its proper place and send the first part (the 'friend') to the very end of the sentence.

e.g. **(sich ausweisen) ich weise mich jetzt aus.**

or **Peter weist sich aus.**

Now you! (They are in the correct order of appearance.)

1) sich umsehen
2) **aufziehen**
3) aufmachen
4) anmachen
5) anrufen
6) durchwählen
7) einlösen
8) ansehen
9) ansehen
10) vorschlagen

1) Er _ _ _ _ _ **sich im Zimmer** _ _ .

2) Sie _ _ _ _ _ _ **die Vorhänge** _ _ _ .

3) Ich _ _ _ _ _ _ **das Fenster** _ _ _ .

4) Er _ _ _ _ _ **das Licht** _ _ .

5) Um fünf Uhr _ _ _ _ **Frau Meyer** _ _ .

6) Peter telefoniert nach England. Er _ _ _ _ _ _ **direkt** _ _ _ _ _ .

7) Der alte Herr _ _ _ _ **seine Reisechecks** _ _ _ .

8) Peter _ _ _ _ _ **Hilde** _ _ .

9) Peter _ _ _ _ _ **sich die Hemden** _ _ .

10) Ich _ _ _ _ _ _ _ **jetzt etwas** _ _ _ .

The correct answers are at the back of the book

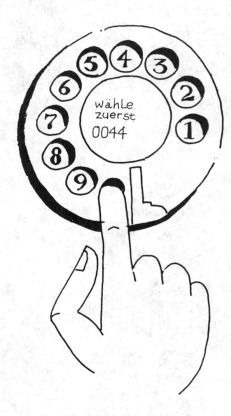

Sie können direkt
durchwählen

63

Teil fünf : Spiele, Rätsel und Reime

1.   Personenbeschreibung - Description of a person

In this game you are asked to make a photofit picture for somebody over the phone. Imagine that the person to whom you are talking has only a few various pieces to put together. You could start with:

Die Augen sind groß / klein or:

Er/sie hat große / kleine Augen.

Here you go now, have a try:

Augen:
Eyes

big
groß

small
klein

round
rund

dark
dunkel

Haare:
Hair

bald,
eine Glatze

light **hell,** long **lang**

short
kurz

dark
dunkel

Er ist:
Sie ist:

old
alt

young
jung

slim
schlank

fat
dick

Er ist:
Sie ist:

tall
groß

medium
mittelgroß

small
klein

2.   Lots of useful expressions are in your possession by now.
     Do you remember them?
a)   Look at the expressions in the balloons below
     Can you find an answer to each question or statement? (as in A and B)
b)   How fast can you respond to each of these expressions?
     You will find that often more than one response is possible.

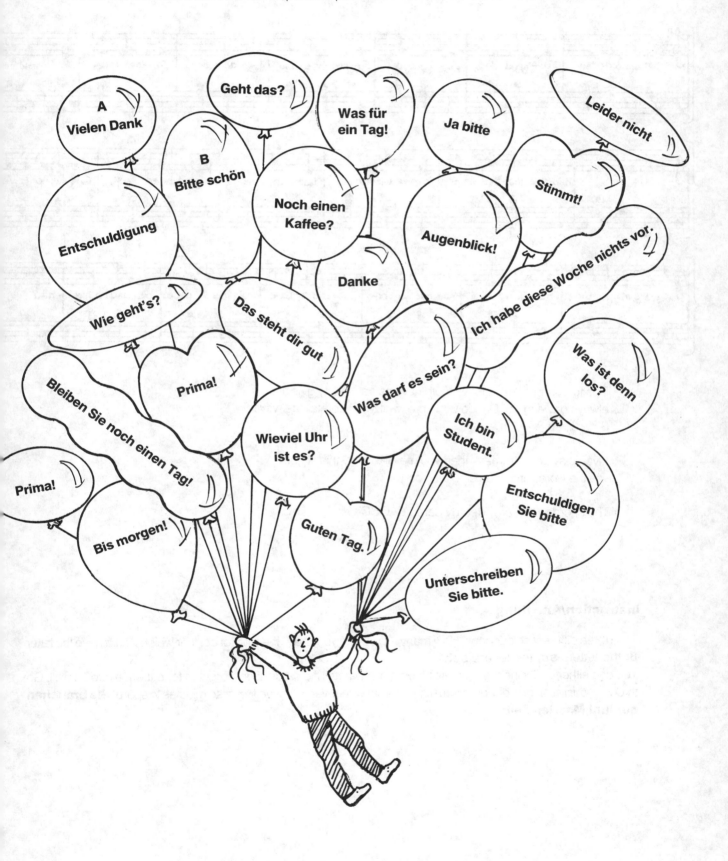

3.   Laß doch der Jugend ihren Lauf!

Laß doch der Ju--gend, der Ju--gend, der Ju--gend ihr--en Lauf. Laß doch
der Ju--gend, der Ju--gend ihr--en Lauf.
Hüb--sche Mäd--chen wach--sen imm--er wie--der auf, laß doch der
Ju--gend ihr--en Lauf. Tanz mit der Lor--e,
walz mit der Lor--e bis nach Schwei--nau mit der Lor--e, tanz mit der
Lor--e, walz mit der Lor--e bis nach Schwei--nau.

This folk song asks us to let youth have its day. Pretty girls are
always growing up. Dance with Lore, waltz with Lore all the way to
Schweinau.

If you play an instrument, then you may like to try this. If not,
say the words first, then sing the song.

The chords were provided by Sara VEACOCK.

Instruction/Anleitung

Take three different colour pens. How many words can you find in the story of act four which which have the letter
ß, the letters **ss,** the letters **sch**?
You can either underline them or write them on separate little cards. Don't forget to read them aloud as well. Go
through your list or 'pile' of words from time to time, whenever you have five or so minutes to spare! **Sie brauchen
nur fünf Minuten Zeit!**

Akt 5

	Scene 1 In a café	**Szene 1** **Im Café**

Erzähler — Hilde and Peter have gone to a café. / **Hilde und Peter sind in ein Café gegangen.**

Tables and chairs stand in front of it on the pavement. / **Tische und Stühle stehen davor auf dem Bürgersteig.**

Peter — Where would you like to sit, outside or inside? / **Wo möchtest du sitzen, draußen oder drinnen?**

Hilde — I'd rather sit outside, it's not too windy. / **Lieber draußen, es ist nicht zu windig.**

I'm going to put on my sunglasses. Then I can watch the people passing by. / **Ich setze meine Sonnenbrille auf. Dann kann ich die Leute beobachten.**

eine Tasse Kaffee

Tee mit Zitrone

Erzähler — The café is busy. / **Das Café ist gut besucht.**

The waiter is coming. / **Der Kellner kommt.**

Kellner — What would you like? / **Was wünschen Sie bitte?**

Tea of coffee? / **Tee oder Kaffee?**

Hilde — I prefer tea. / **Ich trinke lieber Tee.**

But not like the English with milk and sugar, I prefer it with lemon. / **Aber nicht wie die Engländer mit Milch und Zucker, sondern mit Zitrone bitte.**

Peter — All right; one tea with lemon and a little jug of coffee please. / **Also, einmal Tee mit Zitrone und ein Kännchen Kaffee, bitte.**

Kellner — If you want cake or gateau, order at the counter please. / **Wenn Sie Kuchen oder Torte wünschen, bestellen Sie am Büfett bitte.**

Erzähler — They go to the long counter. / **Sie gehen zu dem langen Kuchenbüfett.**

Hilde orders a piece of strawberry tart without cream, and Peter orders a piece of chocolate gateau with cream. / **Hilde bestellt ein Stück Erdbeertorte ohne Sahne, und Peter bestellt ein Stück Schokoladentorte mit Sahne.**

The waiter brings the cakes. / **Der Kellner bringt ihnen den Kuchen.**

Peter — Could you please pass me the sugar? / **Könnten Sie mir bitte noch den Zucker geben?**

Erzähler — They love the taste. / **Sie essen mit Genuß.**

Suddenly Peter looks at Hilde. / **Plötzlich sieht Peter Hilde an.**

Peter — What is in the parcel? / **Was ist in dem Paket?**

Erzähler — Hilde looks serious. / **Hilde wird ernst.**

Hilde — Only papers! / **Nur Papiere!**

Was ist in dem Paket?

Nur Papiere

| | Scene 2 | Szene 2 |
| | Plans for the Evening | **Pläne für den Abend** |

Peter
What shall we do this evening? / **Was machen wir heute abend?**
Do we want to go to the cinema / **Wollen wir ins Kino**
or to the theatre? / **oder lieber ins Theater gehen?**
I'm sure we'll still get tickets. / **Wir können bestimmt noch Karten bekommen.**
But we could also go dancing. / **Aber wir könnten auch tanzen gehen.**

Hilde
I like anything, / **Ich mag alles,**
ballet or theatre. / **Ballett oder Theater.**
I also like going to the cinema; / **Ins Kino gehe ich auch gern;**
you choose, / **du kannst wählen,**
what to do. / **was wir machen.**
I just want to have a night out. / **Ich möchte einfach mal ausgehen.**

Erzähler
Peter remembers how / **Peter denkt daran, wie knapp**
hard up he is! / **bei Kasse er ist!**
But he can't suggest watching television. / **Aber Fernsehen kann er nicht vorschlagen!**
They borrow the newspaper from the man sitting at the table next to them and look for the theatre programme. / **Sie leihen sich die Zeitung von dem Mann am nächsten Tisch und suchen das Theaterprogramm.**
They find nothing suitable, and decide to go to a restaurant. / **Sie finden nichts Passendes und beschließen, zusammen in ein Restaurant zu gehen.**

Hilde
I'll take you, of course. / **Selbstverständlich lade ich dich ein.**
I know a good restaurant. It's fairly small and not expensive. / **Ich kenne das Restaurant. Es ist ziemlich klein und nicht teuer.**
Service is good and the food tastes excellent. That is the most important thing, don't you think? / **Die Bedienung ist gut, und das Essen schmeckt ausgezeichnet. Das ist doch das Wichtigste, nicht wahr?**

Peter
Yes, thank you. / **Ja, danke.**
I can wear the shirt that I bought a minute ago, and the tie, which you gave me as a present. / **Ich kann das Hemd tragen, das ich vorhin gekauft habe und auch den Schlips, den du mir geschenkt hast.**

Hilde
We should go now. / **Wir sollten jetzt gehen.**
The shops close at 6 and I still want to buy something. / **Die Geschäfte schließen um 18 Uhr und ich will noch was kaufen.**

Peter
Waiter, the bill please! / **Herr Ober, zahlen bitte!**

Kellner
A little jug of coffee, one lemon tea and 2 pieces of cake; that comes to 9 marks 70. / **Ein Kännchen Kaffee, ein Tee mit Zitrone und zwei Kuchen; macht zusammen neun Mark siebzig.**
Here's your bill. / **Bitte schön, hier die Rechnung.**

Peter
Should I give a tip? / **Soll ich Trinkgeld geben?**

Hilde
Only 30 Pfennigs, if you want to. / **Nur dreißig Pfennig, wenn du willst.**
In Germany, service is always included. / **Bedienung ist in Deutschland immer inklusive.**

	Scene 3	Szene 3
	In the Department Store	**Im Kaufhaus**

Erzähler	They arrange to meet at 7 o'clock.	**Sie verabreden sich für neunzehn Uhr.**
	Hilde goes to a department store. She has seen a dress, the day before yesterday, which she now would like to buy.	**Hilde geht zu einem Kaufhaus. Dort hat sie vorgestern ein Kleid gesehen, das sie jetzt kaufen möchte.**
	Yesterday it was still there.	**Gestern war es noch da.**
	She is lucky!	**Sie hat Glück!**
	It is still there!	**Da hängt es noch!**
	It is dark red and has an elegant white pattern.	**Es ist dunkelrot und hat ein elegantes, weißes Muster.**
	Size 14!	**Größe 40!**
	Hopefully it will fit!	**Hoffentlich paßt es!**
	She goes to a changing room and takes off her skirt and blouse.	**Sie geht zu einer Kabine und zieht ihren Rock und ihre Bluse aus.**
	Then she puts on the dress.	**Dann zieht sie das Kleid an.**
	She looks in the mirror.	**Sie sieht in den Spiegel.**
	It fits exactly and suits her well.	**Es paßt genau und steht ihr gut.**
	She is pleased.	**Sie freut sich.**
	She buys the dress and matching tights.	**Sie kauft das Kleid und passende Strumpfhosen.**
	And what is Peter doing?	**Und was macht Peter?**
	He has a headache and is looking for a chemist.	**Er hat Kopfschmerzen und sucht eine Apotheke.**
	He finds one and goes in.	**Er findet eine und geht hinein.**
Peter	Have you got anything for headaches?	**Haben Sie etwas gegen Kopfschmerzen?**
Verkäuferin	Is it very bad?	**Haben Sie starke Schmerzen?**
Peter	Not really.	**Eigentlich nicht.**
Verkäuferin	I'll give you some aspirins then.	**Dann gebe ich Ihnen Aspirintabletten.**
Verkäuferin	These are soluble and contain Vitamin C.	**Diese hier sind wasserlöslich und haben Vitamin C.**
	6 marks please.	**Sechs Mark bitte.**
Peter	How many tablets are in this box?	**Wieviele Tabletten sind in dieser Packung?**
Verkäuferin	20.	**Zwanzig.**

Kopfschmerzen

Wieviele Tabletten sind in dieser Packung?

Zwanzig

Erzähler	Peter takes the box,	**Peter nimmt die Packung,**
	pays and leaves the chemist.	**bezahlt und verläßt die Apotheke.**
	Goodness gracious, he thinks.	**Meine Güte, denkt er.**
	That is dreadfully expensive!	**Das ist ja entsetzlich teuer!**
	He calculates:	**Er rechnet:**
	He divides and substracts,	**Er dividiert, er subtrahiert,**
	he multiplies and adds.	**er multipliziert und addiert.**
	He looks around.	**Er sieht sich um.**
	Where is the Hotel?	**Wo ist das Hotel?**
	He has lost his way.	**Er hat sich verlaufen.**
	There is a kiosk.	**Da ist ein Kiosk.**
	The woman in the kiosk explains	**Die Frau am Kiosk erklärt**
	which way to go and	**ihm den Weg,**
	eventually he finds the hotel.	**und schließlich findet er das**
	The receptionist calls him.	**Hotel. Die Empfangsdame ruft ihn.**
Empfangsdame	Hello Mr Wilson!	**Hallo Mr. Wilson!**
	Here is a letter for you.	**Hier ist ein Brief für Sie.**
	It arrived by messenger.	**Er kam per Bote.**
Erzähler	She gives him the letter.	**Sie gibt ihm den Brief.**
	How strange! There is his name	**Wie seltsam! Da steht sein Name**
	and the address, but there is	**und die Adresse, aber da ist**
	no stamp.	**keine Briefmarke.**
	He opens the letter.	**Er öffnet den Brief.**
	In the envelope are 5	**Im Umschlag sind fünf**
	blue 100 DM notes!	**blaue Hundertmarkscheine!**
	There is also a note there.	**Da ist ein Zettel.**
	"For expenses in Germany.	**„Für Spesen in Deutschland.**
	Wilhelm Holz."	**Wilhelm Holz."**
	Peter's headache has gone.	**Peters Kopfschmerzen sind weg!**

$$12 \div 2 = 6 \text{ DM}$$
er dividiert

$$18 - 12 = 6 \text{ DM}$$
er subtrahiert

$$3 \times 2 = 6 \text{ DM}$$
er multipliziert

$$5 + 1 = 6 \text{ DM}$$
er addiert

Cafe

Tisch

Stühle

Bürgersteig

Sie sind in ein Cafè gegangen

Ich setze meine Sonnenbrille auf

Ich kann die Leute beobachten

Der Kellner kommt

ein langes Kuchenbüfett

Stück Erdbeertorte

eine Tasse Kaffee

Tee mit Zitrone

Sahne

Was ist in dem Paket?

Nur Papiere

koladentorte

Sie essen mit Genuß

Akt 5, 2

KLEIDER

Sie hat ein Kleid gesehen

Größe Vierzig

Kopfschmerzen

Hilde zieht ihren Rock aus

ASPIRIN TABLETTEN

Wieviele Tabletten sind in dieser Packung?

Zwanzig

$$12 \div 2 = 6 \text{ DM}$$
Er dividiert

$$18 - 12 = 6 \text{ DM}$$
Er subtrahiert

$$3 \times 2 = 6 \text{ DM}$$
Er multipliziert

$$5 + 1 = 6 \text{ DM}$$
Er addiert

Peter hat sich verlaufen

Hotel

Schließlich findet er das Hotel

Können Sie ihm helfen?

73

Aussprache/Intonation

Let us now concentrate on how to pronounce the letter **'r'** in German. At the end of a word and sometimes in the middle of a word it has no sound at all just as in English **'butter'**, **'bar'**, **'marmalade'**.

---

1.   Listen and imitate:

Wer hat die Butter? -- Natürlich Peter! -- Die Butter ist auf Peters Teller. -- Peter hat immer ein Abenteuer. -- Sie hat blondes Haar. --

---

At the beginning and often in the middle of a word, the **'r'** is pronounced in the throat. We make a short little gurgling sound: **'rrr'**. Now you try:

schwarze Kirschen   2.   **rr, rrr, rrrr --**   Birnen

Warum? -- Birnen. -- Hmm, herrlich! -- Birnen schmecken herrlich! -- Brauchen Sie Birnen? -- Wir haben schwarze Kirschen. -- Birnen und Kirschen. -- Auf dem Markt gibt es rote Geranien. -- Was sucht der Herr? -- Ein Geschäft für Herrenbekleidung. -- Adresse bitte? -- Königstraße drei. --

---

Note: when a word is written with two **'rs'** then the preceding vowel is always short, e.g. **Herr, herrlich** but: **sehr, wer?**

---

3.   Now listen and imitate the following sounds:

Ah! Salami? -- Ja, Salami bitte.-- Was? -- Das ist das Badetuch? -- Und das Badezimmer? Na da, dahinten! --

Oh! -- So groß! -- Wo ist das Brot? -- Wir wollen Brot und rote Tomaten. -- Honig bitte. --   rote Tom

Uh! -- Ich habe Hunger! -- Kuchen, Wurst und hundert Gurken bitte! Wir gehen zu Fuß.--

Augenblick -- Paul? -- Paul hat blaue Augen. -- Deine sind braun und meine grau.

Er ist kein Deutscher. -- Er wohnt in Deutschland. -- Er spricht gut Deutsch. -- Sie ist Deutsche. -- Das ist ein Abenteuer!

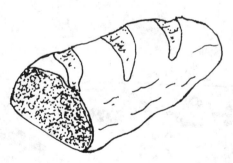

Wo ist das Brot?

Teil zwei: Dialoge

	Dialogue 1	**Dialog 1**
	On the phone; arranging a date	**Am Telefon; eine Verabredung**
Heike	Can we meet this morning?	**Können wir uns heute morgen treffen?**
Bernd	Yes, that's possible.	**Ja, das geht.**
	At 9 o'clock perhaps?	**Um neun vielleicht?**
Heike	No, that won't do.	**Nein, das geht nicht.**
	I want to go shopping first and the shops open at 8.30.	**Ich will erst einkaufen und die Geschäfte öffnen um 8.30.**
	Half past ten is fine.	**Um halb elf geht es.**
Bernd	All right then. At 10.30.	**Na gut. Um zehn Uhr dreißig.**
Heike	Where shall we meet?	**Wo treffen wir uns?**
Bernd	Perhaps in front of the Volksbank?	**Vor der Volksbank vielleicht?**
Heike	Oh no, not there.	**Ach nein, nicht da.**
	Better opposite, in the "Café Schöneberg".	**Lieber gegenüber, im „Café Schöneberg".**
Bernd	All right. I'll be there at half past ten.	**Gut; also um halb elf bin ich da.**

Um halb elf

	Dialogue 2	**Dialog 2**
	In the Café Schöneberg, ordering a cup of coffee	**Im Café Schöneberg, Kaffee bestellen.**
Andreas	May I invite you to a cup of coffee?	**Darf ich Sie zu einer Tasse Kaffee einladen?**
Bettina	Thank you. That's nice of you.	**Danke. Das ist nett von Ihnen.**
Andreas	The cakes here are very good.	**Die Kuchen sind sehr gut hier.**
	Would you like a piece?	**Möchten Sie ein Stück?**
Bettina	No thank you. Only a cup of black coffee, please.	**Nein danke. Nur eine Tasse schwarzen Kaffee bitte.**
Andreas	Waiter! A cup of coffee without cream and a little jug of coffee, please.	**Herr Ober! Eine Tasse Kaffee ohne Sahne und ein Kännchen Kaffee, bitte.**
Bettina	Could you please pass the sugar?	**Könnten Sie mir bitte den Zucker geben?**
Andreas	Here you are.	**Hier bitte.**

ein Kännchen Kaffee

eine Tasse Kaffee

	Dialogue 3	**Dialog 3**
	In the street, asking for help	**Auf der Straße, um Hilfe bitten**
Frau A	Hello, Mrs. B. How are you?	**Hallo, Frau Becker. Wie geht's?**
Frau B	Fine. Thanks.	**Gut. Danke.**
	How are you?	**Und Ihnen?**
Frau A	Not so well.	**Leider nicht so gut.**
Frau B	Oh dear. What is the matter then?	**Ach. Was ist denn los?**
Frau A	My credit card has gone.	**Meine Kreditkarte ist weg.**
	I can't find it anywhere.	**Ich kann sie nicht finden.**
Frau B	When did you last have it?	**Wann haben Sie sie zuletzt gehabt?**
Frau A	Only yesterday.	**Gestern.**
	I paid for something with the card.	**Ich habe mit der Karte bezahlt.**
Frau B	Go to the bank straight away.	**Gehen Sie gleich zur Bank!**
Frau A	Do come with me please.	**Kommen Sie doch bitte mit.**
	I have a bad headache.	**Ich habe starke Kopfschmerzen.**
Frau B	Of course I'll come with you. Then	**Selbstverständlich komme ich mit.**
	we'll go to a café and	**Dann gehen wir in ein Café und**
	have a cup of coffee.	**trinken einen Kaffee.**
	I have some aspirin tablets and	**Ich habe Aspirin, und im**
	in the cafe we can get	**Café gibt es auch**
	some water.	**ein Glas Wasser.**

	Dialogue 4	**Dialog 4**
	Plans for the evening	**Pläne für den Abend**
Gabriele	What shall we do this evening?	**Was sollen wir heute abend machen?**
Bernd	Let's go dancing or would you rather	**Laß uns tanzen gehen oder möchtest du**
	go to the theatre?	**lieber ins Theater?**
Gabriele	I am hard up.	**Ich bin knapp bei Kasse.**
	Let's watch television.	**Laß uns fernsehen.**
Bernd	What's on then?	**Was gibt es denn?**
	Where is the paper?	**Wo ist die Zeitung?**
Gabriele	Here's the program.	**Hier ist das Programm.**
Bernd	Goodness me! Is that boring!	**Meine Güte! Das ist ja langweilig!**
Gabriele	No; why? At 7 there's a ballet.	**Nein; warum? Um 19 Uhr gibt's ein Ballett.**
	I like that.	**Das mag ich gern.**

	Dialogue 5	**Dialog 5**
	In the Department Store;	**Im Kaufhaus;**
	to try something on	**etwas anprobieren**
Kundin	This dress is size 40.	**Dieses Kleid ist Größe 40.**
	That is too small for me.	**Das ist zu klein für mich.**
	Have you not got it in 42?	**Haben Sie's nicht in Größe 42?**
Verkäuferin	No, I'm sorry.	**Leider nicht.**
	But do try it on.	**Aber probieren Sie es doch mal an!**
	It might fit.	**Vielleicht paßt es.**
Kundin	All right then.	**Na gut.**
	Where is the changing room?	**Wo ist die Kabine bitte?**
Verkäuferin	Over there, next to the large	**Da drüben, neben dem großen**
	mirror.	**Spiegel.**
Kundin	Thank you.	**Danke.**

Teil drei: Dialoge

Dialog 1   Im Hotel

You have invited a German business contact for a drink to your hotel. The hotel has a terrace and a garden. Your guest arrives. It's time for you to practise your German.

You	Good evening! How are things? Would you like to sit inside or outside?
Gast	**Lieber drinnen. Heute abend ist es ziemlich kühl. Aber möchten Sie vielleicht lieber draußen sitzen?**
You	No, no. The bar inside is nice. The service is friendly.
Gast	**Wie gefällt Ihnen das Hotel?**
You	I like it. I have breakfast here too.
Gast	**Hat das Hotel ein Restaurant?**
You	No, but there is a dining room. Next to the hotel is a restaurant. I always eat there.

Dialog 2   Am Telefon

Your business friend wants to take you out for dinner.

Fritz B.	**Hallo Mrs. Wilson! Fritz Braun hier. Darf ich Sie für heute abend zum Essen einladen?**
You	Thank you very much. That is very kind of you.
Fritz B.	**Ich kenne ein gutes, kleines Restaurant. Es ist aber gut besucht, und ich muß einen Tisch bestellen. Wann können wir uns treffen?**
You	At seven o'clock perhaps?
Fritz B.	**Dann bestelle ich den Tisch für halb acht und komme um sieben Uhr zu Ihnen ins Hotel.**
You	Yes, 7 o'clock will be all right, 'til seven then.

Dialog 3   Bei der Rezeption

You are returning to your hotel, when the receptionist calls you.

Rezeptionist	**Hallo, Miss Brown. Da war ein Telefonanruf für Sie. Ich habe die Nummer hier. Hier auf dem Zettel.**
You	Thank you very much. (You have to ring back and ask) Where is a telephone please?
Rezeptionist	**Das Telefon ist neben der Treppe zum Speisesaal.**
You	Thanks.

Wo ist ein Telefon
bitte?

Dialog 4   **In der Apotheke**

You have been sightseeing all day and finished up with a dreadful headache. Fortunately, you have found an „Apotheke"

Apotheker	**Was darf es sein?**
You	I have got a bad headache. Have you got aspirin tablets?
Apotheker	**Ja. Diese hier sind sehr gut. Die sind wasserlöslich und haben auch Vitamin C. Möchten Sie die große oder die kleine Packung?**
You	How many tablets are in the small box?
Apotheker	**In der kleinen Packung sind zehn Tabletten.**
You	I'll take the small box.
Apotheker	**Drei Mark bitte. Möchten Sie ein Glas Wasser? Dann können Sie gleich eine Tablette nehmen.**
You	Thank you very much. Yes please.

Dialog 5   **Im Hotel beim Fernsehen**

You are back at your hotel and sit in the lounge watching TV. Another guest comes to join you.

Gast	**Entschuldigen Sie bitte. Ich möchte das Fernsehprogramm sehen. Wissen Sie, wo eine Zeitung ist?**
You	The newspaper? Yes, there is one in the bar.
Gast	**Ich war schon in der Bar. Da liegt die Zeitung von gestern.**
You	Perhaps the newspaper is at the reception?
Gast	**Ah, gute Idee! Danke.**
You	You're welcome.

Dialog 6   **Im Speisesaal im Hotel.**

You are having breakfast in the dining room and would like another cup of tea.

You	(Mr) Waiter!
Kellner	**Ja bitte?**
You	I would like another cup of tea. Tea with milk please.
Kellner	**Bitte schön.** (Puts it down on the table)

The dining room is very busy, so you don't want to call him back. There is no sugar on your table. The people at the next table have a bowl and seem not to use it.

You (louder)	Excuse me please. Could you please pass me the sugar?
Dame	**Bitte schön.**
You	Thank you very much.

(Answers are at the back of the book.)

Könnten Sie mir
bitte den Zucker
geben?

Teil Vier: übungen - Das Himmlische Spiel Nummer drei.

Die Sternkinder von, zu, mit. (The star children **von, zu, mit.**)

Please look out the sheet of word cards for Akt 5. Now put all the cards face up on the table. From the Akt 3 pack of Heavenly Game cards, take the two which say **Er geht zu** and **den großen Fenstern** and add them to your cards for this third game.

There are three different genders in German (masculine, feminine and neuter words), corresponding to the three different ways of saying "the", i.e. **der, die, das.**

The little table below makes it clear that the gender of the noun changes the ending of words like **ein,** or **mein,** as well as adjectives. Or put the other way, the ending of an adjective must always agree with the gender of the noun.

Masculine	Feminine	Neuter
der Kellner	die Bluse	das Stück
ein Kellner	eine Bluse	ein Stück
mein Vater	meine Mutter	mein Stück
der junge Kellner	die junge Dame	das kleine Stück
ein junger Kellner	eine junge Dame	ein kleines Stück
ein roter Rock	eine rote Bluse	ein rotes Kleid
ein kleiner roter Rock	eine kleine rote Bluse	ein kleines rotes Kleid

An easy way to remember **die** endings is that "the sign of femininity is 'e' " (a nice rhyme). And when **der** or **das** (the) becomes **ein** (a), then this happens:

        der junge Kellner   **das kleine Stück**

becomes   becomes

        ein junger Kellner   **ein kleines Stück**

The way this Accelerated Learning Course is constructed means that already you will have begun, subconsciously, to recognise the point, but now we wanted to draw your specific attention to it.

Having appreciated the above, we are ready to play some new Heavenly Games.

You will notice that all the 26 word cards in these Heavenly Games have the same symbol on them - the star ✡

Game One
Spiel Eins Your job (having cut up the cards!) is to match up one of the phrases from the top half of the page to one of the words or phrases from the bottom half. You will find each corresponds to a sentence from Akt 5.

When you have found a match, lay the two cards side by side and read it out loud.

    e.g. **Haben Sie Hemden mit** _ _ _ _ _ _ _ _ **extra langen Ärmeln**

    or **Peter telefoniert und spricht mit** _ _ _ _ _ **seinem Onkel**
                                              seiner Mutter
                                              seinem Hotel

When you have matched up all the cards, then <u>write</u> down the sentences.

Game Two

Spiel Zwei So far all the matches make sense, because you have reproduced sentences from the text of the Akt. But other combinations are possible - some sensible, some bizarre. <u>Grammatically</u> the following combination makes sense:

dieser Schlips passt gut zu	**dem nächsten Tisch** **der modernen Volksbank** **dem langen Kuchenbüffet**

But unless you want your tie to match the next table, or the modern bank, I don't think you would want to team up these cards!

Now make up as many combinations as you can (comical as well). Each time read them out loud.

What have you noticed in playing the first two Heavenly Games?

Game Three

Spiel Drei It would help if you put all the matched phrases from the Akt on the table, one pair of cards under the other. You will end up with a table top that looks like this:

dieser Schlips passt gut <u>zu</u>	**dem neuen Rock** **der neuen Bluse** **dem neuen Hemd**

ich bezahle <u>mit</u>	**einem Reisescheck** **einer Kreditkarte** **einem Fünfmarkstück**

ich habe es <u>von</u>

etc.

	meinem Onkel **meiner Mutter** **meinem Aupair Mädchen** **meinen Kollegen**

Let us look closely at the last matched set. Why is it **ich habe es von ... meinem Onkel?** Why it is not **ich habe es von mein Onkel.** Why is it **ich bezahle mit eine<u>r</u> Kreditkarte,** and not **eine Kreditkarte?**

Have you puzzled out the answer yet?

The point of these heavenly Games is that there are some words in German that change the endings you would normally use.

They are the "star children": **von, zu, mit**

So it is <u>not</u> **von der Mann** . . . . . . it is **von dem Mann**
   it is <u>not</u> **zu die Dame** . . . . it is **zu der Dame**
   it is <u>not</u> **mit das Mädchen** . . . it is **mit dem Mädchen**

If you have seen this, you have "cracked" just about the most difficult point you will come across in German!

Game Four

Spiel Vier Look back through Akt 5 and write out the sentences that include the verbs **geben, zeigen, gehen, schenken** and **gefallen** - or a form of these words, e.g. **gibt, zeigt, geht, schenkt** or **gefällt.**

This game teaches you the fact that there are a few verbs (and some common phrases), that should also be classified as "star children".

There is a logical reason because these verbs mean:

to give (to), to show (to), to go (to), to present (to) and to be pleasing (to). In each case the verb implies the sense of "to", which in German is **zu.** AND **zu** is a star child.

This Heavenly Game teaches us that after the ✡ words **zu, von** and **mit,** the normal endings are changed. In fact you will notice other words in later Akts. They will be **nach, bei, neben** and **aus.**
                                                          (to)   (at) (beside)   (from)

DO NOT TRY TO LEARN ANY OF THIS. Just read it through and understand it thoroughly. Then you will subconsciously and automatically absorb when to say **der** and when to say **dem,** because you understand the principle involved.

Game Five

Spiel Fünf Do you remember in Akt 3 you had three heavenly symbols?

✡ You know the significance of the star now.

☀ The Sun just means you use the normal endings.

☽ The Moon has a simple meaning. Look back to the word cards in Akt 3 and try to work out what is the significance of the Moon sign. (Thankfully it's a small effect!)

You will see that after certain verbs there is a change to the endings of **der** words (but not **die** or **das** words). So if you get out the word cards for Akt 3 you will find the following match:

Dann macht sie   Salat
den grünen

You will deduce that after **machen** you say **sie macht den grünen Salat,** not **macht der grüne Salat.**

The main verbs that cause the "moon" effect are:

machen,	**nehmen,**	**haben,**	**trinken**	**können**
(make)	(take)	(have)	(drink)	(be able)
essen,	**möchten,**	**kaufen,**	**tragen**	
(eat)	(would like)	(to buy)	(to carry or wear)	

Just as the above verbs cause a change of **der** to **den,** you will later see that certain other words do too. They are:

bis	**durch**	**für**	**gegen**	**ohne** and **um**
(until)	through)	(for)	(against)	(without) (around)

Remember the whole point of the way this Accelerated German Course has been constructed is that you will subconsciously *absorb* the "rules". SO IT IS NOT NECESSARY TO MEMORISE THESE POINTS. Now they have been highlighted, you will see and learn the ✡ or ☽ effects automatically.

We also firmly believe that learning a language must be both realistic and a pleasure. The truth is that even if you were sometimes to get the endings wrong, everyone will perfectly well understand you!

Torten, Kuchen and Gebäck

Berliner

Aachener Printen

Dresdener Christstollen

Frankfurter Kranz

Nürnberger Lebkuchen

Schwarzwälder Kirschtorte

Apfelstrudel

Here are a few famous cakes which carry the names of the towns from which they originate. We also included **Apfelstrudel** which can be found all over Austria. **Aachener Printen** and **Nürnberger Lebkuchen** are sold in beautiful boxes. If you only want one, ask for **eine Aachener Printe** or **einen Nürnberger Lebkuchen,** or **einen Berliner.** Larger cakes are sold by the **Stück,** e.g. **ein Stück Obsttorte.**

Übung 1: Take a friend to a café for a treat.
Offer all the cakes which you see on the map.
Start with: **Möchten Sie einen Berliner?** or
Möchten Sie ein Stück Christstollen?
Then give the order to the waiter.

Teil fünf: Spiele, Rätsel und Reime.

Ein Geschenk kaufen – Buying a present

If you know somebody with a sweet tooth, why not make them a present of one of the many delicious sweetmeats?

Go into a Café and ask at the counter for each of the items shown on this page. Don't forget to ask for the price as well!

Eine Packung Nürnberger Nuß-Mürbegebäck

Ein Königsberger Marzipanbrot

Ein Stück Lübecker Marzipan

Eine Tafel Schweizer Schokolade

Eine Mozartkugel

Nürnberger Nuß-Mürbegebäck

Echt Königsberger Marzipanbrot

Lübecker Marzipan

Schweizer Schokolade

Mozartkugel

Laß doch der Jugend . . . ?

Here is the tune of the song from Act 4. Do you remember the words? Write them underneath the notes.

(The correct answers are at the back of the book.)

84

Akt 6

Scene 1
A Pleasant Evening

Szene 1
Ein gemütlicher Abend

Erzähler	On the dot of seven Peter arrives at Hilde's.	**Pünktlich um sieben ist Peter bei Hilde.**
	She is ready to go out.	**Sie ist schon fertig.**
Peter	Shall we take a taxi?	**Sollen wir ein Taxi nehmen?**
Hilde	Yes. The restaurant is in the old part of the town. Unfortunately my car is still at the garage being repaired.	**Ja. Das Restaurant ist in der Altstadt. Mein Auto ist leider noch bei der Reparatur in der Werkstatt.**
Erzähler	They go by taxi into the old part of town.	**Sie fahren mit dem Taxi in die Altstadt.**
	Peter pays the taxi driver and they go into the restaurant.	**Peter bezahlt den Taxifahrer, und sie gehen in das Restaurant.**
	It is fairly busy.	**Es ist ziemlich voll.**
	A waiter shows them to a table for two.	**Ein Kellner führt sie zu einem Tisch für zwei.**
	On the table there are flowers and a candle, which the waiter lights.	**Auf dem Tisch stehen Blumen und eine Kerze; der Kellner zündet sie an.**
Peter	What a festive atmosphere!	**Was für eine festliche Atmosphäre!**
Hilde	Waiter, the menu please.	**Ober, die Speisekarte bitte.**
Erzähler	The waiter brings the menu and the wine list.	**Der Kellner bringt die Speisekarte und die Weinliste.**

Er zündet die Kerze an

Blumen

Scene 2
What shall we eat?

Szene 2
Was sollen wir essen?

Hilde	Let's look at the menu together. What do you like best?	**Laß uns zusammen die Speisekarte ansehen. Was ißt du denn am liebsten?**
	They do good starters here.	**Hier gibt es gute Vorspeisen.**
Peter	What does this mean: Rollmops on country bread?	**Was bedeutet denn dieses hier: Rollmops auf Landbrot?**
Hilde	Rollmops means pickled herring.	**Rollmops bedeutet saurer Hering.**
	Do you like herrings?	**Magst du Heringe?**
Peter	Not particularly.	**Nicht besonders.**
Erzähler	In the end Hilde chooses a stuffed egg and Peter a bowl of onion soup.	**Schließlich wählt Hilde ein gefülltes Ei, und Peter einen Teller Zwiebelsuppe.**
Hilde	For the main course I'll take Kasseler Rippchen.	**Als Hauptgericht nehme ich Kasseler Rippchen.**
	That's a German speciality.	**Das ist eine deutsche Spezialität.**
	I can recommend it.	**Die kann ich dir auch empfehlen.**
	It's made from pork chop.	**Es ist aus Schweinekotelett gemacht.**
	The British produce the best beef, The Italians the best veal, the French perhaps the best lamb, but the Germans have the best pork dishes!	**Die Engländer machen das beste Rindfleisch, die Italiener das beste Kalbfleisch, die Franzosen vielleicht das beste Lammfleisch, aber die Deutschen machen die besten Schweinefleischgerichte!**
Peter	That may be so, but I rather want to try the fish.	**Das mag sein, aber ich will lieber den Fisch probieren.**
	Fried trout for me please.	**Gebratene Forelle für mich bitte.**
Erzähler	The waiter comes and they give the order.	**Der Kellner kommt und sie bestellen.**

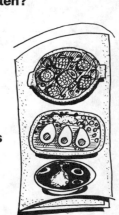

Laß uns zusammen die Speisekarte ansehen

Hilde	Which white wine do you recommend?	**Welchen Weißwein empfehlen Sie?**
Kellner	Mosel wines go well with the dishes you have ordered.	**Moselweine passen gut zu den Speisen, die Sie bestellt haben.**
Hilde	All right. Bring us a bottle of Mosel wine then, please.	**Gut. Dann bringen Sie uns bitte eine Flasche Moselwein.**
Erzähler	The waiter brings the wine and Hilde tastes it. The waiter fills the glasses. Peter and Hilde raise their glasses, look at each other and say:	**Der Kellner bringt den Wein und Hilde probiert einen Schluck. Der Kellner füllt die Gläser. Peter und Hilde heben ihr Glas, sehen sich an und sagen:**
Peter & Hilde	Cheers!	**Prost!**

	Scene 3	**Szene 3**
	Hilde talks about herself	**Hilde erzählt von sich**

Peter	Now tell me about yourself Hilde. I would like to know more about you	**Erzähle mir von dir, Hilde. Ich möchte gern mehr über dich wissen.**
Hilde	My mother and father came to Hanover after the war and married here. I was born here, but went to school in Berlin. My parents moved to Berlin when I was 5 years old. At the moment I live here at my uncle's. My parents aren't in Berlin any longer. They are retired now and have moved to Franken, Oh, that is a wonderful place! There are woods and meadows, and by car it's not too far to the mountains and lakes in Bavaria. My parents started an import-export business 20 years ago. It has been very successful, and is still successful today. It trades mostly with firms in Africa. My parents don't work any more, but I do a lot of hard work. Uncle William is the head of the firm. He is the general manager. His office is here. The other important shareholder was an Englishman. Unfortunately, a month ago he was killed in a plane crash.	**Mein Vater und meine Mutter sind nach dem Krieg nach Hannover gekommen und haben hier geheiratet. Ich bin hier geboren, aber in Berlin zur Schule gegangen. Meine Eltern sind nach Berlin gezogen, als ich fünf Jahre alt war. Zur Zeit wohne ich hier bei meinem Onkel. Meine Eltern sind nicht mehr in Berlin. Sie sind jetzt im Ruhestand und sind nach Franken gezogen. Ach, das ist eine herrliche Gegend! Da sind Wälder und Wiesen, und mit dem Auto sind die Berge und Seen in Bayern auch nicht weit. Meine Eltern haben vor zwanzig Jahren ein Import-Export Geschäft gegründet. Das war sehr erfolgreich; es ist auch heute noch erfolgreich. Die Firma handelt vor allem mit Firmen in Afrika. Meine Eltern arbeiten nun nicht mehr, aber ich arbeite ganz schön viel! Der Chef der Firma ist Onkel Wilhelm. Er ist der Generaldirektor. Sein Büro ist hier. Der andere wichtige Teilhaber war ein Engländer. Leider ist er vor einem Monat bei einem Flugzeugunglück umgekommen.**
Peter	Oh, I am sorry!	**Oh, das tut mir leid!**
Hilde	Well, I didn't know him very well, but it was of course a sad time for the family	**Nun, ich habe ihn nicht sehr gut gekannt, aber es war natürlich eine traurige Zeit für die Familie.**

ich bin hier geboren

das Flugzeugunglück

| | Scene 4 | **Szene 4** |
| | Peter talks | **Peter erzählt** |

Peter	What do you do in the firm?	**Welche Stelle hast du in der Firma?**
Hilde	I am the sales manager. That is a good job, because I meet many people. I also have to travel quite a lot. And you? What kind of plans have you? I don't believe that you want to deliver parcels for the rest of your life.	**Ich bin Verkaufsdirektorin. Das ist eine gute Stelle, weil ich viele Leute kennenlerne. Ich muß auch ziemlich viel reisen. Und du? Was für Pläne hast du? Ich glaube nicht, daß du immer nur Pakete abliefern möchtest!**
Peter	Oh no; I am looking for a job. I have just completed my studies in Business Management at the London School of Economics.	**Oh nein; ich suche eine Stelle. Ich habe gerade mein Studium in Geschäftsführung beendet, an der Londoner Hochschule für Wirtschaft.**
Hilde	How interesting! I studied the same subject at the Free University of Berlin.	**Wie interessant! Das Gleiche habe ich studiert, an der Freien Universität in Berlin.**
Peter	Have you any brothers and sisters?	**Hast du Geschwister?**
Hilde	No. I'm an only child. Have you got any?	**Nein. Ich bin ein Einzelkind. Hast du welche?**
Peter	Yes. My parents live in North London. My brother is a doctor. He is married and has two children. A boy and a girl. I have a sister as well. She works for a dentist, as a nurse. She is younger than I am.	**Ja. Meine Eltern wohnen in Nord-London. Mein Bruder ist Arzt. Er ist verheiratet und hat zwei Kinder. Einen Jungen und ein Mädchen. Ich habe auch eine Schwester. Sie arbeitet bei einem Zahnarzt als Sprechstundenhilfe. Sie ist jünger als ich.**
Hilde	How nice when one has a family and gets on well with them!	**Wie schön, wenn man eine Familie hat und sich gut versteht!**

ein Zahnarzt

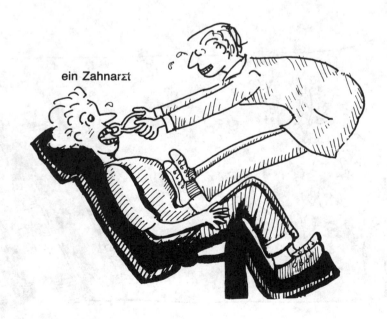

Akt 6, 1

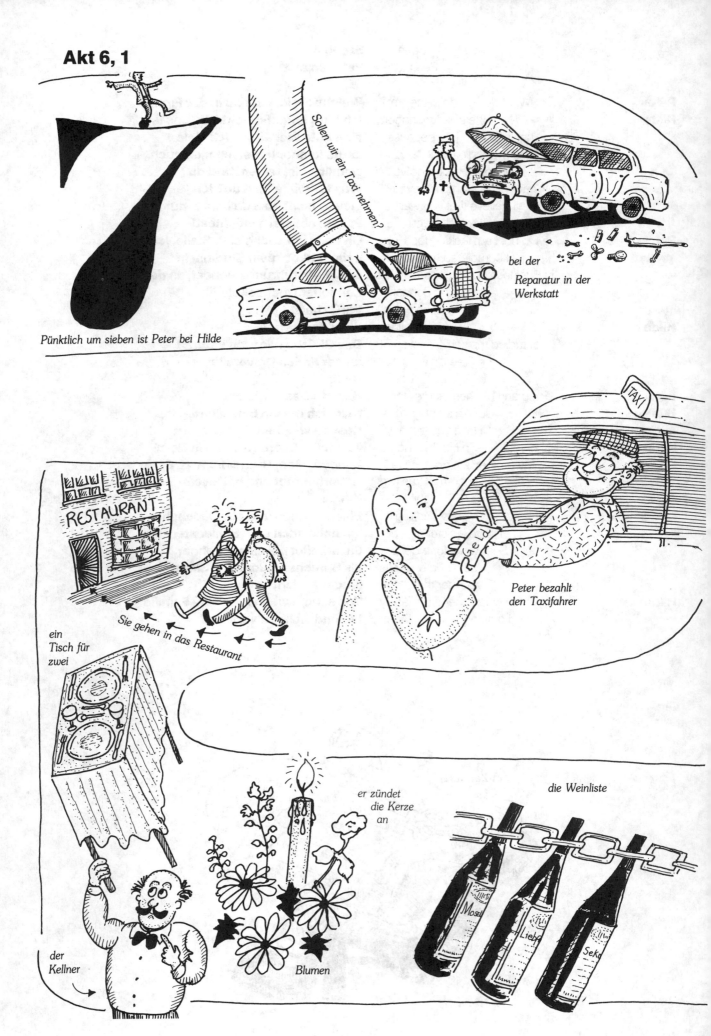

Pünktlich um sieben ist Peter bei Hilde

Sollen wir ein Taxi nehmen?

bei der Reparatur in der Werkstatt

Peter bezahlt den Taxifahrer

Sie gehen in das Restaurant

ein Tisch für zwei

der Kellner

Blumen

er zündet die Kerze an

die Weinliste

88

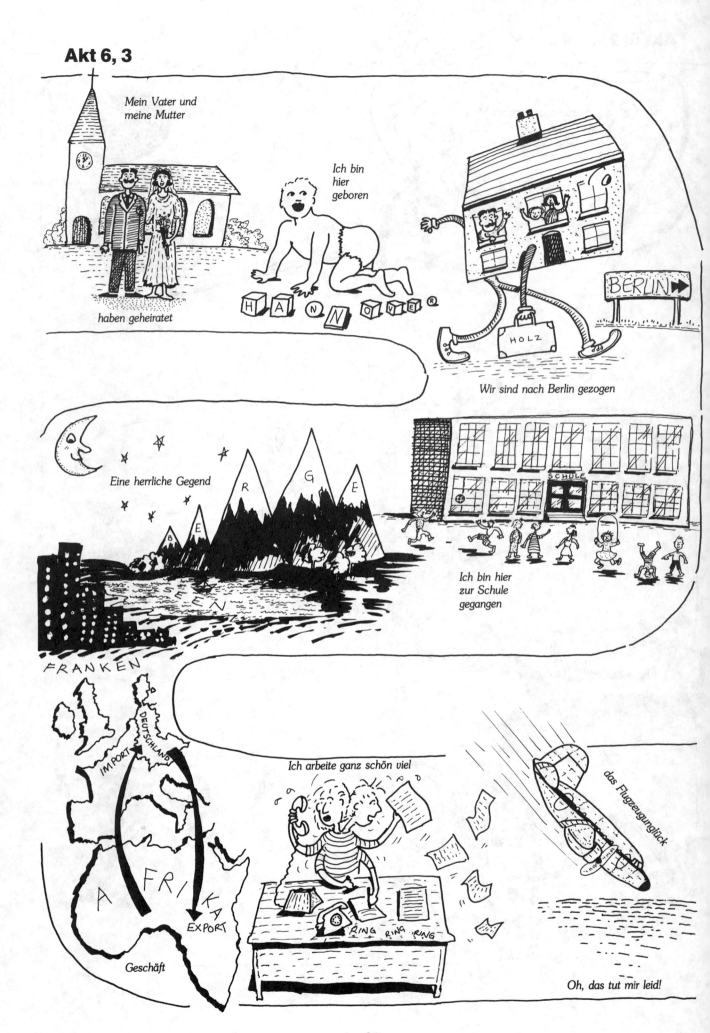

Ich muß auch viel reisen

Pakete abliefern

mein Studium in

Geschäfts-führung

beendet

zwei Kinder

Einen Jungen

Ein Mädchen

Mein Bruder ist Arzt

ein Zahnarzt

Meine Schwester arbeitet als Sprechstundenhilfe

91

Aussprache und Intonation

1. Now a few more German sounds which need your special attention.
   Listen to the long '-e-' sound and repeat:

> **Erdbeere -- geben -- zehn --**
> **Geben Sie mir bitte zehn Erdbeeren --**
> **Der Bodensee ist kein Meer --**

2. Compare this long '-e-' with the following much more open '-e-' sound:

> **zuerst -- gern -- Ersatzteil --**
> **Zuerst möchte ich gern ein Ersatzteil für mein Auto.**

3. Remember that an '-e-' at the end of a word is always unstressed and much more closed.
   Say:

> **habe -- alle -- Damen -- Blumen --**
> **Alle Damen lieben Blumen --**
> **Nette alte Herren habe ich gern --**

You can probably think of many examples which contain all three types of the letter '-e-', for example:

> **In Berlin gehe ich immer gern spazieren.**
> or   **Im Herbst esse ich gern hellblaue Heringe**

This is the final exercise in this format. For the following Acts we have incorporated pronunciation and intonation in a variety of exercises, such as vocabulary, in rhymes, jingles or tongue twisters, in order to make this important aspect of the German language as interesting and as varied as possible. (You will find the hints for these with the corresponding exercises.)

bei der Reparatur in
der Werkstatt

Teil zwei: Dialoge

	Dialogue 1	**Dialog 1**
	In the office	**Im Büro**

Andreas	How long has the car been in the garage?	**Wie lange ist das Auto schon bei der Reparatur?**
Bärbel	A week today.	**Eine Woche jetzt.**
Andreas	Why don't you telephone them?	**Rufen Sie doch mal die Werkstatt an.**
	It might be ready by now.	**Vielleicht ist es heute fertig.**
Bärbel	I have just rung up.	**Ich habe gerade angerufen.**
	It's still not ready.	**Leider ist es immer noch nicht fertig.**
Andreas	When can we have the car then?	**Wann können wir denn das Auto haben?**
Bärbel	The man on the phone said, either tomorrow morning or in the afternoon.	**Morgen früh oder morgen nachmittag, hat der Mann am Telefon gesagt.**
Andreas	Then I will have to take a taxi.	**Dann muß ich jetzt ein Taxi nehmen.**
Bärbel	I have already ordered one for you.	**Ich habe schon eins für Sie bestellt.**

	Dialogue 2	**Dialog 2**
	On the terrace	**Auf der Terrasse**

Andreas	Where would you like to sit?	**Wo möchten Sie sitzen?**
Berta	It's fairly crowded.	**Es ist ziemlich voll.**
	Where can we sit?	**Wo können wir sitzen?**
Andreas	There is a table by the window.	**Da am Fenster ist ein Tisch.**
	We are lucky, two chairs are still free.	**Wir haben Glück, zwei Stühle sind noch frei.**
Berta	Is there no table for two?	**Gibt es keinen Tisch für zwei?**
Andreas	Let's have a look outside.	**Lassen Sie uns mal draußen sehen. Vielleicht**
	Perhaps there is one out there.	**gibt es da einen.**

	Dialogue 3	**Dialog 3**
	At a Party, talking about the family.	**Auf einer Party**

Angela	We haven't seen each other for ages. How are your children?	**Wir haben uns ja lange nicht gesehen. Was machen Ihre Kinder?**
	You've got two, haven't you?	**Sie haben doch zwei, nicht wahr?**
Bert	That's right. Since we last met my daughter has married.	**Richtig. Meine Tochter hat inzwischen geheiratet.**
Angela	Your daughter is a doctor, isn't she?	**Ihre Tochter ist doch Ärztin, oder?**
Bert	No, my wife is a doctor.	**Nein, meine Frau ist Ärztin.**
	My daughter is still at university, and my son as well.	**Meine Tochter studiert noch und mein Sohn auch.**
Angela	What do they study then?	**Was studieren sie denn?**
Bert	Both the same subject.	**Beide das Gleiche.**
	Business management.	**Geschäftsführung.**
	And your children? What do they do?	**Und Ihre Kinder? Was machen die?**
Angela	I have no children.	**Ich habe keine Kinder.**
	I'm not married, either.	**Ich bin auch nicht verheiratet.**
	You must be thinking of my sister.	**Sie denken sicher an meine Schwester.**
	She has two children.	**Die hat zwei Kinder.**

93

| | Dialogue 4 | **Dialog 4** |
| | Holidays | **Urlaub** |

Andreas	How was your holiday then?	**Wie war denn Ihr Urlaub?**
Angela	Great. We've been to South Germany by car.	**Prima! Wir waren mit dem Auto in Süddeutschland.**
Andreas	I don't know South Germany.	**Süddeutschland kenne ich nicht.**
Angela	Oh, the area is wonderful! Meadows, woods, mountains, mountain lakes. We loved it!	**Oh, die Gegend ist herrlich! Wiesen, Wälder, Berge, Bergseen. Ach, es hat uns gut gefallen!**
Andreas	What was the weather like?	**Wie war denn das Wetter?**
Angela	We had 7 days rain and 3 days of sunshine!	**Sieben Tage Regen und drei Tage Sonnenschein!**

eine herrliche
Gegend

Teil drei: Dialoge

Dialog 1　　Im Restaurant

You have been invited to a restaurant for a meal. Your host discusses the menu with you.

Gastgeber	**Möchten Sie eine Vorspeise? Es gibt Suppen, Eier oder etwas mit Fisch.**
You	What kind of soups?
Gastgeber	**Nudelsuppe oder Zwiebelsuppe.**
You	No thank you. What kind of eggs (are there)?
Gastgeber	**Es gibt russische Eier, das sind gefüllte Eier.**
You	What kind of fish?
Gastgeber	**Sardinen auf Toast.**
You	I would like stuffed eggs.
Gastgeber	**Die Hauptgerichte sind Spezialitäten. Darf ich Ihnen etwas empfehlen?**
You	Yes please. I like pork.
Gastgeber	**Gut. Dann bestelle ich für uns beide ein Schweinefleischgericht und eine Flasche Weißwein. Mögen Sie Weißwein?**
You	I like white wine. Thank you.

Dialog 2　　Über die Familie

You are having a conversation about yourself and your family with your host.

Gastgeber	**Ich wohne in Hannover und bin auch hier geboren. Meine ganze Familie kommt aus Hannover. Woher kommen Sie?**
You	I live in _ _ _ _ _ _ . I was born in _ _ _ _ _ _
Gastgeber	**Haben Sie Geschwister? Ich habe zwei Brüder, aber keine Schwester. Ein Bruder ist verheiratet, aber er hat keine Kinder.**
You	I have a brother and a sister.
Gastgeber	**Meine Frau ist nicht aus Hannover, aber ihr Onkel und ihre Tante wohnen hier. Sind Sie verheiratet?**
You	I am / am not married. I have / have no children.

Dialog 3　　Am Telefon, einen Termin festlegen.

You have a raging toothache. Something needs to be done quickly. Check in the phone book to find a dentist near to your hotel. Ring him up.

Stimme	**Doktor Heinz, guten Morgen.**
You	Good morning, Frau Doktor. I have a bad toothache. When can I come?
Stimme	**Augenblick bitte. Ich bin die Sprechstundenhilfe, nicht Frau Doktor Heinz. Wie ist Ihr Name, bitte?**
You	My name is _ _ _ _ _ . I am on a visit here. I'm staying in the hotel Sonne.
Stimme	**Ach. Sie haben Zahnschmerzen. Starke Schmerzen, haben Sie gesagt?**
You	Yes, very bad. Terrible!
Stimme	**Können Sie gleich kommen?**
You	Yes, of course. I'll come straightaway. Good-bye. Thank you very much.
Stimme	**Bis gleich dann. Auf Wiederhören.**

meine Schwester
arbeitet als
Sprechstundenhilfe

Dialog 4   Auf einer Party

Your firm has business connections with a German firm. You are in Germany and have been invited for a drink. You don't know these people, but fortunately your friend can tell you a bit about them. Your friend works for this company.

Freund   **Sehen Sie die kleine blonde Dame, die mit dem Herrn in Braun spricht? Das ist unsere Chefin. Sie ist Generaldirektorin.**

You   Yes, I see her and two men in brown. Who is the man with the bald head next to her?

Freund   **Der mit der Glatze ist unser Verkaufsdirektor. Der heißt Ebert. Der neben ihm steht, das ist Herr Meier; der hat nur Geld, aber keine Stelle. Er spricht gerade mit Frau Becker. Die ist unsere Chefin.**

You   She looks very friendly.

Freund   **Ja, sie sieht gut aus und arbeiten kann sie auch. Ihr Mann war Teilhaber in der Firma, aber er ist leider vor einem Jahr umgekommen. Mit dem Auto auf der Autobahn. So ein Unglück für die Familie!**

You   Oh, has she children?

Freund   **Ja, sie hat zwei Töchter. Beide gehen noch zur Schule.**

You   I would like to meet Mrs. Becker.

Freund   **Ja natürlich. Kommen Sie mit. Wir sagen ihr ‚guten Tag.'**

eine rosige Glatze

sehr elegant gekleidet

Teil vier: Übungen

Aufschlüsselung (Deciphering)

Talking about the past

I have filled the glasses. **Ich habe die Gläser gefüllt.**

We take the action word to the very end of the sentence, adding **ge _ _ _ _ t** and put into
its usual place a form of **haben**;

e.g. **füllen:**   **Ich habe die Gläser gefüllt** (to fill)
              du hast die Gläser gefüllt
              er, sie, es hat die Gläser gefüllt
              wir haben die Gläser gefüllt
              Sie haben die Gläser gefüllt
              sie haben die Gläser gefüllt

Prost!

Note the length of this sentence:
Ich habe heute morgen um halb acht im Restaurant ‚Sonne' die Gläser gefüllt.
This is how we keep our audience awake! They must wait for the last word to know what is going on.

Übung 1

If you found that sentence amusing, take a piece of paper and make sentences from the following action words
which have occurred so far:

Zum Beispiel:

Ich habe in Berlin gewohnt.
Meine Mutter hat gut gekocht.
Er hat gelächelt.

wohnen	gewohnt	kochen	gekocht
drücken	gedrückt	lernen	gelernt
antworten	geantwortet	wählen	gewählt
suchen	gesucht	wünschen	gewünscht
hören	gehört	rechnen	gerechnet
frühstücken	gefrühstückt	schütteln	geschüttelt
klingeln	geklingelt	führen	geführt
kaufen	gekauft	füllen	gefüllt
zeigen	gezeigt	gründen	gegründet
brauchen	gebraucht	handeln	gehandelt
arbeiten	gearbeitet	lächeln	gelächelt

Übung 2

Read the sentences which you have written. Do not stress the **ge** part of the word, but the syllable following it.

The group of words which end in **....ieren** have no **ge,** but only the **t** when they refer to the past.

e.g. **probieren. Ich habe den Wein probiert.** I have tasted the wine.

In English we cannot say: he has goed, we must say: he has gone. In German, we have the same sort of
irregular behaviour in many action words. Those with close friends have the **ge** part between them,
anmachen, e.g. **er hat das Licht angemacht.** Many do not end in **t** but **en, anrufen,** e.g. **Onkel Wilhelm
hat angerufen.**

Übung 3

Can you put the following sentences into the past? You have heard and read them in the story.

1. Onkel Wilhelm ruft an.   2. Das schmeckt prima.   3. Ich lerne es von meiner Mutter.
4. Ich kaufe das blaue Hemd.   5. Hilde schenkt ihm einen Schlips.   6. Sie sieht ein Kleid.
7. Er verläuft sich.   8. Die Eltern heiraten in Hannover.   9. Sie gründen eine Firma.

Übung 4

You have seen and heard these action words in the present tense. Can you recognise them? If you can, then write the sentences out in the present tense. Here they are in the past.

1. Ich habe im Cafe gesessen.   2. Dann habe ich mit dem Kellner gesprochen.
3. Der Kellner hat den Wein gebracht.   4. Er hat den Wein in mein Glas gegossen.
5. Ich habe den Wein getrunken.   6. Ich habe mir die Zeitung von dem Mann am
nächsten Tisch geliehen.

In English we can say: I have gone. In German we must say: **Ich bin gegangen,** I am gone.

Action words which imply movement, and a few which do not, are combined with **bin, ist, sind** instead of **habe, hat, haben** when they refer to the past. Here are those which have occurred so far:

sein	**ich bin in Berlin**	**gewesen**
	er ist in Berlin	**gewesen**
gehen	**du bist**	**gegangen**
springen	**er ist**	**gesprungen**
bleiben	**sie ist**	**geblieben**
aufwachen	**wir sind**	**aufgewacht**
ausgehen	**ich bin**	**ausgegangen**
fahren	**ich bin nach Hannover**	**gefahren**
ziehen	**sie sind nach England**	**gezogen**
umkommen	**er ist**	**umgekommen**
aufspringen	**sie ist**	**aufgesprungen**

Übung 5
Can you put these sentences into the past tense?

e.g. **Ich gehe ins Haus. Ich bin ins Haus gegangen.**

1. Ich gehe ins Cafe.   2. Die Tür springt auf.   3. Er bleibt im Hotel.
4. Peter wacht auf.   5. Hilde geht aus.   6. Wir fahren in die Altstadt.
7. Sie ziehen nach Berlin.   8. Gestern war mein Geburtstag. Wir gehen aus.

Übung 6

With the morning mail you have received a letter from your sister Lore. Her daughter Helga is your favourite niece and since you know about the new man in Helga's life, the elegant Ralf, you eagerly open the letter to find out how things are progressing. Read aloud:

Wien, den 26.5.198 __

Liebe Erika!

Heute hat unsere Helga wirklich Pech gehabt. Im Kaufhaus hat sie ein schönes, weißes Kleid gesehen. Sie hat es anprobiert und es hat gepaßt. Leider war es sehr teuer.

Es hat ihr aber sehr gut gefallen, und sie hat es gekauft. Sie hat es gleich angezogen. Um 7 Uhr war sie mit Ralf verabredet, und sie ist in das Restaurant gegangen. Er war noch nicht da, und sie hat sich an einen Tisch gesetzt und hat auf ihn gewartet. Das Restaurant war ziemlich voll. Im Spiegel hat sie ihr hübsches, neues Kleid gesehen. Sie hat sich darüber gefreut. Dann ist ein Kellner gekommen. Der hat sie leider nicht gesehen. Er hat zwölf, ja wirklich 12 Gläser Rotwein getragen! Plötzlich ist eine Dame aufgestanden. Der Kellner hat den Rotwein über das schöne, weiße Kleid gegossen. So ein Pech! Helga ist gleich mit dem Taxi nach Hause gefahren. Ralf hat angerufen. Er hat Zahnschmerzen gehabt und war beim Zahnarzt.

Viele Grüße und ein Küßchen von Deiner Schwester

Lore

Übung 7

What a disaster! You are reliving Helga's day. Read the letter again as if everything is happening just now.
Start with: **Heute hat unsere Helga wirklich Pech. Im Kaufhaus sieht sie....**

(The correct answers are at the back of the book)

REMINDER

This is a gentle, yet important reminder.

Have you got the Steps in front of you? You should *always* follow each one through faithfully. Always include the visualisation exercise — the step where you close your eyes and visualise the Acts and speak as many words out loud as you can remember. This is a powerful memory device.

Don't forget your activities as you go through this course. By activities we mean not only playing as many of the games and solving as many of the puzzles as possible, but also that you should physically 'work with' the text and/or illustrations. Underlining, highlighting, jotting down any words, phrases, expressions that you particularly want to fix in your memory (or which for some reason have specific significance for you), is important.

Always remember that active involvement is the best method to store new material in your long-term memory.

You should ideally always have writing material ready while you are learning and/or listening to the cassettes.

We recommend you to have a look at these Steps as you progress through this course from time to time.

Teil fünf: Spiele, Rätsel und Reime

Die Familie

Ingrid and Georg Braun have invited you for a glass of wine to their home. During the evening they talk about their family and show you the family photo album. You realise that you have met all these people separately, not knowing that they were related!

Here are some more words associated with family and relatives:

die Großeltern = the grandparents
die Schwiegereltern = the parents-in-law
das Enkelkind = the grandchild
die Nichte = the niece
der Neffe = the nephew

Übung 1

Can you deduce who is who? Look at the family tree after each statement. This is what they have said to you during previous conversations:

a) Ich habe einen Bruder und eine Schwester. Die Schwester ist älter als ich. Sie hat einen Sohn und eine Tochter. Mein Bruder ist jünger als ich. Er ist auch verheiratet und seine Tochter ist noch sehr jung, nur ein Baby.

Wer ist a? = _____

b) Wir haben nur einen Sohn.

Wer ist b? = _____

c) Unsere Tochter ist das jüngste Enkelkind meiner Schwiegereltern.

Wer ist c? = _____

d) Ich habe eine Nichte und zwei Neffen.

Wer ist d? = _____

e) Ga-ga-ga!

Wer ist e? = _

f) Meine Großeltern wohnen in Hannover. Meine Tante Lisa mag ich gern, aber ihr Sohn, mein Vetter Hans, der ist entsetzlich!

Wer ist f? = _

g) Ich habe vor fünf Monaten ein kleines Kusinchen bekommen. Diese Kusine ist das hübscheste Baby! Einen Vetter habe ich auch und auch einen Bruder. Der Bruder ist jünger als ich.

Wer ist g? = _

h) Ich habe zwei Kusinen und einen Vetter. Die große Kusine ist sehr nett.

Wer ist h? = _

i) Ich bin verheiratet und habe zwei Töchter und einen Sohn. Mein Mädchenname war Böll. Ich habe auch vier Enkelkinder. Zwei sind Enkeltöchter und zwei sind Enkelsöhne.

Wer ist i? = _

j) Meine Frau und ich waren Einzelkinder. Unsere Familie hat jetzt zwölf (12) Personen.

Wer ist j? = _

k) Mein Mädchenname war Müller. Jetzt bin ich verheiratet und wir haben eine Tochter und einen Sohn.

Wer ist k? = _

l) Wir haben zwei Kinder. Einen Jungen und ein Mädchen.

Wer ist l? = _

Übung 2

Why not draw up the family tree of someone you know and name all the relations?

DEUTSCHE DEMOKRA-TISCHE

BUNDES

Die größte Messe
Hannover

Die meisten Messen
Berlin

REPUBLIK

REPUBLIK

Düsseldorf

Köln

Die älteste Messe

DEUTSCH-LAND

Leipzig

Bad Orb

Frankfurt

Offenbach

Wien

ÖSTERREICH

Basel

BERN

LIECHTENSTEIN

SCHWEIZ

Trade Fairs (Not all fairs could be included)

Übung

You are a busy businessman or woman. Tell your secretary about your travel plans for next year.

Start with: **Im Januar fahre ich zur grünen Woche nach Berlin. Dann fahre ich zur Möbelmesse nach Köln.**

Look at the map. Can you see
  1) Where most trade fairs are held?
  2) Where the largest trade fair is held?
  3) Which is the town where the first trade fairs were held?

Und dann zur Wiener Modemesse

Note: we add **-er** to the name of the place, and the word **-messe** at the end.

MONAT	STADT	MESSE
Januar	Berlin	**Grüne Woche** (Green Week Agricultural Fair)
	Köln	**Möbel** (Furniture)
Februar	Offenbach	**Lederwaren** (Leather goods)
März	Leipzig	**Allgemeine Messe** (General Fair)
	Düsseldorf	**Damenmoden** (Ladies Fashions)
	Wien	**Mode, Technik** (Fashions, Technical goods)
	Köln	**Eisenwaren, Haushaltswaren** (Iron goods, Household goods)
April	Frankfurt	**Pelz** (Fur)
Mai	Hannover	**Maschinenbau, Optik** (Machine building, Optical goods)
	Basel	**Mustermesse** (all Swiss industries)
	Düsseldorf	**Interpack** (Packing materials)
Juni	Frankfurt	**Interstoff** (Clothing industries)
Juli	Bad Orb	**Kur** (take the waters at the Spa)
August	Offenbach	**Leder** (leather)
	Köln	**Herrenmoden** (Men's fashions)
September	Wien	**Moden** (Fashions)
	Köln	**Haushaltswaren** (Household goods)
Oktober	Düsseldorf	**Damenmoden (Ladies fashions)**
	Köln	**Photokina** (Photographic equipment)
November	Frankfurt	**Interstoff** (Clothing ind.)
Dezember		**keine Messen!**

Akt 7

	Scene 1 Hilde and Peter's Hobbies	**Szene 1** **Hilde und Peters Hobbies**
Erzähler	Hilde and Peter have eaten their starters and the waiter brings the main course. Hilde has chosen kohlrabi and peas cooked with carrots to go with the Kasseler Rippchen. She didn't want any potatoes. Peter has ordered a green salad to go with his trout. They did not want a dessert, but both ordered a cup of coffee and a liqueur. During the meal they talk about their hobbies.	**Hilde und Peter haben die Vorspeise gegessen und der Kellner bringt das Hauptgericht. Hilde hat Kohlrabi und Erbsen mit Karotten zu den Kasseler Rippchen gewählt. Sie wollte keine Kartoffeln. Peter hat einen grünen Salat zu seiner Forelle bestellt. Sie wollten keinen Nachtisch, aber jeder bestellt sich noch eine Tasse Kaffee und einen Likör. Während der Mahlzeit unterhalten sie sich über ihre Hobbies.**
Hilde	Sport and languages. That is my change from the office. What do you do?	**Sport und Sprachen. Das ist meine Abwechslung vom Büro. Was machst du?**
Peter	On Sundays I play golf, but I also like swimming.	**Sonntags spiele ich Golf, aber ich schwimme auch gern.**
Hilde	I like playing tennis. It's all the same to me whether I win or lose. I always feel good when I have played. At the moment I'm also learning Italian. I find it easy to read but not so easy to write.	**Ich spiele gern Tennis. Es ist mir egal, ob ich gewinne oder verliere. Ich fühle mich immer so wohl, wenn ich gespielt habe. Zur Zeit lerne ich auch Italienisch. Ich finde, es ist leicht zu lesen, aber nicht so leicht zu schreiben.**

	Scene 2 Plans for the next day	**Szene 2** **Pläne für den nächsten Tag**
Erzähler	Peter looks at Hilde. An attractive intelligent woman, he thinks. How long will this stay in Hanover last? He would like to stay here for a long time. But why is this business with the uncle so mysterious? Hilde smiles.	**Peter sieht Hilde an. Eine aparte, intelligente Frau, denkt er. Wie lange dauert wohl dieser Aufenthalt in Hannover? Er würde gerne lange hier bleiben. Warum ist die Sache mit dem Onkel nur so geheimnisvoll? Hilde lächelt.**
Hilde	What are you thinking about?	**Woran denkst du Peter?**
Peter	About how much I like it here. If your uncle is still away tomorrow, perhaps we could drive into the country. Only if you have the time, of course.	**Daran, wie gut es mir hier gefällt. Wenn dein Onkel morgen noch weg ist, könnten wir vielleicht aufs Land fahren. Natürlich nur, wenn du Zeit hast.**

der Onkel so geheimnisvoll?

Hilde	Yes, tomorrow I have got time. Let's go to Berlin. There is a lot to see. But we would have to stay there overnight. It's too far for just one day. We could hire a car. There is a car hire firm next to the hotel. The replacement part for my car still hasn't come.	**Ja, morgen habe ich Zeit. Laß uns nach Berlin fahren. Da gibt es viel zu sehen. Wir müßten aber dort übernachten. Für einen Tag ist es zu weit. Wir könnten ein Auto mieten. Da ist eine Autovermietung neben dem Hotel. Das Ersatzteil für mein Auto ist immer noch nicht da.**
Erzähler	They pay the bill and take a taxi. Hilde's home is first on the way.	**Sie bezahlen die Rechnung und nehmen ein Taxi. Hilde ist zuerst zu Hause.**
Hilde	'Bye Peter, till tomorrow morning.	**Tschüß Peter, bis morgen früh.**
Erzähler	She blows him a little kiss and the taxi drives on.	**Sie wirft ihm ein Küßchen zu, und das Taxi fährt weiter.**

Scene 3	**Szene 3**
Peter hires a car	**Peter mietet ein Auto**

Erzähler	At seven o'clock the next morning Hilde goes into the Hotel Sonne. She is wearing a yellow summer dress. Peter is waiting already in the lobby. He is wearing the casual shirt which he bought yesterday.	**Um sieben Uhr am nächsten Morgen geht Hilde ins Hotel Sonne. Sie trägt ein gelbes Sommerkleid. Peter wartet schon im Foyer. Er trägt das Freizeithemd, das er gestern gekauft hat.**
Hilde	Good morning, Peter. Are you ready? Have you got your passport? We'll be driving through the GDR and you cannot do that without a passport.	**Guten Morgen, Peter. Bist du fertig? Hast du deinen Reisepaß? Wir fahren durch die DDR und ohne Reisepaß geht das nicht.**
Peter	I am ready and so let's go.	**Ich bin fertig und von mir aus können wir gehen.**
Erzähler	The car hire office is already open. The man is sitting at the desk. He wants to see Peter's driving licence and his passport. Peter would like to take out comprehensive insurance. He fills out the forms and signs them. Then he takes the car. The tank is full. Peter checks the oil level.	**Die Autovermietung ist schon geöffnet. Da sitzt ein Mann am Schreibtisch. Er möchte Peters Führerschein und seinen Reisepaß sehen. Peter möchte Vollkaskoversicherung. Er füllt die Formulare aus und unterschreibt sie. Dann übernimmt er das Auto. Der Tank ist voll. Peter prüft den Ölstand.**
Peter	Is the tyre pressure all right?	**Ist der Reifendruck in Ordnung?**
Mechaniker	Yes. Have a good trip!	**Ja, natürlich! Gute Reise!**

Der Tank ist voll

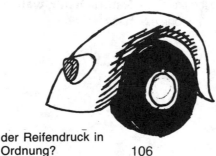

der Reifendruck in Ordnung?

	Scene 4	**Szene 4**
	The trip to Berlin	**Die Fahrt nach Berlin**
Erzähler	At this time in the morning the traffic is very heavy. There are simply too many cars, motorbikes, bicycles and trams on the road. Peter and Hilde look for the approach road for the motorway to Berlin.	**Morgens um diese Zeit ist der Verkehr sehr stark. Es gibt einfach zu viele Autos, Motorräder, Fahrräder und Straßenbahnen auf den Straßen. Peter und Hilde suchen die Auffahrt zur Autobahn nach Berlin.**
Hilde	Be careful, Peter. You have to turn off any minute now. You see the blue signs? They are there for the motorways. On the motorway we may drive as fast as we want to. There is no speed limit.	**Paß auf, Peter. Gleich mußt du abbiegen. Siehst du die blauen Schilder? Die sind für die Autobahnen. Auf der Autobahn dürfen wir so schnell fahren, wie wir wollen. Eine Geschwindigkeitsbegrenzung gibt es da nicht.**
	But please be careful!	**Aber bitte sei vorsichtig!**
Erzähler	They drive along the flat landscape, past villages and fields. After only an hour they arrive at the border. They show their papers. Luckily it doesn't take long. Then they drive through the GDR. Here they are only allowed to drive at a maximum of 100 km per hour. To the left and right there are potato fields. Hilde looks at the sky.	**Sie fahren durch die flache Landschaft, vorbei an Dörfern und Feldern. Nach einer Stunde sind sie schon an der Grenze. Sie zeigen ihre Papiere. Zum Glück dauert es nicht lange. Dann fahren sie durch die DDR. Hier dürfen sie nur hundert Kilometer pro Stunde fahren. Links und rechts sind Kartoffelfelder. Hilde sieht zum Himmel.**
Hilde	Oh dear! There are grey clouds gathering. We had planned a picnic, hadn't we? I hope it won't rain. That would be dreadful!	**O je! Da kommen graue Wolken. Wir wollten doch ein Picknick machen, nicht wahr? Hoffentlich regnet es nicht! Ach, das wäre schrecklich!**
Peter	Oh no. the weather will stay nice. In an hour's time we will be in Berlin. Surely the sun will be shining there. Have a look at the map. How do we get to West-Berlin then? Our border crossing is at Zehlendorf, isn't it?	**Ach nein. Das Wetter bleibt schön. In einer Stunde sind wir in Berlin. Dort scheint bestimmt die Sonne. Sieh mal auf die Landkarte. Wie kommen wir denn nach West-Berlin? Unser Grenzübergang ist bei Zehlendorf, nicht wahr?**
Hilde	Yes, we will be there soon. Here are the first signposts for the town already: 'Berlin, capital of the GDR'.	**Ja, bald sind wir da. Hier kommen schon die ersten Schilder für die Stadt: ‚Berlin, Hauptstadt der DDR'.**

keine Geschwindigkeitsbegrenzung

der Grenzübergang

Erzähler	At the border into West-Berlin they have to show their papers again. Not many cars are waiting and therefore everything is over fairly quickly.	**An der Grenze West-Berlin müssen sie wieder ihre Papiere zeigen. Es warten nicht viele Autos, deshalb geht alles ziemlich schnell.**
Hilde	And now let's have our picnic. I know a nice little spot. At the next traffic light you turn right, past a hospital, then we must turn off to the left.	**Und jetzt machen wir erst einmal Picknick. Ich kenne ein schönes Plätzchen. Biege an der nächsten Verkehrsampel rechts ein, an einem Krankenhaus vorbei, dann müssen wir nach links abbiegen.**
	After that we'll pass a little factory. Next to it is a shop, where we can go shopping for our picnic.	**Danach kommen wir an einer kleinen Fabrik vorbei. Daneben ist ein Geschäft, wo wir für das Picknick einkaufen können.**
Erzähler	They find the shop eventually and Peter parks the car by the side of the road.	**Sie finden das Geschäft, und Peter parkt das Auto am Straßenrand.**

Erbsen mit Karotten

grünen Salat Forelle

meine Abwechslung vom Büro

Sie unterhalten sich über ihre Hobbies

Sonntags

spiele ich Golf

Italienisch

es ist leicht zu lesen

aber nicht so leicht zu schreiben

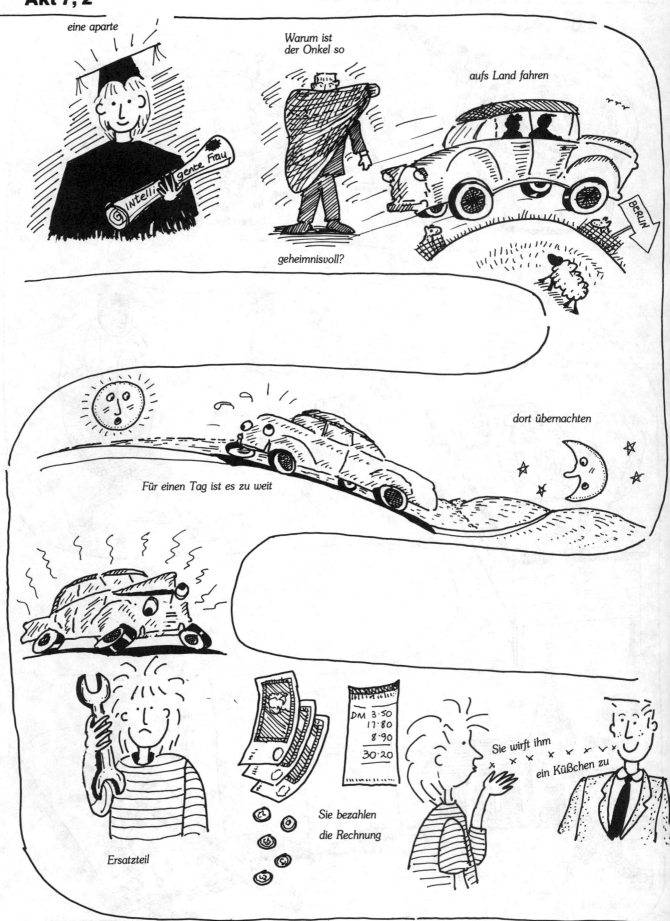

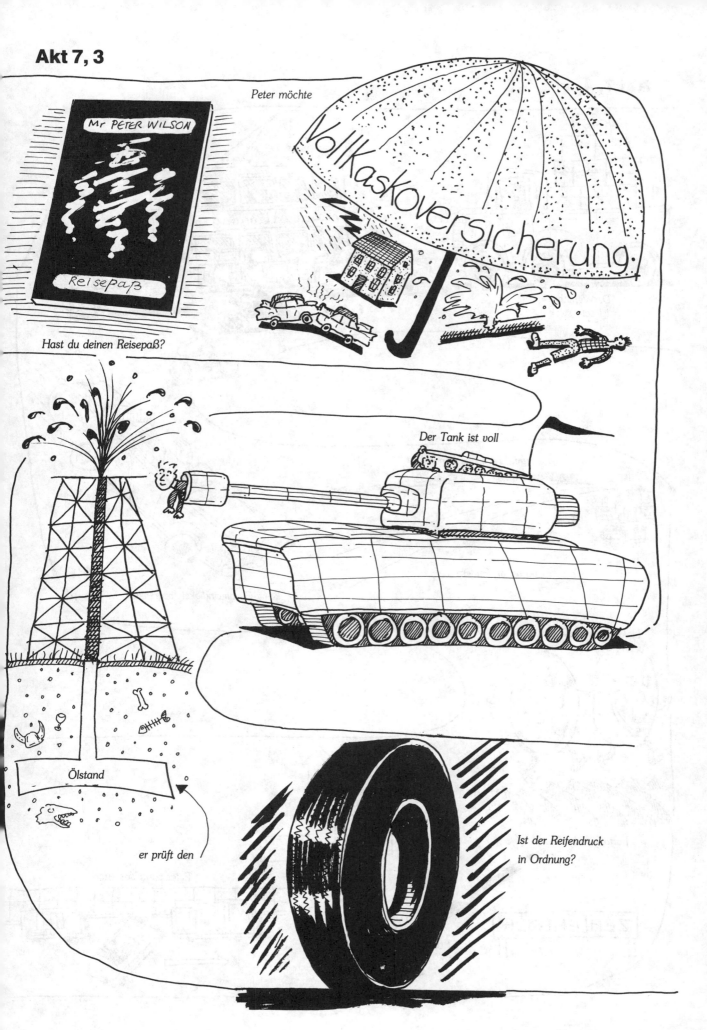

Peter möchte

Mr PETER WILSON

Reisepaß

Hast du deinen Reisepaß?

Vollkaskoversicherung

Der Tank ist voll

Ölstand

er prüft den

Ist der Reifendruck
in Ordnung?

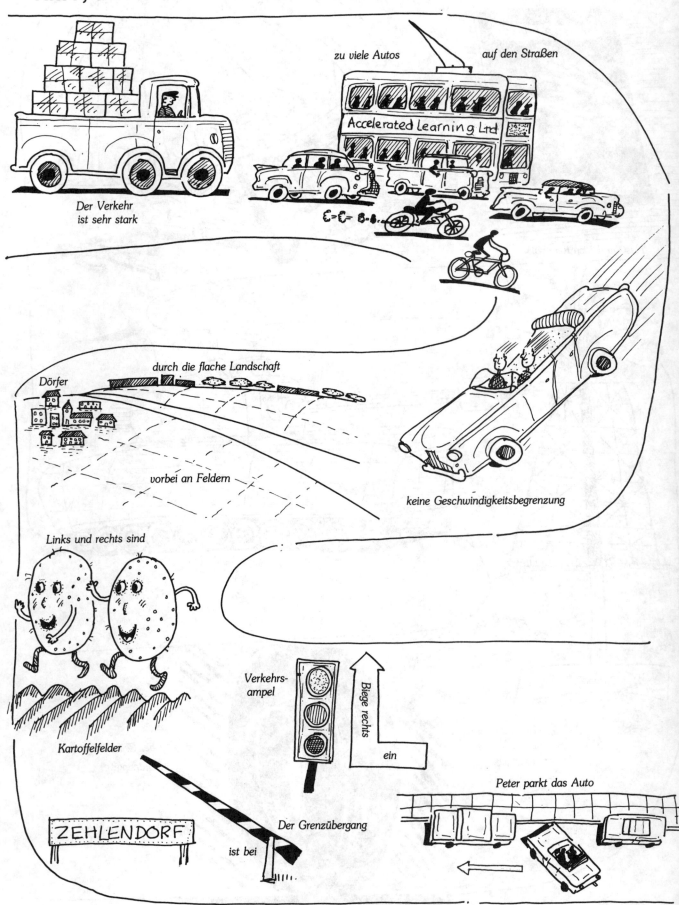

Der Verkehr
ist sehr stark

zu viele Autos

auf den Straßen

Accelerated Learning Ltd

durch die flache Landschaft

Dörfer

vorbei an Feldern

keine Geschwindigkeitsbegrenzung

Links und rechts sind

Kartoffelfelder

Verkehrs-
ampel

Biege rechts
ein

Peter parkt das Auto

ZEHLENDORF

Der Grenzübergang

ist bei

Teil zwei: Dialoge

	Dialogue 1	**Dialog 1**
	In the car on the motorway, giving orders.	**Im Auto auf der Autobahn, Anweisungen geben.**
Peter	I need a break.	**Ich brauche eine Pause.**
	Let's have something to drink.	**Laß uns etwas trinken.**
	A beer perhaps?	**Ein Bier vielleicht?**
Hilde	Be careful! You are driving.	**Sei vorsichtig! Du fährst Auto.**
	We'd better have a coffee.	**Laß uns lieber einen Kaffee trinken.**
Peter	That's a very good idea.	**Prima Idee!**
Hilde	Three more kilometres, then comes the service area.	**Noch drei Kilometer, dann kommt schon eine Raststätte.**
	Watch out.	**Paß auf!**
	Any minute you'll have to turn off to the right.	**Gleich mußt du rechts abbiegen.**
	There is the sliproad already.	**Da ist schon die Einfahrt.**
Peter	Thank goodness!	**Ein Glück!**
	Coffee at last!	**Endlich Kaffee!**

schwarzen Kaffee

	Dialogue 2	**Dialog 2**
	Anyone for tennis?	**Tennis?**
Heike	When do you play tennis?	**Wann spielst du Tennis?**
Andreas	Whenever I have the time.	**Wenn ich Zeit habe.**
Heike	When do you have the time?	**Wann hast du Zeit?**
Andreas	Whenever it's raining.	**Wenn es regnet.**
Heike	It's raining now; are you free, do you want to play?	**Es regnet jetzt; hast du Zeit, willst du spielen?**

	Dialogue 3	**Dialog 3**
	In the Restaurant	**Im Restaurant**
Gabi	What tastes better, peas or carrots?	**Was schmeckt besser, Erbsen oder Karotten?**
Andreas	I don't mind whether I eat peas or carrots. I am hungry.	**Es ist mir egal, ob ich Erbsen oder Karotten esse. Ich habe Hunger.**
Gabi	Then we'll take Kasseler and potatoes.	**Dann nehmen wir Kasseler und Kartoffeln.**
Andreas	No, I'd rather not have potatoes.	**Nein, lieber keine Kartoffeln.**
	Carrots please.	**Karotten bitte.**

zwei Kartoffeln

	Dialogue 4	**Dialog 4**
	At the Petrol Station	**An der Tankstelle**
Tankwart	What can I do for you?	**Bitte schön?**
Heike	Fill it up please.	**Volltanken bitte.**
Tankwart	Super or regular?	**Super oder Normal?**
Heike	Super please.	**Super bitte.**
Tankwart	Anything else?	**Sonst noch etwas?**
Heike	Would you please test the tyre pressure?	**Bitte prüfen Sie den Reifendruck.**
Tankwart	The tyre gauge is over there.	**Der Reifendruckmesser ist da drüben.**
	Please help yourself.	**Bitte bedienen Sie sich selbst.**
Heike	Thank you very much.	**Vielen Dank.**
	Where can I pay?	**Wo kann ich bezahlen?**
Tankwart	The office is also over there.	**Die Kasse ist auch da drüben.**
	Good bye. Have a nice journey.	**Auf Wiedersehen. Gute Fahrt.**
Heike	Thank you. Good bye.	**Danke. Auf Wiedersehen.**

Teil drei: Dialoge

1. You talk about hobbies.

Andreas	**Haben Sie ein Hobby?**
You	Yes. I play golf on Sundays.
Andreas	**Nur am Sonntag?**
You	Yes, but I also like swimming.
Andreas	**Spielen Sie auch Tennis?**
You	Yes, but only if I win.

Sonntags

spiele ich Golf

2. Now you are talking about learning a foreign language.

Heike	**Können Sie eine Fremdsprache?**
You	I'm learning Italian at the moment.
Heike	**Wie finden Sie das?**
You	I find it easy to read but not so easy to write.
Heike	**Könnten Sie eine Zeitung auf Italienisch lesen?**
You	Yes, I can read it but not understand everything.

3. Next you are talking about an outing to Berlin.

Gabi	**Haben Sie morgen Zeit?**
You	Yes, I have got time tomorrow.
Gabi	**Kennen Sie Berlin?**
You	No, I don't know Berlin.
Gabi	**Laß uns nach Berlin fahren.**
You	That's a splendid idea!
Gabi	**Es gibt dort so viel zu sehen!**
You	Could we hire a car there?
Gabi	**Aber sicher. Warum?**
You	By car we can see more.

4. You are on the road, telling your friend which way to go.

Heike	**Fahr bitte vorsichtig!**
You	Yes, O.K., but I may not drive too slowly.
Heike	**Du mußt gleich abbiegen.**
You	May we turn right here?
Heike	**Nein, nur nach links.**
You	And we have to turn right!
Heike	**Sei vorsichtig! Fahr hier geradeaus und dann rechts.**

114

Teil vier: Übungen

1. Vocabulary and Pronunciation. **Wortschatzübung und Aussprache**

Go through the story again and find the missing word in each sentence. As soon as you have found it - there's only one solution to each sentence - write it down and read it aloud. Pay attention to the correct stress of each word and underline or mark those sounds which you find difficult.
Check against the text for the correct pronunciation. One dot for each letter:

1) **Er möchte** . . . .
2) **Er sucht eine** . . . .
3) **Auf der Autobahn gibt es keine** . . . .
. . .
4) **Das Auto braucht ein neues** . . . .
5) **An der Tankstelle prüft er den** . . . .
6) **Halt! Die** . . . . **zeigt, rot'.**
7) **Wir fahren jetzt am** . . . . **vorbei.**
8) **Ich parke das Auto am** . . . .
9) **Am** . . . . **müssen sie ihre Papiere zeigen.**

Clues to help you along:
1)   In order to be safe when driving.
2)   You can hire a car there.
3)   Do you like fast driving?
4)   One of its parts has gone wrong.
5)   It must be "even" for safe driving.
6)   Green is what you hope for here.
7)   Unlucky drivers may have to be taken there.
8)   It separates pedestrians from motorists.
9)   You have to pass here before you get into West-Berlin.

(The answers are at the back of the book.)

die Verkehrsampel

2. Reime

You have already met the words **dürfen** - may
müssen - must, have to
können - to be able to, can

in this exercise you will learn how to use them in a broader context.

dürfen
Ich darf
du darfst
und er, sie, es darf auch
wir dürfen es probieren

müssen
Ich muß
du mußt
und er, sie, es muß auch
wir müssen das studieren

können
Ich kann
du kannst
und er, sie, es kann auch
wir können gut addieren
Wir dürfen nicht
wir möchten gern
die Rechnung reduzieren.

Wir möchten gern telefonieren.
Probieren geht über studieren!

eine aparte

Now try to make up your own sentences stating what you may not or cannot do.

parken, schwimmen, bezahlen, schreiben, fühlen, kochen, lernen, finden, studieren, probieren.

e.g. **Er ist erst 13. Er <u>darf</u> noch <u>nicht</u> Auto fahren.**
Es ist zu laut. Ich <u>kann nicht</u> schlafen.
Ich <u>möchte</u> nach Berlin fahren. Ich habe keinen Reisepaß.
Ich <u>darf nicht</u> nach Berlin fahren, ich muß fliegen.
<u>Müssen</u> Sie auch fliegen? Nein, ich <u>darf</u> mit dem Auto fahren.
Ich habe einen Reisepaß.
Ich kann auch mit dem Bus fahren, aber ich <u>darf nicht</u> einschlafen.

3.

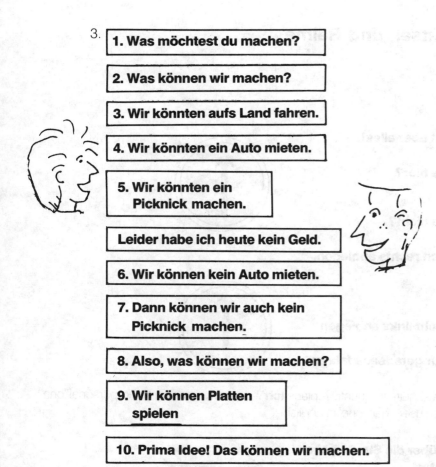

1. Was möchtest du machen?

2. Was können wir machen?

3. Wir könnten aufs Land fahren.

4. Wir könnten ein Auto mieten.

5. Wir könnten ein
   Picknick machen.

Leider habe ich heute kein Geld.

6. Wir können kein Auto mieten.

7. Dann können wir auch kein
   Picknick machen.

8. Also, was können wir machen?

9. Wir können Platten
   spielen

10. Prima Idee! Das können wir machen.

Now make some changes from **3.** onwards, instead of **aufs Land fahren** say, **in die Stadt fahren.**

Likewise for **4.** substitute **Ein Taxi nehmen** and for **5. Essen gehen; 6. kein Taxi nehmen;
7. Nicht essen gehen; 8. Also, was können wir machen?**

Now you suggest something for 9.

Teil fünf: Spiele, Rätsel und Reime

Safety First   **Sicherheit geht über alles!**

Was dürfen Sie hier?
or:

Was dürfen Sie nicht?

You: **Hier darf ich rechts abbiegen.**

oder:

Hier darf ich nicht links abbiegen.

Hier darf ich nur geradeaus fahren.

Note in German we quite frequently replace **ich** with **man,** meaning the impersonal 'one': **man** is more often used than 'one' in English.

Hier darf man über die Straße gehen.
Ich habe Vorfahrt!

Sicherheit geht über alles!

Imagine you are in Munich at various places and crossings.
Try to answer the questions, using the same action words as in the questions.

Now make up your own questions and answers, stating what you can, may, cannot or may not do by using the other signs on the map.
(If you have a partner, play it in pairs and try to 'exploit' the signs as much as possible).

Übung

1. Gehen Sie in die Schellingstraße, Ecke Türkenstraße.
    Was dürfen Sie dort? . . . .
    Dürfen Sie dort auch geradeaus fahren? . . . .

2. Gehen Sie in die Görresstraße.
    Sie wollen geradeaus fahren.
    Geht das? . . . .
    Sie möchten nach rechts in die Adelheidstraße fahren.
    Geht das auch? . . . .

3. Sie sind am Zirkus Krone (am Punkt X) und möchten nach links abbiegen.
    Können Sie das? . . . .
    Wie können Sie fahren? . . . .

4. Sie kommen am Bahnhof an und müssen über die Straße gehen. Wo können Sie die Straße überqueren? (3 possibilities)
    a) . . . .
    b) . . . .
    c) . . . .

5. Sie sind in der Arcisstraße, Ecke Schellingstraße.
    Was darf man dort nicht? (Start your answer with ‚man'): . . . .
    Und was kann man? Man . . . .

    Well done! Do you think you will ever get lost in Munich? We don't.

Straßenplan von München

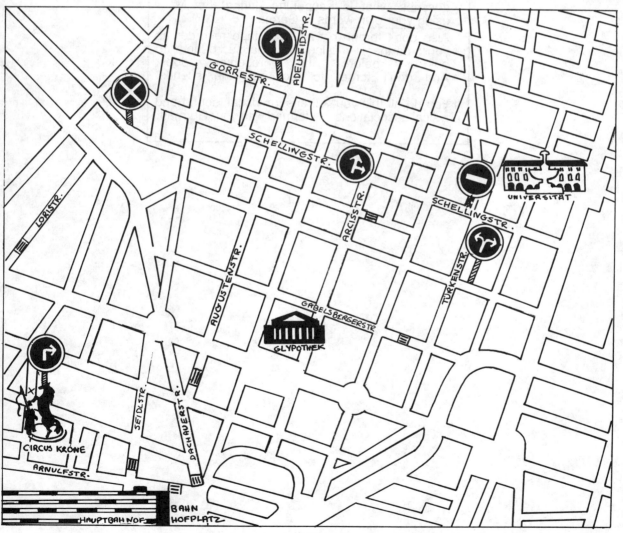

119

Teil fünf: Word cards

Please find the word cards for Akt 7 You can play with one (or ideally) more players.

Cut up the paper to make playing cards, so you'll end up with a pack of cards. Divide equally between the players, (if there's more than one player). Put the pack face down, pick up the first card and ask the question - either to yourself or to your partner(s) - „**Haben Sie ein Hobby?**" Answer with the sentence on your first card. After this question has been answered by all the players, for the second and subsequent rounds ask: „**Haben Sie noch ein Hobby?**" Should the answer on the card be negative, e.g. **ich mache nichts** , then the next question to that person (or to yourself) is: **Haben Sie kein Hobby?** (no hobby).

See how fluently you can ask in the end: „**Haben Sie ein Hobby?**" The more players you can get for this game, the more interesting it will become.

REMINDER

* Are you following the Step by Step instruction sheet?
* Don't forget the visualisation exercise - the exercise where you close your eyes and describe what is happening during the Akt - using your own words in German.
* Also don't forget to treat your tape recorder as your partner - using the pause button to answer before the presenter does.
* And don't forget to 'act out' the scenes.

If you do all this you will ensure visual, sound and physical associations are formed with your German.

Akt 8

<table>
<tr><td>Scene 1</td><td>**Szene 1**</td></tr>
<tr><td>Court Charlottenburg and a Picnic</td><td>**Schloß Charlottenburg und ein Picknick**</td></tr>
</table>

Erzähler	Hilde and Peter have arrived at Berlin and are now in a street called 'Nehringstraße'. It is very close to the Charlottenburg court. You are allowed to park there between 8 a.m. and 6 p.m., and at weekends. In the small shop they buy bread, two rolls, cheese, sliced sausage, two bottles of beer and some mineral water. Then they walk from Nehringstreet into Schloß Street. Charlottenburg court is opposite. They walk across the 'Spandauer Damm', cross the courtyard and walk to the main entrance. The sky is blue. The grey clouds have gone. Therefore they decide to have their picnic in the court gardens first and to visit the court afterwards.	**Hilde und Peter sind jetzt in Berlin, in der ‚Nehringstraße'. Die ist ganz in der Nähe vom Schloß Charlottenburg. Dort ist das Parken zwischen 8 und 18 Uhr und an den Wochenenden erlaubt. In dem kleinen Laden kaufen sie Brot, zwei Schrippen*, Käse, Aufschnitt, zwei Flaschen Bier und Mineralwasser. Dann gehen sie zu Fuß von der Nehringstraße in die Schloßstraße. Schloß Charlottenburg ist gegenüber. Sie überqueren den Spandauer Damm und gehen über den Schloß-hof zum Haupteingang. Der Himmel ist blau. Man sieht keine grauen Wolken mehr. Deshalb beschließen sie, zuerst im Schloßgarten Picknick zu machen und sich dann das Schloß anzuschauen.**

* A typical Berlin expression for crispy rolls

Aufschnitt

<table>
<tr><td>Scene 2</td><td>**Szene 2**</td></tr>
<tr><td>A surprise</td><td>**Eine Überraschung**</td></tr>
</table>

Hilde	Are you hungry?	**Bist du hungrig?**
Peter	I'm not only hungry but also thirsty.	**Ich bin nicht nur hungrig, sondern auch durstig.**
Hilde	Can you open the beer?	**Kannst du die Bierflaschen öffnen?**
Erzähler	Peter opens the bottles and Hilde takes a beautiful little booklet out of her bag.	**Peter öffnet die Flaschen und Hilde nimmt ein kleines, schönes Buch aus ihrer Tasche.**
Hilde	I bought a present for my cousin, a booklet with poems in it.	**Ich habe ein Geschenk für meinen Cousin gekauft, ein Buch mit Gedichten.**
Hilde	Listen to this:	**Hör mal zu:**
liest	This is an autumn day, such as I never saw. The air is still as if one scarcely breathed, and yet, nearby and far with rustling falls most luscious fruit from every tree.	**Dies ist ein Herbsttag, wie ich keinen sah. Die Luft ist still, als atmete man kaum und dennoch fallen raschelnd fern und nah, die schönsten Früchte ab von jedem Baum.**

die schönsten Früchte

	Oh don't disturb this celebratory feast of gathering which nature holds herself; For only such fruit leaves its branch today, as falls before the mild rays of the sun. How do you like it?	O stört sie nicht, die Feier der Natur Dies ist die Lese, die sie selber hält, denn heute löst sich von den Zweigen nur, was vor dem milden Strahl der Sonne fällt. Wie gefällt dir das?
Peter	It's wonderful! Is it by Goethe?	**Wunderbar! Ist es von Goethe?**
Hilde	A good guess, but it is by Friedrich Hebbel.	**Gut geraten, aber es ist von Friedrich Hebbel.**
Peter	Today is exactly a day like that!	**Genauso ein Tag ist heute!**
Hilde	You are right. How very pleasant and quiet it is round here!	**Stimmt. Wie ruhig und angenehm es hier ist!**
Erzähler	They relax from their car journey. From the court gardens they can see the summer residence 'Belvedere'. It really looks very romantic!	**Sie erholen sich von der Autofahrt. Vom Schloßgarten aus können sie die Sommerresidenz Belvedere sehen. Sie ist wirklich sehr romantisch!**
Hilde	By the way, at two o'clock we have a meeting there with my cousin. After our picnic we'll go to meet him.	**Übrigens, um zwei haben wir dort eine Verabredung mit meinem Cousin. Nach unserem Picknick gehen wir, um ihn zu treffen.**
Erzähler	Peter was astonished. What a surprise, once again! After the picnic they walked across the lawn towards Belvedere. A young man of about 25 was standing at the entrance and came towards them.	**Peter ist erstaunt. Was für eine Überraschung; schon wieder! Nach dem Picknick gehen sie über den Rasen auf Belvedere zu. Ein junger Mann, er ist ungefähr 25, steht am Eingang und kommt auf sie zu.**

	Scene 3 Another surprise	**Szene 3 Noch eine Überraschung**
Hans (der Cousin)	Ah, here she is, my cousin. Punctual as ever. Hello Hilde, how are you? Nice to see you again.	**Ah, da kommt ja meine Cousine. Pünktlich wie immer. Guten Tag, Hilde, wie geht's? Nett dich wiederzusehen.**
Hilde	Hello Hans. May I introduce you: this is Peter Wilson, from London. Peter, this is my cousin Hans Holz.	**Tag Hans. Darf ich vorstellen: das ist Peter Wilson aus London. Peter, das ist mein Cousin Hans Holz.**
Hans	Hello Peter; welcome to Berlin. Shall we go into the castle? There is a marvellous porcelain collection inside.	**Guten Tag, Peter; willkommen in Berlin. Sollen wir ins Schloß gehen? Drinnen gibt es eine wunderschöne Porzellansammlung.**
Peter	Oh yes; that's a great idea.	**Oh ja; das ist eine gute Idee.**
Erzähler	Hans pays the entrance fee for the three of them, and they enter a room with very large, high windows.	**Hans bezahlt den Eintritt für alle drei, und sie gehen in einen Raum mit sehr großen, hohen Fenstern.**

Hans	What do you do, Peter? Are you studying or working?	**Was machen Sie, Peter? Studieren Sie noch oder arbeiten Sie?**
Peter	I've just finished my studies. I don't know yet what I want to do. I would like to work in an import/export company like Hilde.	**Ich habe gerade mein Studium beendet. Ich weiß noch nicht, was ich machen will. Ich würde gern in einer Import/Export Firma arbeiten, wie Hilde.**
Erzähler	Hans asks a lot of questions about Peter's family, his hobbies and interests. Then comes the next surprise for Peter:	**Hans hat noch viele Fragen. Er will mehr über Peters Familie, seine Hobbies und Interessen wissen. Dann kommt die nächste Überraschung für Peter:**
Hans	I also work in an import/export company.	**Ich arbeite auch in einer Import/Export Firma.**
Peter (erstaunt)	Ah, exactly like Hilde!	**Ach, genau wie Hilde!**
Hans	Yes of course. We work in the same company!	**Ja natürlich. Wir arbeiten doch zusammen!**

Scene 4	**Szene 4**
The next surprise	**Die nächste Überraschung**

Peter	Why didn't you tell me that the two of you work together?	**Warum hast du mir nichts davon gesagt, daß ihr zusammen arbeitet?**
Hilde	Oh, sorry; I completely forgot about that. But I'm so glad that you have met Hans.	**Oh entschuldige, das habe ich ganz vergessen. Aber ich bin froh, daß du Hans jetzt kennengelernt hast.**
Erzähler	Hilde and Peter walked back to their car and drove to the hotel Astoria in Spichernstraße. They had booked the rooms by telephone. When they got there they found a message from Mr. Wilhelm Holz: "Will arrive one day later than planned; please ask Peter to stay. My suggestion: why not go on a sightseeing tour of Berlin tomorrow?"	**Hilde und Peter gingen zum Auto zurück und fuhren zum Hotel Astoria in der Spichernstraße. Sie hatten die Zimmer telefonisch bestellt. Als sie dort ankamen, fanden sie eine Nachricht von Herrn Wilhelm Holz: „Werde einen Tag später ankommen; bitte aber Peter noch zu bleiben. Mein Vorschlag: macht morgen eine Stadtbesichtigung von Berlin!"**
Peter (dachte)	This is all very strange! First Hilde's cousin Hans and now this message. But three days spent together with Hilde, that's not too bad at all.	**Dies ist alles höchst seltsam! Zuerst der Cousin Hans und jetzt diese Nachricht. Aber drei Tage mit Hilde zusammen ist auf jeden Fall ganz schön.**

eine
Stadtbesichtigung

123

Akt 8, 1

Es ist ganz nah

Parken zwischen acht
und achtzehn Uhr erlaubt

8 am   6 pm

Käse

In dem
kleinen
Laden

Aufschnitt

Kaufen sie

zwei Flaschen Bier

zuerst Picknick im

gegenüber

Schloßgarten

die Bierflaschen öffnen

Hilde nimmt

ein kleines Buch

aus ihrer Tasche

O stört sie nicht

die schönsten Früchte

Baum

ein Herbsttag

fallen raschelnd

Wunderbar! von F. Hebbel.

Sie gehen über den Rasen

Sie erholen sich von der Autofahrt

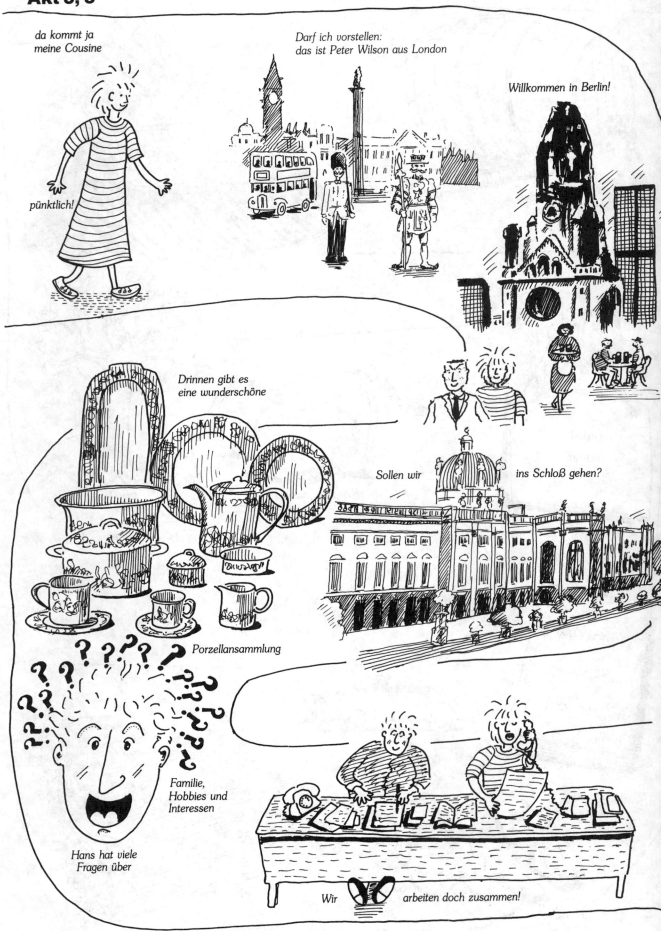

da kommt ja
meine Cousine

pünktlich!

Darf ich vorstellen:
das ist Peter Wilson aus London

Willkommen in Berlin!

Drinnen gibt es
eine wunderschöne

Sollen wir   ins Schloß gehen?

Porzellansammlung

Familie,
Hobbies und
Interessen

Hans hat viele
Fragen über

Wir   arbeiten doch zusammen!

126

Teil zwei: Dialoge

1.

| | Plans for a picnic | **Pläne für ein Picknick** |
| | Making suggestions | **Vorschläge machen** |

Hilde	Are you hungry? Or not yet?	**Bist du hungrig, oder noch nicht?**
Peter	I'm hungry and thirsty.	**Ich bin hungrig und durstig.**
Hilde	Shall we have our picnic?	**Sollen wir Picknick machen?**
Peter	That's a great idea. Where shall we have the picnic?	**Das ist eine prima Idee. Wo sollen wir picknicken?**
Hilde	I suggest in the court gardens.	**Im Schloßpark schlage ich vor.**
Peter	Yes, that's grand. Afterwards we can go inside and have a look around. I would like to see the porcelain collection.	**Oh ja, und dann können wir hineingehen und uns das Schloß anschauen. Ich möchte gern die Porzellansammlung sehen.**
Hilde	It's very famous. It contains all the original pieces from the 18th century.	**Die ist sehr berühmt. Es sind alles Originalstücke aus dem achtzehnten Jahrhundert.**
Peter	I've heard about that. I hope we won't break anything.	**Davon habe ich gehört. Ich hoffe, wir machen nichts kaputt!**
Hilde	Don't worry! It's all behind glass.	**Keine Sorge! Ist alles hinter Glas ausgestellt.**

die Porzellansamm

2.

| | Hotel Astoria | **Hotel Astoria** |
| | To reserve a room (by telephone) | **Ein Zimmer bestellen (per Telefon)** |

Empfangsdame	Hotel Astoria, Berlin, can I help you?	**Hotel Astoria Berlin; was kann ich für Sie tun?**
Peter	Have you any vacancies?	**Haben Sie Zimmer frei?**
Empfangsdame	Yes, we have. When would you want them?	**Ja, für wann bitte?**
Peter	Tomorrow night until Thursday, for one night.	**Für morgen, die Nacht von Mittwoch auf Donnerstag also.**
Empfangsdame	Yes, we've still got rooms. What kind of rooms would you like?	**Ja, da sind noch Zimmer frei. Was für Zimmer möchten Sie?**
Peter	Two single rooms with bathroom, please.	**Zwei Einzelzimmer mit Bad bitte.**
Empfangsdame	Two singles with bath, O.K. What's the name please?	**Zwei Einzel mit Bad, ist in Ordnung. Auf welchen Namen bitte?**
Peter	Wilson and Holz. It's for Miss Holz and myself.	**Wilson und Holz. Für Fräulein Holz und mich.**
Empfangsdame	I've written it down, Mr. Wilson. Please report at the reception by 2 p.m. tomorrow. Otherwise we do not guarantee the booking.	**Ich habe das notiert, Herr Wilson. Melden sie sich bitte morgen bis um 14 Uhr an der Rezeption an. Sonst können wir die Zimmer nicht garantieren.**
Peter	Thank you; good-bye.	**Vielen Dank. Auf Wiederhören.**

3.   A telegram; reading a message.   **Ein Telegramm; eine Nachricht lesen**

Hilde	Here is a telegram for you.	**Hier ist ein Telegramm für dich.**
Anne	For me? How strange. Who sent it?	**Für mich? Seltsam. Von wem?**
Hilde	How should I know? Open it and read it!	**Das weiß ich doch nicht. Mach mal auf und lies!**
Anne	Arrive one day later - stop -	**Komme einen Tag später - stop -**
	please stay in Berlin - stop -	**bitte bleibe noch in Berlin - stop -**
	sightseeing perhaps? - stop -	**Stadtbesichtigung vielleicht? - stop -**
	See you later - stop Peter H.	**Bis später - stop Peter H.**
Hilde	Well, are you staying?	**Also, bleibst du noch?**
Anne	Of course I am!	**Aber natürlich!**

4.   Another message...   **Noch eine Nachricht...**

Reading a bizarre message.

Anne	Have a listen: Do I come? - or	**Hier, hör mal zu: Komme ich? - oder**
	do you come? Over the weekend or	**kommst du? Am Wochenende oder am**
	on Friday? In the castle or in	**Freitag? Im Schloß oder im**
	the court gardens? -	**Schloßgarten? -**
	Where shall we meet?	**Wo treffen wir uns denn?**
Andreas	Who's sent that then?	**Wer hat denn das geschickt?**
Anne	I don't know, no idea. Perhaps a	**Weiß ich doch nicht, keine Ahnung. Ein**
	ghostwriter?	**Ghostwriter vielleicht?**
Andreas	Very strange!	**Höchst seltsam!**
	Exactly as in a thriller.	**Genau wie im Krimi.**

5.   No parking -   **Parken verboten -**

what you can and can't do.   **was können Sie und was dürfen Sie nicht?**

Politesse	There's no parking here!	**Hier ist parken verboten!**
Peter	I didn't know that. I will drive off	**Das habe ich nicht gewußt. Ich fahre**
	immediately.	**sofort weg.**
Politesse	On weekends you can	**Am Wochenende können Sie hier**
	park here.	**parken.**
Peter	And what day is it today?	**Und was ist heute?**
Politesse	Today is Wednesday.	**Heute ist Mittwoch.**
Peter	What a pity! But I can't	**Schade! Aber zwei Tage kann**
	wait for 2 days!	**ich nicht warten!**
Politesse	And you are not allowed to	**Das dürfen Sie**
	do so either!	**auch nicht!**

Parken
verboten

Teil drei: Dialoge

1. You reserve a room by telephone.

Empfangs-dame	**Hier Hotel Sonne, kann ich Ihnen helfen?**
You	Yes, please. I would like to reserve a room, a single room.
Empfangsd.	**Mit Bad oder Dusche?**
You	With shower please.
Empfangsd.	**Für wann möchten Sie das Zimmer?**
You	For tomorrow; for one night please.
Empfangsd.	**Geht in Ordnung. Auf welchen Namen bitte?**
You	For _ _ _ _ _ _ _ _ _ _ (say your name).
Empfangsd.	**Habe ich notiert. Auf Wiederhören, bis morgen dann.**

Ich möchte ein Zimmer reservieren

2. You enquire about the way.

Empfangsd.	**Hotel Sonne, ja bitte?**
You	I can't find the hotel.
Empfangsd.	**Sind Sie mit dem Auto hier? Und wo genau sind Sie bitte?**
You	Yes, by car; I'm at Kennedy Square, at the Rathaus Schöneberg.
Empfangsd.	**Am Kennedyplatz? Das ist ja ganz in unserer Nähe; wir sind in der Apostel-Paulus-Straße.**
You	How do I get there?
Empfangsd.	**Ganz einfach: Fahren Sie die Salzburger Straße entlang, die zweite Straße rechts ist schon die Apostel-Paulus-Straße; Nummer 35, rechts. Alles klar?**
You	I hope so. Thank you very much and see you soon.

3. At a party, you ask someone about his studies.

Person	**Was machen Sie? Studieren Sie noch?**
You	I've just finished my studies. And you?
Person	**Ich studiere noch.**
You	What do you study?
Person	**Ich studiere Elektronik.**
You	Oh, is that interesting?
Person	**Manchmal schon, aber nicht immer.**
You	And where do you study?
Person	**Hier in Berlin, natürlich, an der Freien Uni.** (**Uni.** is short for **Universität**).

4.   You buy a ticket to go round the museum.

Kasse	**Ja bitte?**
You	I would like to see the porcelain collection.
Kasse	**Die ist zur Zeit leider geschlossen.**
You	What a pity! Why?
Kasse	**Die wird renoviert; nicht die Sammlung, sondern der Raum.**
You	Oh, I see. I hope they won't break anything.
Kasse	**Keine Sorge. Möchten Sie vielleicht die Gemäldesammlung sehen?**
You	Yes please. One ticket please. Where is it?
Kasse	**Hier bitte. Sie ist im ersten Stock.**

5.   You talk about hobbies

Haben Sie
ein Hobby?

A.	**Haben Sie ein Hobby?**
You	Of course, everybody has a hobby.
A.	**Was ist denn Ihr Hobby?**
You	I like listening to music and I like sport. And what is your hobby?
A.	**Andere Leute nach ihren Hobbies fragen. Aber ich höre auch gern Musik, besonders Pop-Musik.**
You	I prefer Jazz.
A.	**Kennen Sie ein Jazzlokal in Berlin?**
You	No. I don't know Berlin that well. Can you recommend one?
A.	**Ja, ich kann Ihnen die „Eierschale" empfehlen. Da gibt's jeden Sonntagmorgen Jazz, zum Frühstück sozusagen. Der Eintritt ist frei.**
You	Thanks for the tip.

1. Sprichwörter und Redensarten - proverbs and sayings

a) **Wenn einer eine Reise tut, dann kann er was erzählen.**
(Travel broadens the mind)

b) **Eine Überraschung kommt selten allein; oder auch:**
Ein Unglück kommt selten allein!
(It never rains but it pours!)

c) **Ich lache mich kaputt, und er weint wie ein Schloßhund.**
(He's crying his eyes out)

2. Reime - (nonsense rhymes)
Lesen Sie laut:

a) **Zwei Bierflaschen sprangen in die Taschen;**
da mußten sie lachen, bis die Griffe brachen.
(du machst Sachen!)

(The original expression is really: **sich kaputt lachen** - to laugh oneself silly).

b) **Im Magen lagen viele Fragen,**
im Keller hat er manche gute Lagen.
(d.h. = das heißt, gute Lagen Wein,
z.B. = zum Beispiel: Jahrgang 1982 war ein besonders guter Wein).

Teil vier: Übungen

Wie gut kennen Sie Berlin?

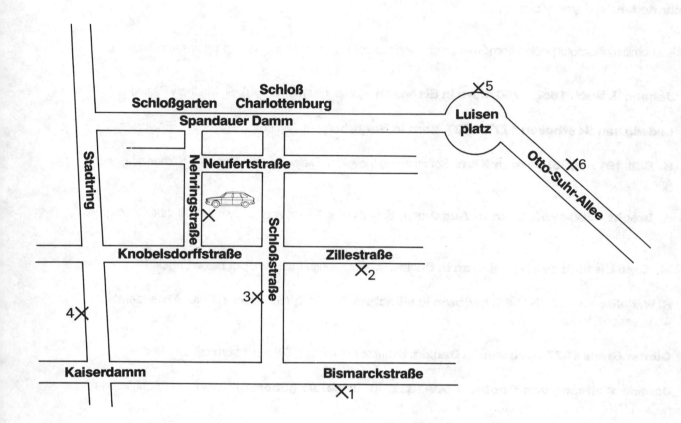

Do you remember Peter and Hilde had parked the car in Nehringstraße?

From there they walked to the Schloß Charlottenburg.

Now imagine they had parked their car at all those places marked with a X. Could you tell them the way to the Schloß if they asked you: **Wir sind hier in der Bismarckstraße. Wie kommen wir zum Schloß bitte?**

As a variation, you are visiting Berlin and want to get to the Schloß from all the X marked places. How would you ask the way? **Ich bin (hier) in _ _ _ _ _ _ _ _ _ _ _ _ _**

(The answers are at the back of the book)

The Name Game

> You would now benefit a lot from reading through the Name Game again — including Parts 2 and 3. Are you remembering to make up a mnemonic dictionary for these words where there are no linguistic associations?

Teil fünf: Spiele, Rätsel und Reime.

Berühmte Leute - Famous people.

Here is a number of famous people from German speaking countries, mainly from the world of arts and literature.

1. **Johann S. Bach 1658-1750, born in Eisenach,** Komponist (composer), St. Matthew Passion.

2. **Ludwig van Beethoven 1770-1827, born in Bonn,** Komponist (composer), Eroica, Pastorale.

3. **H. Böll 1917-1985, born in Köln,** Schriftsteller (novelist), Die verlorene Ehre der Katharina Blum, Ansichten eines Clowns.

4. **B. Brecht 1898-1956, born in Augsburg,** Schriftsteller (writer and playwright), Mutter Courage, Galileo Galilei.

5. **Marlene Dietrich 1901- , geboren in Berlin,** Schauspielerin (actress), Der blaue Engel.

6. **R. W. Faßbinder 1947-1982, geboren in München,** Regisseur (film director),Berlin Alexanderplatz, Angst'essen Seele auf.

7. **Günter Grass 1927-, geboren in Danzig,** Schriftsteller (writer), Die Blechtrommel, Der Butt.

8. **Johann Wolfgang von Goethe 1749-1832, in Frankfurt geboren,** Dichter und Schriftsteller (writer), Götz von Berlichingen der Erlkönig, Faust.

9. **Immanuel Kant 1724-1804, in Königsberg geboren,** Philosoph (philosopher), Kritik der reinen Vernunft.

10. **Käthe Kollwitz 1867-1945, in Königsberg geboren,** Bildhauerin (sculptress), Pieta.

11. **Gottfried Keller 1819-1890, in Zürich geb.,** Schriftsteller (writer), Die Leute von Seldwyla, Der Grüne Heinrich.

12. **Martin Luther 1483-1546, in Wittenberg geb.,** Reformator (church reformer) Bibel-Übersetzung ins Deutsche.

13. **Rosa Luxemburg 1871-1919, in Berlin geb.,** Sozialistische Politikerin, Spartakus-Bund (Spartacus-league)

14. **Wolfgang A. Mozart 1756-1791, in Salzburg geb.,** Komponist (composer), Eine kleine Nachtmusik, Die Hochzeit des Figaro.

15. **Friedrich Schiller 1759-1805, in Marbach geb.,** Dichter und Schriftsteller (writer), Don Carlos, Maria Stuart, Die Glocke.

16. **Johann Strauss 1825-1899, in Wien geb.,** Komponist (composer) Wiener Blut, Kaiserwalzer, An der schönen blauen Donau.

17. **Ulrich Zwingli 1484-1531, in Zürich geb.,** Humanist, Reformator (church reformer) Kirchenreform.

Übung:

1. Can you place the right person to the town which had a special significance for them? We have given you a clue by adding their most famous works or achievements.

2. What else do you know about these people?

3. Try to make a thumbnail sketch of the person(s) you know best; then say aloud his/her lifespan (dates of birth and death) and works, and everything else you know.

   Start, for example, with **Er/Sie ist 1901 (Neunzehnhunderteins) in Berlin geboren.**
                                              (year)   (place)

   Then: **Sie hat im blauen Engel in Berlin die Lola gespielt.**
                 (work or film)   (place/location) (character)

   Das Stück / Der Film ist sehr erfolgreich gewesen
   (nature of work)

N.B. If you wish to check how to make up numbers please refer to the glossary.

DEUTSCHE DEMOKRA-TISCHE

BUNDES

Hannover

• BERLIN

REPUBLIK

REPUBLIK

DEUTSCH-LAND

Cochem

• Limburg

• Katz

Trier

• Heidelberg

• Ludwigsburg

• Nymphenburg

• Sigmaringen

ÖSTERREICH

• Neuschwanstein

• Linderhof

SCHWEIZ

Übung : When you have found the places on the map, try to answer this question for some of them, stating what they are famous for or what they house; **zum Beispiel:**
Wofür ist Schloß Nymphenburg berühmt?
Schloß Nymphenburg / Das Schloß / Es ist berühmt für die
Schönheitsgalerie, oder für die Porzellanfabrik.

Akt 8

Berühmte Schlösser und Burgen - Famous castles

Here are some of the most famous castles in and around Germany and along the river Rhine. Can you ‚place' the following ones into their correct position on the map? Most of them are situated in cities which are as famous as the palaces and castles themselves such as München (Munich)

1. Schloß Herrenhausen und Gärten. Die Schloßgärten sind mit die schönsten in Europa; Freilufttheater.

7. Burg Cochem im Rheinland

2. Schloß Sigmaringen, vormals Sitz der Hohenzollern.

8. Schloß Heidelberg am Neckar

3. Schloß und Kathedrale in Limburg.

9. Schloß Trier an der Mosel. Trier ist die älteste Stadt Deutschlands, von den Römern gegründet.

4. Schloß Charlottenburg; schönstes Zeugnis des Barock-Stil; im Jahre 1695 für die Kurfürstin Sophie Charlotte gebaut.

10. Schloß Linderhof in Oberbayern

5. Schloß Katz am Rhein (in der Nähe gibt es auch ein Schloß Maus!)

11. Schloß Neuschwanstein bei Füssen; diese beiden Schlösser, „Märchenschlösser" genannt, wurden für den „Märchenkönig" Ludwig II von Bayern gebaut.

6. Schloß Ludwigsburg und Gärten

12. Schloß Nymphenburg; Innendekoration im Rokokostil, brillanter Festsaal, „Schönheitsgalerie" König Ludwigs I., Porzellanfabrik

Aufschlüsselung - Deciphering.

Some more talking about the past.

You have already met one form of the past tense in Act 6: **gefüllt, gewohnt, gelernt,** do you remember?

There is, however, another past tense in German. Go back to the story, Scene 4, and underline the words: **gingen, fuhren, hatten, ankamen, fanden,** and their translations.

It's not difficult to see that these action words have been put into the past tense, because the **Erzähler** is telling us what Hilde and Peter did. There is a simple rule when to use this version of the past tense - when someone is reporting about events which took place.

Now, how do you form this tense? Many action words are irregular and therefore the past tense of them simply has to be learnt.

For the regular ones, you simply add **-te** to the stem of the word as in **machen, machte, lachen, lachte,** etc. Fortunately, this tense is only used in the written language, for writing letters, etc. For communication you do not normally use it, so now you know about it you can largely neglect it! As long as you recognise it that will suffice.

Akt 9

	Scene 1 Sightseeing	**Szene 1** **Stadtbesichtigung**

Erzähler — At breakfast the next morning in the Hotel Astoria Peter greets the waitress.

Beim Frühstück am nächsten Morgen im Hotel Astoria begrüßt Peter die Kellnerin:

Peter — Good morning

Guten Morgen.

Kellnerin — Good morning, Mr. Wilson.

Guten Morgen, Herr Wilson.

Peter — Have you a newspaper please? I would like to know what the temperature is going to be like today.

Haben Sie eine Zeitung bitte? Ich möchte gerne nachsehen, wie heiß es heute wird.

Erzähler — Peter reads the weather forecast in the 'Berlin paper'. He is amused to read that it is cool and windy in London. In Berlin, however, it is going to be sunny and hot again. Then he asks Hilde:

Peter liest den Wetterbericht in der ‚Berliner Zeitung'. Er muß lachen, als er liest, daß es in London kühl und windig ist. In Berlin dagegen wird es sonnig und heiß bleiben. Dann fragt er Hilde:

Peter — What shall we do today?

Was sollen wir heute machen?

Hilde — Don't you remember, we wanted to go sightseeing in Berlin. We could go to the National Gallery first. It is at the 'Tiergarten', in Potsdamerstraße, and is open from 10 o'clock today. Let's go there by tube and bus.

Weißt du denn nicht mehr, wir wollten doch eine Stadtbesichtigung machen. Wir könnten zuerst in die Nationalgalerie gehen. Die ist am Tiergarten, in der Potsdamerstraße, und ist heute ab zehn Uhr geöffnet. Laß uns mit der U-Bahn und dem Bus dorthin fahren.

By bus we can at least see a bit of Berlin. And it's cheaper than by taxi.

Mit dem Bus sehen wir wenigstens ein bißchen von Berlin. Und es ist billiger als mit dem Taxi.

wie heiß es heute wird

Erzähler — They walked to the tube station 'Wittenbergplatz', which is very near to their hotel.

Sie gingen zur U-Bahn Station ‚Wittenbergplatz', ganz in der Nähe ihres Hotels.

Hilde — You can buy the tickets. That's good practice for you.

Du kannst die Fahrkarten kaufen. Das ist eine gute Übung für dich.

Peter — Okay. Shall I get singles or returns?

Einverstanden. Soll ich einfache oder Rückfahrkarten kaufen?

Hilde — The best thing to get is a multiple ticket, it's only 9 marks. That gives us five trips altogether. It's practical and we save money.

Am besten kaufst du eine Sammelkarte, die kostet nur neun Mark. Da haben wir fünf Fahrten. Das ist praktisch und wir sparen Geld.

eine

139

Erzähler	Peter goes to the ticket office.	**Peter geht zum Fahrkartenschalter.**
Peter	How do we best get to the National Gallery please?	**Wie kommen wir am besten zur Nationalgalerie bitte?**
Beamter	First you take line 1. It's two stops to the Kurfürstenstraße. There you have to change and take bus No. 48 to the Potsdamer Brücke. The National Gallery is at the corner opposite.	**Mit der Linie eins fahren Sie zwei Stationen bis zur Kurfürstenstraße. Dort steigen Sie in den achtundvierziger Bus und fahren bis zur Potsdamer Brücke. Die Nationalgalerie ist gleich an der Ecke gegenüber.**
Peter	Thanks. A multiple ticket please.	**Danke. Eine Sammelkarte bitte.**
Beamter	One multiple ticket; that's nine marks please.	**So, eine Sammelkarte, die kostet neun Mark bitte.**
Peter	Which platform please?	**Welcher Bahnsteig bitte?**
Beamter	Platform two, for Schlesisches Tor!	**Bahnsteig zwei, Richtung ,Schlesisches Tor'.**
Erzähler	Peter and Hilde go to the platform. A few minutes later the tube arrives. They don't have to wait long for the bus either.	**Hilde und Peter gehen zum Bahnsteig. Ein paar Minuten später kommt schon die U-Bahn. Auch beim Umsteigen in den Bus müssen sie nicht lange warten.**

der Fahrkarten schalter

die U-Bahn kommt schon

	Scene 2 In the National Gallery	**Szene 2 In der Nationalgalerie**
Erzähler	They get off the bus at Potsdamer Brücke, and the National Gallery is directly in front of them.	**Sie steigen an der Potsdamer Brücke aus, und die Nationalgalerie liegt direkt vor ihnen.**
Peter	I would like to see pictures by the expressionists.	**Ich würde gern Bilder von den Expressionisten sehen.**
Hilde	Oh, how intelligent you are! So you know the painters belonging to the 'Brücke' and 'Blauer Reiter' group. Good. Let's go and see the expressionist paintings first and afterwards whatever interests you.	**Ah, was du nicht alles weißt! Du kennst also die Malergruppe ,Brücke' und ,Blauer Reiter'! Gut! Da schauen wir uns zuerst den Expressionismus an und dann, was dich sonst noch interessiert.**
Erzähler	They spent a good two hours at the exhibition and saw pictures by Kandinsky, Franz Marc, by Macke, Beckmann and Schmidt-Rotluff. Peter was very impressed by their strong colours and the enormous size of their canvases.	**Sie verbrachten gut zwei Stunden in der Ausstellung und sahen Bilder von Kandinsky, Franz Marc, von Macke, Beckmann und Schmidt-Rotluff. Peter war sehr beeindruckt von den kräftigen Farben und den großen Flächen.**
Hilde	These paintings give the best effect when you don't stand too close to them. Seen at a very close range, they look very different.	**Diese Bilder wirken am besten, wenn man nicht zu nah davor steht. Von der Nähe gesehen, wirken sie ganz anders.**

zu nah

Peter	Yes you are right. I'm fascinated by these pictures, this exhibition is wonderful. I'm glad that we came here.	**Ja. du hast recht. Ich bin ganz begeistert von diesen Bildern. Ich muß sagen, diese Ausstellung ist großartig. Ich bin so froh, daß wir hierher gekommen sind.**
Hilde	What's the time now?	**Wieviel Uhr ist es jetzt?**
Peter	It's half past two.	**Es ist halb drei.**
Hilde	There is still time left. Now we can go to see the 'Gedächtniskirche'. It's not too far from here.	**Da haben wir ja noch Zeit. Jetzt können wir noch zur Gedächtniskirche gehen. Es ist nicht so weit von hier.**

Scene 3	**Szene 3**
A Car Accident	**Ein Verkehrsunfall**

Erzähler	Hilde and Peter walked along the 'Reichspietschufer', then turned into the Kurfürstenstraße. In the distance they could see the Gedächtniskirche.	**Hilde und Peter gingen am Reichspietschufer entlang und dann in die Kurfürstenstraße. In der Ferne sahen sie die Gedächtniskirche.**
Peter	Will I ever really meet your uncle?	**Werde ich deinen Onkel wirklich jemals treffen?**
Hilde	Don't worry. He wiil certainly be at home this evening. I'm sure you'll like him.	**Sei unbesorgt! Er wird ganz sicher heute abend zu Hause sein. Ich bin sicher, daß du ihn magst.**
Erzähler	Suddenly they saw a lot of people on the road. Two cars had collided, and a man was lying on the road.	**Plötzlich sahen sie viele Leute auf der Fahrbahn. Zwei Autos waren zusammengestoßen, und ein Mann lag auf der Straße.**
Peter	What has happened?	**Was ist passiert?**
Passant	A car crossed the lights on 'red' and collided with another one. Fortunately, only one of the drivers is injured.	**Ein Auto ist bei ‚rot' über die Ampel gefahren und mit dem anderen Auto zusammengestoßen. Zum Glück ist nur der eine Fahrer verletzt.**
Peter	Is he badly injured?	**Ist er schwer verletzt?**

ein Mann lag
auf der Straße

Passant	It looked severe at first, but he is only slightly injured. He is in shock, of course.	**Zuerst sah es schlimm aus, aber er ist nur leicht verletzt. Er hat natürlich einen Schock.**
Peter	Can I help? Shall I call a doctor?	**Kann ich helfen? Soll ich einen Arzt rufen?**
Passant	No, it's not necessary. We have already called an ambulance Perhaps he has broken something?	**Nein, es ist nicht mehr nötig. Wir haben schon einen Krankenwagen angerufen. Vielleicht hat er sich etwas gebrochen?**
Erzähler	Peter and Hilde walked along the famous 'Ku-damm'* and visited the Gedächtniskirche with its bombed-out spire, one of the landmarks of Berlin.	**Peter und Hilde gingen den berühmten Ku-damm* entlang, und besichtigten die Gedächtniskirche mit dem zerstörten Turm, eines der Wahrzeichen von Berlin.**
Hilde	I'm really tired from all this walking! Let's drive home and have a rest.	**Ich bin von dem vielen Laufen ganz müde geworden! Laß uns nach Hause fahren und uns ausruhen.**
Erzähler	When they got home Uncle William was indeed waiting for them!	**Als sie zu Hause ankamen, wartete Onkel Wilhelm tatsächlich auf sie!**

* short for 'Kurfürstendamm' and used much more often than the latter.

Ich bin ganz
müde geworden!

142

eine

wie heiß es heute wird

kühl und windig

es soll sonnig und heiß bleiben

Laß uns mit der U-Bahn fahren

Wir sehen ein bißchen von Berlin

der Fahrkarten-schalter

einfach

Rückfahrkarten

DM 9.-

Rückfahrkarten

Sie steigen aus

Kandinsky

große Flächen

zu nah
davor steht

Kräftige farben

3 +3=6

Wievel Uhr
ist es jetzt?

es ist halb drei

du hast recht

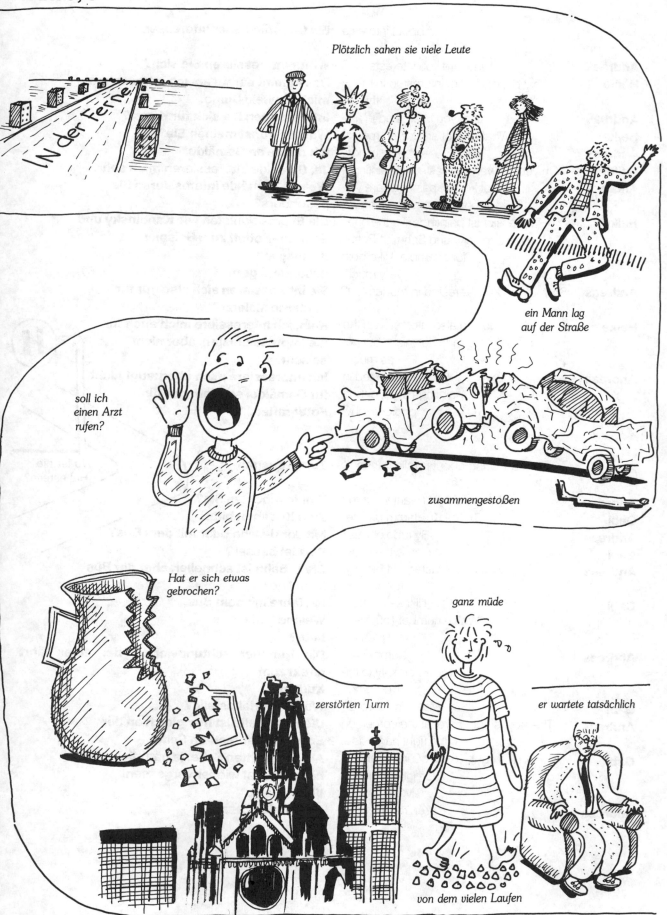

Plötzlich sahen sie viele Leute

In der Ferne

ein Mann lag
auf der Straße

soll ich
einen Arzt
rufen?

zusammengestoßen

Hat er sich etwas
gebrochen?

ganz müde

er wartete tatsächlich

zerstörten Turm

von dem vielen Laufen

eines der Wahrzeichen von Berlin

Teil zwei: Dialoge

1.   Talking about interests   **Ein Gespräch über Interessen**

Andreas	What are you interested in?	**Wofür interessieren Sie sich?**
Heike	That depends. I'm interested in many things.	**Das kommt darauf an. Ich interessiere mich für viele Dinge.**
Andreas	Are you interested in art?	**Interessieren Sie sich für Kunst?**
Heike	What kind of art do you mean?	**Was für Kunst meinen Sie?**
Andreas	Paintings.	**Ich denke an Gemälde.**
Heike	Oh yes, I'm very interested in paintings.	**Ja, Gemälde interessieren mich sehr.**
Andreas	What kind of paintings are you particularly interested in?	**Welche Gemälde interessieren Sie besonders?**
Heike	Expressionist paintings like the ones by Kandinsky and Schmidt-Rotluff for example. I like both very much.	**Die Expressionisten wie Kandinsky und Schmidt-Rotluff zum Beispiel, die mag ich besonders gern.**
Andreas	So you are only interested in modern art?	**Sie interessieren sich also nur für moderne Malerei?**
Heike	No, I'm also interested in the impressionists, but not as much.	**Nein, ich interessiere mich auch für die Impressionisten, aber nicht so sehr.**
Andreas	I'm not interested in paintings at all, only in photography.	**Ich interessiere mich überhaupt nicht für Gemälde, sondern nur für Fotografien.**

Wo ist die Haltestelle?

2.   Enquiring about public transport   **Zum Kudamm**

Andreas	Where do you want to go to?	**Wohin möchten Sie?**
Gabi	To the Ku-damm please.	**Zum Kudamm bitte.**
Andreas	By tube or bus?	**Mit der U-Bahn oder mit dem Bus?**
Gabi	Which is the best?	**Was ist besser?**
Andreas	By tube it's faster, but the bus is cheaper.	**Die U-Bahn ist schneller, aber der Bus ist billiger.**
Gabi	I'll take the bus. Which number (bus) is it, please?	**Ich fahre mit dem Bus. Welche Linie bitte?**
Andreas	Number 48; it goes directly to the Ku-damm.	**Die Nummer achtundvierzig; der 48-er fährt direkt zum Kudamm.**
Gabi	Where is the stop?	**Wo ist die Haltestelle?**
Andreas	The stop is right here, at the corner, on the right hand side.	**Die Haltestelle ist hier gleich an der Ecke, auf der rechten Seite.**
Gabi	On the right, yes of course, I almost forgot about that! Many thanks.	**Auf der rechten Seite, ja natürlich, das hätte ich fast wieder vergessen! Vielen Dank.**
Andreas	You're welcome.	**Bitte, keine Ursache.**

3.

	Talking about the weather	**Wettervorhersage**
Helga	Do you know what the weather is going to be like?	**Wissen Sie, wie das Wetter wird?**
Gisela	Yes, I happen to know it; I've seen the weather report.	**Ja, das weiß ich zufällig. Ich habe den Wetterbericht gelesen.**
Helga	What's the weather like in London?	**Wie ist das Wetter in London?**
Gisela	In London it's cool; but it's going to improve.	**In London ist es kühl; es wird aber besser.**
Helga	And what's the weather in Berlin going to be like?	**Und wie wird das Wetter in Berlin?**
Gisela	Here it's going to stay warm, just as yesterday. It's going to be a lovely summer.	**Hier bleibt es sonnig und warm, so wie gestern. Das wird ein schöner Sommer!**
Helga	You are quite right. It's fairly warm already.	**Da haben Sie recht. Es ist schon jetzt sehr warm.**
Gisela	According to the report, we will get as much as 30° centigrade today.	**Laut Wetterbericht wird es heute 30 Grad geben.**
Helga	Ah, that's the right weather for the Berlin Weiße. 'Bye.	**Da wird die Berliner Weiße gut schmecken! Auf Wiedersehen.**

4.

	Describing an accident	**Ein Autounfall**
Andreas	What was that?	**Was ist denn jetzt passiert?**
Heike	An accident, in Kantstraße.	**Ein Autounfall, auf der Kantstraße.**
Andreas	How did it happen?	**Wie ist denn das passiert?**
Heike	The traffic lights at the crossing are not working. Three cars have collided.	**Die Ampel an der Kreuzung hat nicht funktioniert. Drei Autos sind zusammengestoßen.**
Andreas	Is somebody injured?	**Ist jemand verletzt?**
Heike	Yes, two drivers are badly injured; the other passengers only slightly, thank goodness.	**Ja, zwei Fahrer sind schwer verletzt; die anderen zum Glück nur leicht.**
Andreas	When did it happen then?	**Wann ist es denn passiert?**
Heike	Ten minutes ago. Somebody rang the ambulance. It will be here soon.	**Vor zehn Minuten. Jemand hat den Krankenwagen angerufen. Er wird gleich kommen.**
Andreas	I hope so. The traffic looks like chaos, don't you think?	**Das hoffe ich auch. Der Verkehr hier ist chaotisch, nicht wahr?**

REMINDER

Have you got the Steps in front of you? You should *always* follow each one through faithfully. Always include the visualisation exercise — the step where you close your eyes and visualise the Acts and speak as many words out loud as you can remember. This is a powerful memory device.

Don't forget your activities as you go through this course. By activities we mean not only playing as many of the games and solving as many of the puzzles as possible, but also that you should physically 'work with' the text and/or illustrations. Underlining, highlighting, jotting down any words, phrases, expressions that you particularly want to fix in your memory (or which for some reason have specific significance for you), is important.

Always remember that active involvement is the best method to store new material in your long-term memory.

You should ideally always have writing material ready while you are learning and/or listening to the cassettes.

We recommend you to have a look at these Steps as you progress through this course from time to time.

Teil drei: Dialoge

Dialog 1

You are visiting the National Gallery in Berlin and on that day an opinion poll takes place.

Andreas	**Darf ich Sie etwas fragen: Sind Sie zum ersten Mal hier?**
You	Yes, I'm here for the first time.
Andreas	**Warum Sind Sie in die Nationalgalerie gekommen?**
You	I'm interested in art and paintings.
Andreas	**Welche Gemälde interessieren Sie besonders?**
You	The expressionists; from the 20th century.
Andreas	**Haben Sie einen Lieblingsmaler?**
You	Yes, my favourite German painter is Kandinsky.
Andreas	**Welche Maler mögen Sie außerdem noch?**
You	I also like Turner and Constable very much.
Andreas	**Wo kann man Gemälde von diesen Malern sehen?**
You	In the Tate Gallery and the National Gallery in London.
Andreas	**Vielen Dank für das interessante Gespräch. Und viel Spaß!**
You	Thank you. You're welcome!

große Flächen

Dialog 2   **Beim Frühstück im Hotel**

Before you go sightseeing in Berlin you would like to know what the weather is going to be like.

Gabi	**Guten Morgen. Wie geht's?**
You	Good morning. I'm fine, thanks.Do you know what the weather is going to be like?
Gabi	**Das weiß ich leider nicht, tut mir leid.**
You	Have you a newspaper? I'd like to look it up.
Gabi	**Hier bitte. Also, wie wird das Wetter?**
You	In Berlin it's going to be sunny and warm, around 30 degrees centigrade.
Gabi	**Das wird ja ganz schön heiß. Zu heiß für mich. Wo ist es kühler?**
You	In London, of course.
Gabi	**Bleibt es dort kühl?**
You	Yes, it's going to stay cool, windy and wet, according to the weather report.
Gabi	**Ein Pech, daß wir in Berlin und nicht in London sind!**

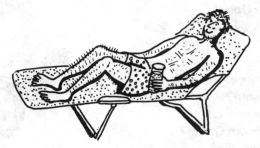

es soll sonnig und heiß bleiben

Dialog 3   **Im Hotel; nach dem Frühstück**

You had breakfast in the hotel with coffee but you would have preferred tea.

Heike	**Wie hat Ihnen das Frühstück geschmeckt?**
You	I liked it very much, but I would have preferred tea to coffee.
Heike	**Warum haben Sie nichts gesagt? Sie hätten Tee bestellen können.**
You	I didn't know that.
Heike	**Möchten Sie noch einen Tee bestellen?**
You	I'd love one.
Heike	**Ein Kännchen kostet 3 Mark.**
You	Then I just take a cup of tea please.

eine
Tasse Tee

Dialog 4   Ein Unfall

You happened to be on a street in Berlin when an accident happened.

Andreas	**Haben Sie den Unfall gesehen?**
You	Yes, I happened to see it.
Andreas	**Wie ist das passiert?**
You	The blue car drove through the red traffic light.
Andreas	**Ist jemand verletzt?**
You	Only one person is injured.
Andreas	**Wissen Sie, ob er schwer verletzt ist?**
You	Fortunately he is only slightiy injured. Here comes the ambulance!

Dialog 5   Der mysteriöse Onkel

Are you sure? Talking about certainties and uncertainties.

You	This is all very strange.
Gabi	**Was ist so seltsam?**
You	The thing about your uncle.
Gabi	**Was ist mit meinem Onkel?**
You	Shall/Will I ever meet him?
Gabi	**Sei unbesorgt. Du wirst ihn heute abend treffen.**
You	Are you sure?
Gabi	**Ich bin ganz sicher. Er wird heute abend zu Hause sein.**
You	You said that yesterday already.

Teil vier: Übungen

Ausdrücke und Sprüche, die sich aufs Wetter beziehen; und andere.
Expressions and sayings related to the weather; and others.

Es gießt in Strömen.
It's pouring

Es schüttet wie aus Kannen/Eimern.
It's raining cats and dogs

Es ist knallheiß.
It's boiling hot

Heute herrscht wieder eine brüllende Hitze / eine Affenhitze. It's steaming / roasting hot

Bei dem Mistwetter jagt man ja keinen Hund vor die Tür!
In such weather you wouldn't put a dog out

Was ich nicht weiß, macht mich nicht heiß.
Ignorance is bliss

Übung macht den Meister!
Practice makes perfect

Sie macht ein Gesicht wie sieben Tage Regenwetter.
She looks as miserable as sin

Donnerwetter!
Fabulous!

Zum Donnerwetter!
Blow it!

Abzählreim - counting out rhyme

Ich und du
Müllers Kuh   **Wie du mir**
Müllers Esel   **So ich dir**
das bist du!   Tit for tat

Go back to the story, Scene 1 and to Teil zwei, Dialog 3, and underline the words **wird, werden, wirst.** (8 altogether).

It's not difficult to see that they indicate events that take place in the future.

Now do this little exercise. Fill in the right word:

1. Wie _ _ _ _ das Wetter morgen?

2. Morgen _ _ _ _ es wieder sonnig und warm.

3. Hilde und Peter _ _ _ _ _ _ nächstes Jahr wieder in die Nationalgalerie gehen.

4. Peter _ _ _ _ Hildes Onkel heute abend treffen.

5. – – – – du Peter mögen?

6. Er _ _ _ _ ihm wichtige Informationen geben.

7. Es _ _ _ _ sehr spät sein.

Die Wettervorhersage - The Weather forecast

Imagine you are a meteorologist (**ein Meteorologe oder eine Meteorologin**) and are asked to read the weather forecast for a late spring day in Germany and some foreign cities. (As they are usually announced via radio).

Go through the list of major cities in Germany beside the map, and start your announcement by saying:
Die Vorhersage für morgen. In Hamburg wird es bedeckt, 13 Grad .

Then pick some foreign cities as well. Choose the ones where it is warmest and coldest at this time of year.

DasWetter

Lage: Ein Hoch mit Schwerpunkt über Norditalien bestimmt das Wetter in Deutschland, nur der Norden wird von Wolkenfeldern ostwärts ziehender Tiefausläufer überquert.
Vorhersage: Am Wochenende im Norden Deutschlands wolkig, aber niederschlagsfrei, sonst überwiegend sonnig und Erwärmung auf Temperaturen zwischen 17 und 22 Grad. Meist schwachwindig.
Aussichten: Teils heiter, teils wolkig. Temperaturrückgang.

Deutscher Wetterdienst

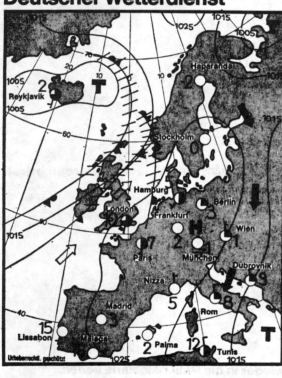

Die Vorhersagekarte für den 21. April 1985 8 Uhr

Zeichenerklärung:	
◖	wolkenlos
◗	heiter
◐	halb bedeckt
◕	wolkig
●	bedeckt
()	Windstille
⤴	Nordwind 10 km/h
�	Ostwind 20 km/h
⟱	Südwind 30 km/h
⤵	Westwind 40 km/h
Temperatur in Grad Celsius	
≡	Nebel
⦁	Nieseln
●	Regen
✳	Schnee
▼	Schauer
⚡	Gewitter
⧄	Niederschlagsgebiet
⌒⌒	Warmfront
△⌒△	Okklusion
▲▲▲	Kaltfront am Boden
△△△	Kaltfront in der Höhe
⇨	Luftströmung warm
⬛⇨	Luftströmung kalt
H	Hochdruckzentrum
T	Tiefdruckzentrum
—	Isobaren

Deutschland:

Sylt	bedeckt	10
Schleswig	wolkig	12
Norderney	wolkig	11
Hamburg	bedeckt	13
Lübeck	bedeckt	12
Greifswald	bedeckt	12
Osnabrück	bedeckt	14
Hannover	bedeckt	15
Berlin	heiter	13
Düsseldorf	wolkig	12
Leipzig	heiter	12
Köln-Bonn	wolkig	13
Koblenz	heiter	10
Bad Hersfeld	heiter	12
Trier	heiter	11
Feldberg/Ts.	heiter	8
Frankfurt/M.	heiter	13
Stuttgart	heiter	11
Nürnberg	*wolkenl.	12
Freiburg	wolkenl.	12
Freudenst.	heiter	9
München.	wolkenl.	11
Passau	wolkenl.	10
Feldb./Schw.	heiter	5
Konstanz	wolkenl.	9
Oberstdorf	wolkenl.	9
Zugspitze	wolk'l.	—3
Garmisch	wolkenl.	13

Ausland:

Helsinki	heiter	8
London	heiter	12
Kopenhagen	bedeckt	12
Amsterdam	heiter	13
Ostende	heiter	13
Zürich	wolkenl.	9
Locarno	wolkig	12
Paris	heiter	15
Nizza	heiter	16
Barcelona	wolkenl.	15
Madrid	wolkenl.	15
Mallorca	heiter	17
Malaga	wolkenl.	15
Wien	heiter	10
Innsbruck	wolkenl.	9
Prag	wolkenl.	11
Warschau	heiter	10
Belgrad	wolkenl.	13
Konstanza	bedeckt	10
Bozen	wolkenl.	11
Venedig	wolkenl.	13
Rom	heiter	15
Athen	bedeckt	14
Istanbul	bedeckt	8
Moskau	heiter	7
Las Palmas	bedeckt	19
Tokio*	heiter	16
Peking*	heiter	17
Kairo*	heiter	20

Wetter und Temperaturen in Grad Celsius vom Freitag, 11 Uhr

*7.00 Uhr MEZ

Heute: Sonnenaufgang:	6.15 Uhr	Mondaufgang:	2.31 Uhr
Sonnenuntergang:	20.28 Uhr	Monduntergang:	9.48 Uhr

*Wolkenlos

P.S. Do you know where the **„Zugspitze"** is?

MEZ = Mitteleuropäische Zeit (= Central European Time)

Die 24 - Stunden - Uhr

Ist es 15 Uhr oder 24 Uhr?
Oder 15.24, oder 3 Uhr?

Am Flughafen Berlin-Tegel

All scheduled flights and the world airline companies - except Lufthansa, the German national airline - arrive and depart from Berlin-Tegel, West Berlin's airport situated in the north west of Berlin.

(The British, French and Americans have their own sections on the airport, according to the **4 Sektoren** of Berlin).

Airports are always fascinating and attract large crowds; as you have a few hours to spare before your flight is due, you watch the "arrival" and "departure" boards, with the different flight numbers and times on it:

Flug-Nr.	Ankunft von	Landung
LH 621	Frankfurt	13:20
PA 734	New York	13:40
BA 807	London Heathrow	14:05
KLM 09	Amsterdam	16:15
CAL 654	London Luton	16:55
LH 070	München	17:25
DA 030	Palmas	18:25

* (Nr. = Nummer)

1. Look out for the flights/arrivals from London, say aloud
   a) the flight number and
   b) the landing time
   as indicated on the schedule.
2. You are asked to give some information:

Frage   **Wann landet die Maschine aus Frankfurt?**

You   **Um _ _ _ _ _ _ Uhr _ _ _ _ _ _ .**

Frage   **Und wieviel Uhr ist es jetzt?**

You   **Es ist _ _ _ _ _ _ _ _ _ _ _ _ _ _ .**

.... richtig oder falsch?

3.   Read the sentences aloud, and correct the time(s) where necessary:

	Richtig / Falsch	

1)   **Die Maschine aus Palmas landet um 18:25.**

2)   **Das Flugzeug aus München landet um 17:20.**

3)   **Der Flug von Frankfurt ist um 13:20 in Berlin.**

4)   **Die Maschine aus Amsterdam landet um 16:20.**

5)   **Das Flugzeug aus New York kommt um 13:40 an.**

6)   **Die Maschine aus London landet um 14:15.**

7)   **Der Flug von London, Luton ist um 16:05 in Berlin.**

As an alternative, if the plane landed earlier or later than the scheduled times, say:

Die Maschine / Das Flugzeug kommt 5 Minuten früher / später an;

or:

Die Maschine / Das Flugzeug kommt fünf Minuten früher / später.

The Name Game

You would now benefit a lot from reading through the Name Game again — including Parts 2 and 3. Are you remembering to make up a mnemonic dictionary for these words where there are no linguistic associations?

Teil fünf: Spiele, Rätsel und Reime

The Weather Game - **Das Wetterspiel**

Wie wird das Wetter?

Do you remember what the weather was like in Berlin when Hilde and Peter went sightseeing, and in London at the same time?

In Berlin wird es sonnig und warm.

As the weather is very changeable and very different in different places, find the sheet with the weather pictures on it and say what the weather is going to be like in a particular place. Each time start with a question:

e.g.: **Wie wird das Wetter in London?**

        (name of place)

Antwort: **In London wird es**

      (name of place)   (nature of the weather)

Note: If you don't get it right, don't forget that the weather forecaster doesn't always get it right either!

    Variation: a) **Wie war das Wetter gestern in Berlin?**

            (name of place)

        b) **Wie ist das Wetter heute in Hannover?**

            (name of place)

Ausdrücke zum Wetter:

**sonnig, heiter, warm, wolkenlos
kühl, windig, kalt, naß
Nebel, neblig
Schnee, es schneit
Donner und Blitz, es donnert, es blitzt
Hagel, es hagelt**

sonnig, heiter.

Schnee

es blitzt

Akt 10

Scene 1: / Szene 1:
Uncle William / Onkel Wilhelm

Erzähler

At last Peter had the opportunity to get to know Uncle William. Uncle William was very tall. To be honest he was rather fat. One could see that for many years he had lived well, perhaps too well. He was elegantly dressed, about 6′ tall and wore glasses. He was pleased to see Peter and Hilde at last.

Jetzt endlich bekam Peter die Gelegenheit, Onkel Wilhelm kennenzulernen. Onkel Wilhelm war sehr groß. Um ehrlich zu sein, er war ziemlich dick. Man sah, daß er viele Jahre gut, vielleicht zu gut gelebt hatte. Er war elegant gekleidet, ungefähr 1 Meter 80 groß und trug eine Brille. Er freute sich, Hilde und Peter endlich zu sehen!

Onkel Wilhelm

Good evening! I hope that you liked Berlin. I am sorry I have come so late, but I have been very busy.

Guten Abend! Ich hoffe, daß euch Berlin gefallen hat. Es tut mir leid, daß ich so spät gekommen bin, aber ich war sehr beschäftigt.

Peter

That doesn't matter. We really had a good time in Berlin. As a matter of fact I, enjoy being a tourist!

Das macht überhaupt nichts! Wir haben uns gut amüsiert in Berlin. Ich muß sagen, meine Rolle als Tourist gefällt mir!

Onkel Wilhelm

I'm afraid you'll have to become a courier again. There is a lot of work for you tomorrow.

Leider müssen Sie aber wieder Kurierdienst machen. Morgen gibt es viel Arbeit für Sie.

Peter

What a pity! But one can't be on holiday forever. All good things come to an end!

Schade! Aber man kann nicht immer auf Urlaub sein. Alle schönen Tage gehen einmal zu Ende!

Ich war sehr beschäftigt

Scene 2: / Szene 2:
Two parcels / Zwei Pakete

Erzähler

Uncle William then walked to his desk. He took out two parcels: the one that Peter had brought to Hanover and a second one, a new one.

Dann ging Onkel Wilhelm zu seinem Schreibtisch. Er nahm zwei Pakete heraus: eins, das Peter nach Hannover gebracht hatte und ein zweites, ein neues.

Onkel Wilhelm

Peter, I would like you to take these two parcels to Zurich tomorrow. I will give you an address. Please deliver them by 1 o'clock tomorrow. I will give you the money for the airfare, of course, and your expenses.

Peter, ich möchte, daß Sie diese beiden Pakete morgen nach Zürich bringen. Ich gebe Ihnen eine Adresse. Liefern Sie bitte die Pakete morgen mittag vor 13 Uhr dort ab. Natürlich gebe ich Ihnen das Geld für den Flug und die Spesen.

zwei Pakete

Peter	I hope you don't think I'm impolite, but why can't you send the parcels by post? Is it not much more expensive if I take them there by plane? I must also tell you that I'm a bit worried. I don't even know what is inside those parcels.	Hoffentlich finden Sie mich nicht unhöflich, aber warum können Sie die Pakete nicht mit der Post schicken? Ist es nicht viel teurer, wenn ich sie mit dem Flugzeug dorthin bringe? Und um ganz ehrlich zu sein, ich habe auch ein bißchen Angst. Ich weiß ja nicht, was in den Paketen drin ist.

Mit der Post schicken

Erzähler	Peter did expect Uncle William to be annoyed now, but he only smiled.	Eigentlich erwartete Peter, daß Onkel Wilhelm jetzt ärgerlich reagieren würde, aber er lächelte nur.
Onkel Wilhelm	Don't worry, Peter. Please trust me. I do understand you, but everything will be all right. However, first you must deliver the parcels in person to Mr. Harald Zuckermann. Here is the address.	Haben Sie keine Angst, Peter. Vertrauen Sie mir bitte. Ich verstehe Sie, aber es wird schon alles in Ordnung gehen. Doch zuerst müssen Sie die Pakete persönlich bei Herrn Harald Zuckermann abliefern. Hier ist die Adresse.
Erzähler	Although Peter was still doubtful he agreed. Mr. Holz put the two parcels in a very expensive leather briefcase and handed it over to Peter. Then they had something to eat and afterwards Peter soon returned to his hotel. Mr. Holz had told him that the flight was already booked. That meant he had to get up early to pick up the ticket at the airport.	Peter war zwar immer noch skeptisch, aber dann doch einverstanden. Herr Holz packte die zwei Pakete in eine sehr wertvolle Aktentasche aus Leder und gab sie Peter. Dann aßen Sie noch etwas zusammen und danach kehrte Peter gleich in sein Hotel zurück. Herr Holz hatte ihm gesagt, daß der Flug bereits gebucht war. Er mußte also früh aufstehen, um das Ticket am Flughafen abzuholen.

die Aktentasche

	Scene 3: The flight to Zurich	Szene 3: Der Flug nach Zürich
Erzähler	Next morning Peter paid the hotel bill. Then he drove to the airport by taxi and went directly to the Swiss Air desk.	**Am nächsten Morgen bezahlte Peter die Hotelrechnung. Dann nahm er ein Taxi zum Flughafen und ging direkt zum Swiss Air Schalter.**
Peter	Can you help me please? You have a ticket for Peter Wilson, is that correct? A return flight to Zurich, at 10.15.	**Können Sie mir helfen, bitte? Sie haben ein Ticket auf den Namen Peter Wilson, nicht wahr? Ein Rückflug nach Zürich, um 10 Uhr fünfzehn.**
Angestellte	Yes, we have your ticket. How would you like to pay? By credit card or cash?	**Ja, wir haben Ihr Ticket hier. Wie möchten Sie bezahlen? Mit Kreditkarte oder in bar?**
Peter	I'll pay cash, please. Do you know if the flight is on time?	**In bar, bitte. Wissen Sie, ob der Flug pünktlich ist?**
Angestellte	Yes, absolutely. Check-in is half an hour beforehand, at 9.45 at the Swiss Air check-in desk. You still have one hour.	**Ja, auf die Minute sogar. Einchecken ist eine halbe Stunde vorher, also um 9.45 Uhr am Swiss Air Schalter. Sie haben noch eine Stunde Zeit.**
Peter	Thanks. Can I book the return flight now? I think there is a flight from Zurich to Hanover at 5 this evening, is that correct?	**Vielen Dank. Kann ich den Rückflug jetzt schon buchen? Ich glaube, es gibt einen Flug von Zürich nach Hannover um 17.00 Uhr heute abend, nicht wahr?**
Angestellte	Yes; the plane arrives at Hanover at 18.15. I can confirm this flight for you, Mr. Wilson, if you want me to.	**Ja, die Maschine kommt um 18.15 Uhr in Hannover an. Ich kann Ihnen den Flug bestätigen, Herr Wilson, wenn Sie wollen.**
Erzähler	Peter still had 45 minutes left until check-in. He bought a postcard of Berlin and some stamps. He wrote the card to his mother to tell her that he would stay in Germany until the weekend. Then he found a letterbox, went to the check-in desk, took his ticket and handed it to the official.	**Peter hatte noch 45 Minuten Zeit bis zum Einchecken. Er kaufte eine Ansichtskarte von Berlin und Briefmarken. Er schrieb die Karte an seine Mutter, um ihr mitzuteilen, daß er bis zum Wochenende in Deutschland bleiben würde. Dann warf er die Karte in einen Briefkasten, ging zum Check-in-Schalter, nahm sein Ticket und gab es dem Beamten.**

Nr: 01 25369706

RÜCKFLUG-TICKET
PASSENGER RETURN TICKET
Lufthansa

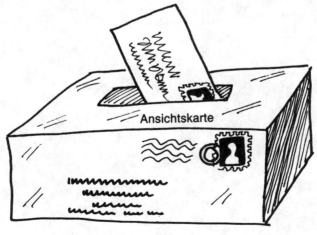

Ansichtskarte

Angestellte	Where would you like to sit? Smoking or non-smoking? Have you any luggage, sir?	**Wo möchten Sie sitzen? Raucher oder Nichtraucher? Haben Sie Gepäck?**
Peter	I would like a window seat please, non-smoking. I have only hand luggage and would like to take it with me.	**Ich möchte einen Fensterplatz bitte, Nichtraucher. Ich habe nur Handgepäck und würde es gern mit ins Flugzeug nehmen.**
Angestellte	Yes, that's all right. You have window seat 10 A. Here is your boarding card.	**Ja, in Ordnung. Sie haben Fensterplatz 10 A. Hier ist Ihre Bordkarte, bitte schön.**
Erzähler	Peter put his ticket and the boarding card into his wallet. With his briefcase he walked to the passport control.	**Peter steckte sein Ticket und die Bordkarte in seine Brieftasche. Mit seiner Aktentasche ging er zur Paßkontrolle.**

Nichtraucher?

Raucher?

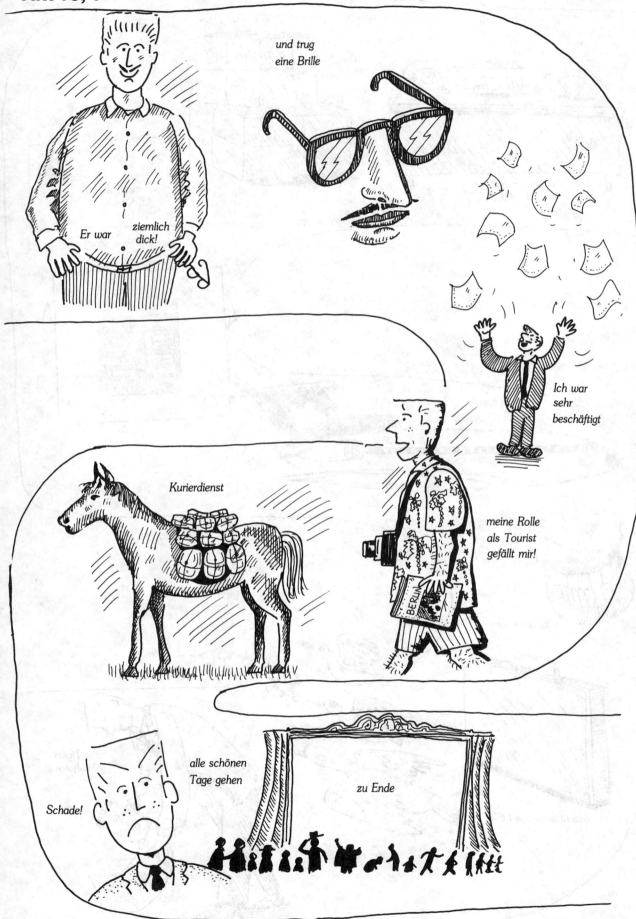

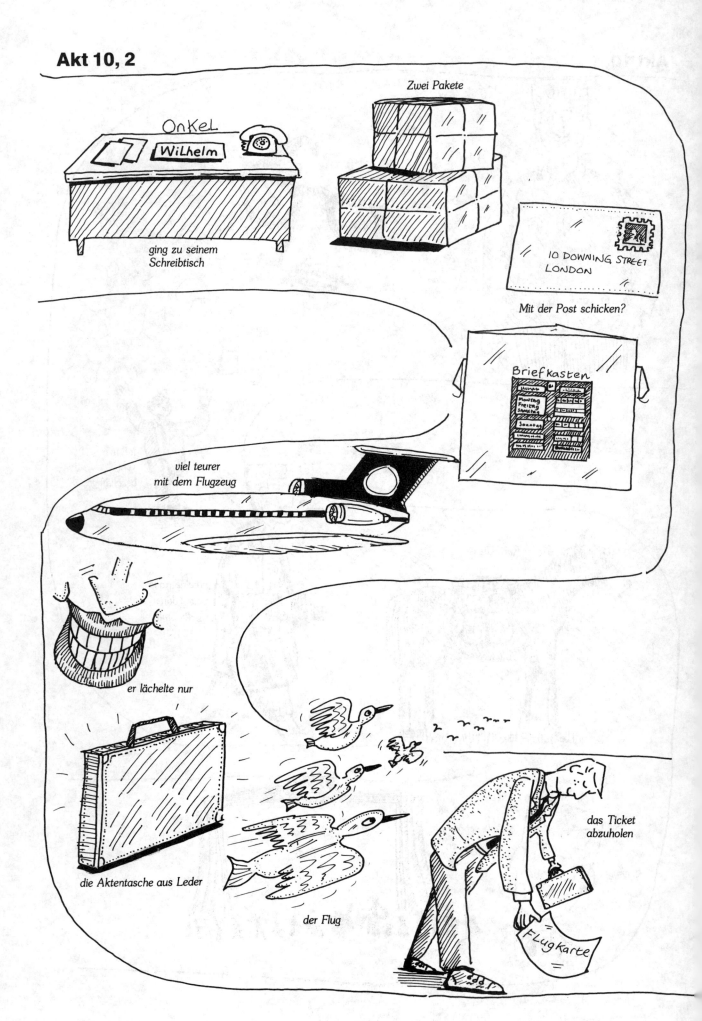

Zwei Pakete

ging zu seinem
Schreibtisch

Mit der Post schicken?

viel teurer
mit dem Flugzeug

er lächelte nur

die Aktentasche aus Leder

der Flug

das Ticket
abzuholen

Teil zwei: Dialoge

Dialog 1   To express likes   **Ich wohne in Berlin!**

Helga	Do you like Berlin?	**Gefällt Ihnen Berlin?**
Anja	Oh yes, very much.	**Oh ja, es gefällt mir sehr gut.**
Helga	What do you like best?	**Was gefällt Ihnen am besten?**
Anja	I like the National Gallery and Schloß Charlottenburg best. But I also like the Court Gardens.	**Die Nationalgalerie und Schloß Charlottenburg gefallen mir am besten. Aber auch den Schloßgarten mag ich.**
Helga	Would you like to live in Berlin?	**Möchten Sie in Berlin wohnen?**
Anja	Oh yes, that would be good. I would speak German a lot better then.	**Oh ja, das wäre gut. Dann würde ich auch viel besser Deutsch sprechen.**
Helga	Where do you live, then?	**Wo wohnen Sie?**
Anja	I live in London, and you?	**Ich wohne in London, und Sie?**
Helga	I have been living here in the 'Spreemetropolis'* for the past 40 years. I'm a genuine Berliner.	**Ich wohne hier in der Spreemetropole,* schon seit vierzig Jahren. Ich bin eine echte Berlinerin.**

Dialog 2   To discuss methods of payment   **Im Geschäft**

Gabi	That comes to 125 marks 50.	**So, das macht 125 Mark 50.**
Andreas	I haven't got that much on me, sorry.	**Soviel Geld habe ich leider nicht in bar.**
Gabi	That doesn't matter. You can pay by credit card.	**Das macht nichts. Sie können auch mit Kreditkarte bezahlen.**
Andreas	Do you also take cheques?	**Geht es auch mit Scheck?**
Gabi	Yes, if you have a valid cheque card (on you).	**Ja, wenn Sie eine gültige Scheckkarte haben.**
Andreas	Yes, of course.	**Ja natürlich, die habe ich.**
Gabi	All right then. Please make the cheque payable to Zille and Co.	**Gut. Schreiben Sie den Scheck bitte auf den Namen Zille und Co. ****
Andreas	And here is my cheque card.	**Und hier ist die Scheckkarte, bitte sehr.**
Gabi	Ah I see, you are English? You speak German very well. Congratulations!	**Ach, Sie sind Engländer? Sie sprechen aber sehr gut Deutsch. Mein Kompliment!**
Andreas	Thank you very much.	**Danke sehr.**

* Spree = The river which flows through Berlin. Berliner colloquialism for their city.

** Co. = Short for **Companie**, Company

Dialog 3	To express quality	**Geschenke**
Heike	Have a look at the present I bought.	**Sieh mal, was für ein Geschenk ich gekauft habe.**
Gabi	Oh, a wallet, made of leather. Who is it for?	**Oh, eine Brieftasche aus Leder. Für wen ist die denn?**
Heike	For Max, for his birthday.	**Für Max, zum Geburtstag.**
Gabi	I bought a spectacle case made from a nice piece of cloth for him; and from his girlfriend he is getting a genuine silver ring.	**Dem hab' ich ein Brillenetui aus einem schönen Stoff gekauft; und von seiner Freundin bekommt er einen echten silbernen Ring.**
Heike	Really?	**Wirklich?**
Gabi	Yes, made of real silver.	**Ja, aus echt Silber.**
Heike	He is well off this year.	**Dem geht's dieses Jahr aber gut.**

Dialog 4	To describe a person	**Onkel Heinrich**
Anja	Could you please meet my uncle at 12.57? I'm busy.	**Kannst du bitte meinen Onkel um 12.57 abholen? Ich habe keine Zeit.**
Helga	From the station, you mean? Okay, what does he look like?	**Vom Bahnhof, meinst du? Na schön, wie sieht er denn aus?**
Anja	He is very tall, about 6′, and he's rather fat.	**Er ist sehr groß, ungefähr 1.80m und ziemlich dick.**
Helga	Does he wear glasses?	**Hat er eine Brille?**
Anja	Yes, and he is always very elegantly dressed. Most of the time in a dark suit, and he is always carrying a briefcase.	**Ja, und er ist immer sehr elegant gekleidet. Meistens im dunklen Anzug, und er trägt immer eine Aktentasche bei sich.**
Helga	There are hundreds of those types. What's his name then?	**Von denen gibt es doch hunderte! Wie heißt er denn?**
Anja	Heinrich Meier, the same as me.	**Heinrich Meier, genau wie ich.**

Teil drei: Dialoge

Dialog 1:
Am Abfertigungsschalter

You are at the airport in Hanover, at the check-in desk. As your German has improved so much, you want to master the situation in German:

Andreas	**Ihr Ticket bitte. Haben Sie Gepäck?**
You	No. I don't have any luggage, only hand luggage.
Andreas	**Das können Sie mit ins Flugzeug nehmen. Es ist nicht sehr groß.**
You	Yes, I'll be coming back tonight already.
Andreas	**Wo möchten Sie sitzen?**
You	At the window, if possible.
Andreas	**Es gibt nur noch einen Fensterplatz hinten.**
You	Oh, I don't like that! I don't smoke.
Andreas	**Vorn haben wir nur noch einen Platz am Gang. Wir sind fast ausgebucht.**
You	That doesn't matter. I'd rather sit at the gangway than in the back.
Andreas	**Ganz wie Sie möchten! Hier ist Ihre Bordkarte. Einchecken ist dort drüben.**

nur
Handgepäck

Dialog 2:
Am Flugschalter

You have booked a flight to Zurich and you go directly to the airport to collect your ticket; you are paying by cash.

Gabi	**Kann ich Ihnen helfen?**
You	I have booked a flight and would like to collect my ticket.
Gabi	**Wohin fliegen Sie bitte und wann?**
You	To Zurich, a return flight on Saturday.
Gabi	**Wissen Sie, wann Sie gebucht haben?**
You	Yes, yesterday afternoon; in the name of . . . . (your name) I spoke to Mrs. Luthi, I believe.
Gabi	**Ah ja, das war meine Kollegin. Hier ist Ihr Ticket. Wie bezahlen Sie bitte?**
You	Cash. Can you give me a receipt please? Thank you very much.

Dialog 3:
Beim Juwelier

You discuss quality.

Andreas	**Was für einen Ring hätten Sie denn gern? Einen aus Silber oder einen aus Gold?**
You	I prefer silver. Could you show me some?
Andreas	**Ja gern. Für wen soll er denn sein? Für Sie selbst?**
You	Yes, for me. Hm; I like this little one here. How much is it?
Andreas	**Der ist ziemlich preiswert. Nur 99 Mark.**
You	Yes, all right. I think I'll take this one.
Andreas	**Bitte sehr. Ich packe ihn für Sie ein.**

Dialog 4:
Herr Heinrich Zille

You ask a friend of yours to deliver a parcel to Mr. Zille in Berlin. Your friend doesn't know Mr. Zille. You describe him.

Heike	**Also, wie sieht der Herr denn aus?**
You	He is very tall and rather fat.
Heike	**Trägt er eine Brille?**
You	No, he does not wear glasses.
Heike	**Welche Haarfarbe hat er?**
You	He has short dark hair.
Heike	**Was kannst du mir noch über ihn sagen?**
You	He is always very elegantly dressed. In a dark suit most of the time.
Heike	**Das genügt, glaube ich. Wie heißt er übrigens?**
You	His name is Heinrich Zille, he's a genuine Berliner!

Teil vier: Übungen/Silbenrätsel/Syllable Puzzle.

Büste von Nofretete

„Wie gut kennen Sie Berlin?"
(Sind Sie ein Kulturgeier?)

In the following syllables you will find well-known places, streets, locations, tube stations, museums, art collections, all of which are located in Berlin

Find them by combining the right syllables. (Refer to the text and/or the memory map if you have to refresh your memory.)

Bel -- Ber -- berg -- Bran -- Brü -- burg -- burger -- Char -- cke -- dächt -- damer -- damm -- Damm -- dauer -- den -- dere -- fre -- ga -- gar -- garten -- Ge -- kirche -- Ku -- lan -- lerie -- li -- lotten -- lung -- me -- Na -- ner -- nis -- No -- platz -- pole -- Por -- Pots -- samm -- Schloß -- Schloß -- Span -- Spree -- ße -- te -- te -- ten -- ten -- Tier -- tional -- Tor -- tro -- ve -- Wei -- Wit -- zel.

Remember to use the opportunity to check once again the pronunciation and the correct stress of the words you have found.

(The solutions are at the back of the book)

Reim:
Ich steh auf der Brücke
und spuck' in den Kahn, (Boat)
da freut sich die Spucke,
daß sie Kahn fahren kann!

168

1. **Teil vier: Übungen**

Aus welchem Material? -- What is it made from?

Find the most suitable material* for the clothes/items listed below and say whether you like them or not; combine them by saying:

z.B.   **Die Jacke ist aus Wolle. Die gefällt mir.**
       Das Etui ist aus Kunststoff. Das gefällt mir nicht.

das Hemd

der Hut

der Schlips/die Krawatte

das Kleid

die Aktentasche

die Brieftasche

die Handtasche

der Euroscheck

das Geld

die Strumpfhose

die Zeitung

der Ring

die Schuhe (!)

die Hose

*	**Leder**
	Baumwolle
	Papier
	Seide
	Nylon
	Kupfer
	Wolle
	Synthetik
	Stoff
	Baumwollstoff
	Silber
	Gold
	Kunststoff
	Wollstoff

Note that some items can be made from different or more than one material.

Sprichwort: Papier ist geduldig!

2.

MESSEN UND AUSSTELLUNGEN
(Fairs and Exhibitions)

Situation   When Peter arrives at Zurich-Kloten he has to wait before he can go through the passport
control, as it is very busy. He has a good look round, and sees a board announcing all the
forthcoming exhibitions and fairs in Zurich.He reads:

**Zürich
Handels- und Finanzmetropole der Schweiz. Größte Stadt der Schweiz.
Interkontinentaler Flughafen Zürich-Kloten mit direkter Bahnverbindung zum
Messegelände.**

**10.1. - 12.1.   EXPORTORAMA
Informationsmesse für die schweizerische Export-Industrie**

**22.1. - 25.1.   ORNARIS
Fachmesse für Wohndesign, Kunstgewerbe und Boutique-Mode**

29.2. - 5.3.   Schweizerische Bootsschau

**18.3. - 20.3.   MODEXPO
Internationale Fachmesse für Damenbekleidung**

**1.4. - 4.4.   SWISSPO
Einkaufswoche für Wintersportartikel**

28.4. - 6.5.   ANTIC Internationale Kunst und Antiquitäten-Messe

**29.4. - 2.5.   PAP-EX
Papeterie-Fachmesse für Bürobedarf**

**15.5. - 18.5.   SICHERHEIT
Internationale Fachmesse für Sicherheit**

**29.8. - 3.9.   FERA
Internationale Fernseh- Radio- und Hi-Fi- Ausstellung**

**22.8. - 1.9.   NABA
Nationale Briefmarken-Ausstellung**

**20.9. - 30.9.   ZÜSPA
Zürcher Herbstschau für Haushalt, Wohnen, Sport und Mode**

Do the same as Peter and read all the dates with the corresponding events out loud. Imagine you were the
announcer at the airport and had to read this information through the loudspeaker. Therefore try to read as clearly
and distinctly as possible. Again, mark those words you find difficult with a stress and repeat them. (By the way,
there's a lot going on in Zurich, don't you think? It's certainly well worth a visit.)

Teil fünf: Spiele, Rätsel und Reime

Schützenfest

Read the statements on the left one by one. Then 'shoot'
the balloon which contains the most suitable remark, e.g.
In Berlin gibt's keine,Weiße' mehr!   Schade!
Alternatively "shoot" the most appropriate expression
from the column on the right.

In Berlin gibt's keine ‚Weiße' mehr!	**Schade!**
Stell dir vor, morgen besucht uns Onkel Zille aus Berlin.	**Das tut mir leid!**
Sie kommen viel zu spät.	**Was für eine Überraschung!**
Sie haben Geburtstag.	**Ich gratuliere Ihnen!**
Du kannst die Tickets kaufen.	**Herzlichen Glückwunsch!**
Otto hat sich rote Schuhe gekauft.	**Das kann man wohl sagen!**
Lena hat jetzt grüne Haare.	**Ist das jetzt modern?**
Mir geht's heute gar nicht gut.	**Das ist der letzte Schrei.**
Darf ich Sie einladen?	**Das kann doch nicht wahr sein!**
Sie sind heute mein Gast.	**Ich kann's kaum glauben.**
Es ist fünf vor zwölf, Hans ist immer noch nicht da!	**Er hat zu gut gelebt.**
Ich habe nur noch 2 Tage Urlaub.	**Zu einem Glas Wein?**
Machen Sie sich's bequem!	**Aber gern!**
Das sollten wir feiern!	**Das ist sehr nett von Ihnen.**
	Ich mache mir Sorgen.
	Alles geht einmal zu Ende.
	Was Sie nicht sagen!
	Das ist eine gute Übung für dich!

Akt 11

Scene 1	**Szene 1**
On the plane	**Im Flugzeug**

Erzähler	At the passport control Peter didn't have to wait long. Very briefly the official glanced at his passport. Flight No.125 was precisely on time. Peter was looking out of the plane when he heard a voice.	**An der Paßkontrolle brauchte Peter nicht lange zu warten. Der Beamte schaute seinen Paß nur kurz an. Flug Nr.125 war auf die Minute pünktlich. Peter sah gerade aus dem Flugzeug, als er eine Stimme hörte.**
Hans	Good morning, how are you?	**Guten Morgen, wie geht es Ihnen?**
Erzähler	Peter turned round and saw Hans, Hilde's cousin. He was very surprised to see him here.	**Peter drehte sich um und sah Hans, Hildes Cousin. Er war sehr überrascht, ihn hier zu sehen.**
Peter	I'm fine, thanks, and how are you, Hans?	**Gut, danke, und wie geht es Ihnen, Hans?**
Hans	So am I, thanks. There is an empty seat beside me. Would you like to sit here?	**Auch gut, danke. Neben mir ist ein Platz frei. Möchten Sie sich dahin setzen?**
Peter	Yes, why not?	**Ja, warum nicht?**
Hans	What a surprise to meet you here on the plane!	**Was für eine Überraschung, Sie hier im Flugzeug zu treffen!**
Erzähler	A stewardess was walking along the aisle.	**Eine Stewardeß kam den Gang entlang.**
Hans	Excuse me, please, could you bring us something to drink?	**Entschuldigen Sie bitte, können Sie uns etwas zu trinken bringen?**
Peter	No alcohol for me, it's too early in the morning. But I would like a coffee.	**Nichts Alkoholisches für mich, nicht so früh am Morgen. Aber ich würde ganz gern einen Kaffee trinken.**
Hans	And a gin and tonic for me, please.	**Und für mich bitte einen Gin Tonic.**
Peter	Do you have business in Zurich as well?	**Haben Sie auch geschäftlich in Zürich zu tun?**
Hans	Yes, I have a meeting there with one of our important customers. He buys a lot of our products. Then tomorrow I will be flying on to Frankfurt. I often make this trip; on average twice a month. And why do you go to Zurich?	**Ja, ich habe dort eine Verabredung mit einem wichtigen Kunden von uns. Er kauft viele unserer Produkte. Dann fliege ich morgen nach Frankfurt weiter. Ich mache diese Reise öfters, im Durchschnitt zweimal im Monat. Und warum fliegen Sie nach Zürich?**

Er war sehr

überrascht

Erzähler	Peter was certain that Hans knew exactly why. However, he gave a polite answer.	**Peter war sicher, daß Hans genau wußte, warum. Er antwortete trotzdem sehr höflich.**
Hans	Where are you staying overnight? I always stay at the Rex Hotel, it's right at the Zurich lake.	**Wo übernachten Sie? Ich bleibe immer im Hotel Rex, es liegt direkt am Zürich See.**
Peter	I don't intend to stay overnight in Zurich. I will be glad when I have delivered the parcels and be back in Hanover again.	**Ich will nicht in Zürich übernachten. Ich bin froh, wenn ich die Pakete abgeliefert habe und wieder in Hannover bin.**
Erzähler	Hans wanted to reply something, but the stewardess was serving a snack; so they didn't talk about it any further.	**Hans wollte noch etwas erwidern, aber die Stewardeß servierte einen Snack; deshalb sprachen sie nicht mehr darüber.**

übernachten Sie

Scene 2
Arrival in Zurich

**Szene 2
Ankunft in Zürich**

Erzähler	Peter had from the very beginning worried about the parcels. Now, however, he was certain that something was wrong. Perhaps they are all criminals, he thought, but he couldn't really believe that of Hilde. Probably it's only my imagination! Fortunately the flight was very quiet and Peter read a magazine. But he kept thinking again and again, what could be in the briefcase? After a short while the plane landed at Zurich. Peter said goodbye to Hans.	**Peter hatte sich von Anfang an Sorgen wegen der Pakete gemacht. Jetzt war er aber ganz sicher, daß etwas nicht stimmte. Vielleicht sind sie alle Betrüger, dachte er, aber von Hilde konnte er das eigentlich nicht glauben. Wahrscheinlich ist es nur meine Einbildung! Zum Glück war der Flug sehr ruhig, und Peter las eine Zeitschrift. Er dachte aber immer wieder daran, was wohl in der Aktentasche stecken könnte. Kurz darauf landete die Maschine in Zürich. Peter verabschiedete sich von Hans.**
Peter	Excuse me please, but I have to hurry. Otherwise I'll miss my appointment. Goodbye.	**Entschuldigen Sie bitte, aber ich muß mich beeilen. Sonst verpasse ich meine Verabredung. Auf Wiedersehen.**

3+2=6

daß etwas nicht stimmte

	Scene 3	Szene 3
	Delay at the Customs	Verzögerung am Zoll
Erzähler	Peter wanted to walk swiftly through the Customs; he took the green channel as he had nothing to declare.	**Peter wollte schnell durch den Zoll gehen; er nahm die grüne Sperre, denn er hatte ja nichts zu verzollen.**
Zollbeamter	One moment,please. What have you got in your briefcase, sir?	**Einen Augenblick, bitte. Was haben Sie in Ihrer Aktentasche?**
Erzähler	The customs official made Peter stop. Suddenly Peter didn't feel well at all. This was exactly the situation he had been afraid of. He tried to answer as harmless as possible.	**Der Zollbeamte hielt Peter an. Peter spürte plötzlich ein flaues Gefühl im Magen. Dies war genau die Situation, die er befürchtet hatte. Er versuchte, so normal wie möglich zu antworten.**
Peter	Only two small parcels with papers.	**Nur zwei kleine Pakete mit Papieren.**
Zollbeamter	May I see them, please?	**Darf ich die mal bitte sehen?**
Erzähler	Peter opened the briefcase.	**Peter öffnete die Aktentasche.**
Zollbeamter	I see, do you mind unpacking them, sir?	**Aha, können Sie die mal bitte auspacken?**
Erzähler	Poor Peter opened both parcels. Now the catastrophe was bound to happen... But..nothing happened! Uncle William had promised that the parcels contained only papers, and that was exactly what was inside, nothing else! Now Peter was completely confused. He didn't know what to say. The Customs official had suddenly lost all interest in Peter's briefcase...	**Der arme Peter machte also beide Pakete auf. Jetzt mußte die Katastrophe kommen... Aber...nichts passierte! Onkel Wilhelm hatte versichert, daß nur Papiere in den Paketen waren und tatsächlich gab es nur Papiere, nichts als Papiere! Jetzt war Peter total verwirrt. Er wußte nicht, was er sagen sollte. Der Zollbeamte hatte plötzlich kein Interesse mehr an Peters Aktentasche...**
Zollbeamter	That's all right, sir, thanks. You can go now.	**Das wär's also, vielen Dank. Sie können gehen.**
Erzähler	Peter left the Customs and looked at his watch. It was 12.25. He had only 35 minutes left to get to Mr. Zuckermann's office on time.	**Peter ging durch den Zoll und schaute auf seine Uhr. Es war 12.25. Er hatte nur noch fünfunddreißig Minuten Zeit, um pünktlich zu Herrn Zuckermanns Büro zu kommen.**

REMINDER

Have you got the Steps in front of you? You should *always* follow each one through faithfully. Always include the visualisation exercise — the step where you close your eyes and visualise the Acts and speak as many words out loud as you can remember. This is a powerful memory device.

Don't forget your activities as you go through this course. By activities we mean not only playing as many of the games and solving as many of the puzzles as possible, but also that you should physically 'work with' the text and/or illustrations. Underlining, highlighting, jotting down any words, phrases, expressions that you particularly want to fix in your memory (or which for some reason have specific significance for you), is important.

Always remember that active involvement is the best method to store new material in your long-term memory.

You should ideally always have writing material ready while you are learning and/or listening to the cassettes.

We recommend you to have a look at these Steps as you progress through this course from time to time.

Peter sah gerade aus
dem Flugzeug

Er war sehr

überrascht

Neben mir ist ein Platz frei

Eine Stewardeß
kam den Gang
entlang

etwas zu trinken?

es liegt direkt
am Zürich See

die Stewardeß
servierte einen
Snack

Wo übernachten sie?

nicht so früh am Morgen

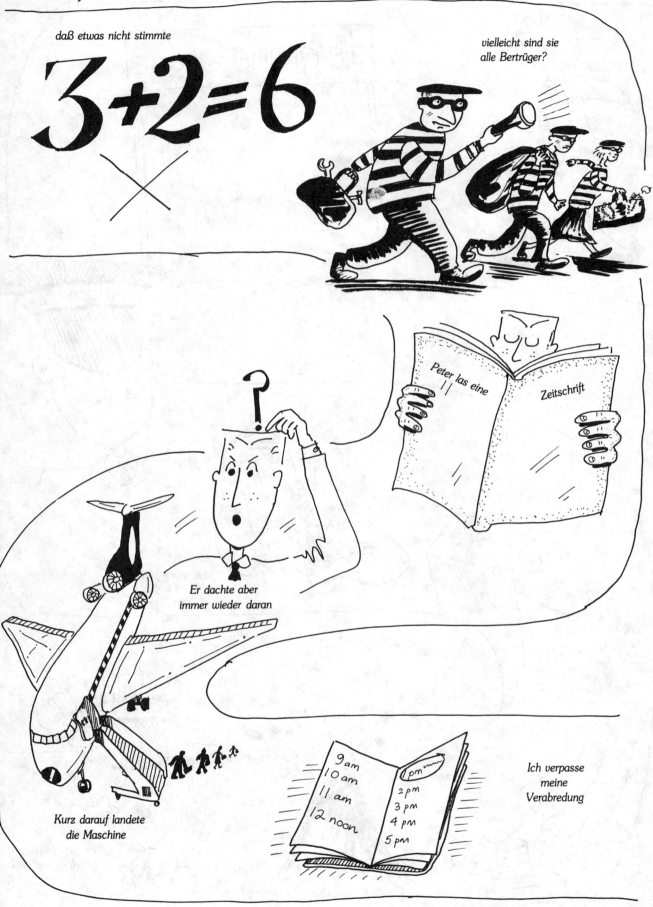

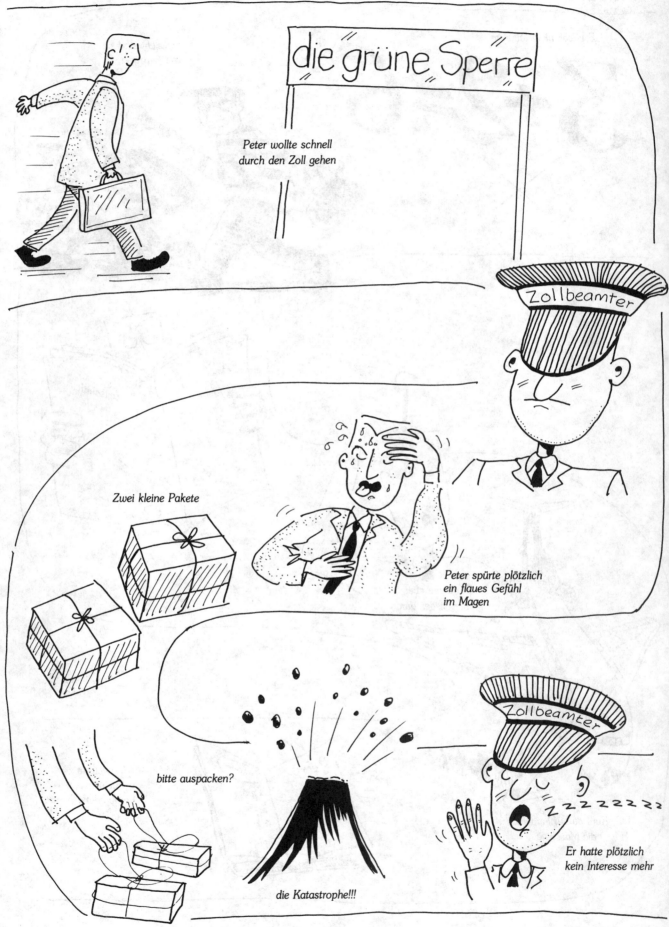

Akt 11

Teil zwei: Dialoge

1. Difficulties on the phone
(To complain about an order)

Schwierigkeiten am Telefon

Sekretärin	Sauer & Co., hello.	**Hallo, hier Sauer & Co.**
Frau Becker	Good morning. Becker fashions. We received your parcel this morning.	**Guten Morgen; hier Modehaus Becker. Wir haben Ihr Paket heute morgen erhalten.**
Sekret.	Which parcel are you talking about?	**Welches Paket meinen Sie?**
Frau Becker	The delivery of socks.	**Die Lieferung mit den Socken.**
Sekret.	Oh yes, now I remember. Good. I'm pleased.	**Ah. Jetzt erinnere ich mich. Gut.**
Frau Becker	No, not good at all. There are as many as 300 pairs of grey socks.	**Nein, nicht gut. Im Paket sind dreihundert Paar graue Socken.**
Sekret.	That's right.	**Stimmt.**
Frau Becker	No, it's not right, Miss...	**Nein, stimmt nicht, Fräulein...**
Sekret.	Mrs., if you please, Mrs. Ernst.	**Frau bitte. Frau Ernst.**
Frau Becker	Mrs. Ernst, we didn't actually order 300 pairs of grey socks.	**Also, Frau Ernst, wir haben keine dreihundert Paar graue Socken bestellt.**
Sekret.	Oh yes, you did. I've got it here in the books.	**Doch. Graue Socken, 300 Paar, steht hier im Buch.**
Frau Becker	Mrs. Ernst, something must be wrong there. We ordered 30 pairs of grey socks, not 300.	**Frau Ernst, irgendetwas stimmt hier nicht. Wir haben dreißig Paar graue Socken bestellt, aber nicht 300.**
Sekret.	Not 300 then? Oh well, send those you don't want back to us. Goodbye.	**Was? Nicht 300 sagten Sie? Na gut, schicken Sie zurück, was Sie nicht wollen. Auf Wiederhören.**
Frau Becker (zu sich)	I don't know what to say, but what can I do?	**Mir verschlägt's die Sprache, aber was will man machen?**

2. Get well wishes

,Gute Besserung'

Gabi	Have you anything planned for today?	**Hast du heute etwas vor?**
Heike	Yes, I have to go to the hospital.	**Ja, ich muß ins Krankenhaus.**
Gabi	Oh, what's happened then?	**Ach! was ist denn passiert?**
Heike	My granddad is in hospital. I'm going to visit him. He's had an accident, you know.	**Mein Großvater liegt im Krankenhaus. Ich will ihn besuchen. Er hat einen Unfall gehabt.**
Gabi	Oh dear, how is he then?	**Oh je, wie geht es ihm denn?**
Heike	He's better now, thank goodness. He has had a car accident, you know. Well, when I think of it, I feel sort of queasy. (lit.)	**Jetzt besser, Gott sei Dank. Es war ein Autounfall, weißt du. Ach, wenn ich daran denke, bekomme ich immer ein flaues Gefühl im Magen.**
Gabi	I'm sorry for him. He meant to fly to Zurich, didn't he?	**Das tut mir leid. Er wollte doch nach Zürich fliegen, oder?**
Heike	Yes today (exactly). He was really unfortunate.	**Ja eben, heute. Er hat wirklich Pech gehabt.**
Gabi	I wish him a speedy recovery.	**Ich wünsche ihm gute Besserung.**
Heike	Thanks. Bye for now.	**Danke. Wiedersehen.**
Gabi	Cheers.	**Tschüs.**

Peter spürte plötzlich ein flaues Gefühl im Magen

3. A meeting on the plane — **Ein Treffen im Flugzeug**

Andreas	Hello, Mrs. Schmidt. What a surprise to meet you here on the plane!	**Hallo, Frau Schmidt. Was für eine Überraschung, Sie hier im Flugzeug zu treffen!**
Frau Schmidt	Yes. Isn't it? How are you?	**Das kann man wohl sagen! Wie geht es Ihnen?**
Andreas	I'm fine thanks, and how are you? Where are you going to?	**Gut, danke; und Ihnen? Wohin geht's denn?**
Frau Schmidt	I'm going to visit my son. He is living in Switzerland now. And what about you?	**Ich will meinen Sohn besuchen. Er wohnt jetzt in der Schweiz. Und Sie, was haben Sie vor?**
Andreas	I'm on business again. I often fly on this route.	**Ich bin mal wieder geschäftlich unterwegs; ich fliege diese Route öfters.**
Frau Schmidt	I see. How often then?	**Ach ja? Wie oft denn?**
Andreas	About 2-3 times per month.	**Etwa zwei bis dreimal im Monat.**
Fr. Schmidt	I'm only flying for the second time today!	**Ich fliege heute erst zum zweiten Mal!**
Andreas	No wonder that we don't meet more often!	**Kein Wunder, daß wir uns nicht öfters treffen!**

4. The mysterious briefcase — **Die geheimnisvolle Aktentasche**

Mann	Well, Mrs. B. I say, your briefcase looks very smart. What have you got in it?	**Oh, Frau Kollegin. Ihre Aktentasche sieht ja sehr schick aus. Was haben Sie denn in der drin?**
Heike	I don't know myself, actually.	**Das weiß ich leider auch nicht!**
Mann	What? Do you mean that you don't know what's in your case?	**Wie bitte? Sie meinen, Sie wissen nicht, was Sie in Ihrer Tasche haben?**
Heike	That's what I said.	**Das sagte ich doch.**
Mann	Don't you want to know it?	**Wollen Sie es nicht wissen?**
Heike	Of course I do. Then I would certainly feel better.	**Natürlich möchte ich das. Dann ging es mir sicherlich besser.**
Mann	Why don't you have a look then?	**Warum schauen Sie dann nicht mal nach?**
Heike	Okay then; here, look for yourself.	**Also gut. Hier, sehen Sie selbst.**
Mann (erstaunt)	Only papers, nothing but papers. Are you feeling better now?	**Hm? Nur Papiere, nichts als Papiere! Geht es Ihnen jetzt besser?**

Teil drei: Dialoge

1.   You are correcting an order

M.M.   **Modehaus Müller, guten Morgen. Kann ich Ihnen helfen?**

You   Yes please. I received your parcel this morning.

M.M.   **Welches Paket meinen Sie?**

You   The parcel with the ties.

M.M.   **Ach so, das. Ist alles in Ordnung?**

You   No, I'm sorry. There is a problem.

M.M.   **Ja bitte, was ist es denn?**

You   I ordered 5 ties. There are 50 in the parcel .

M.M.   **Fünfzig, sagten Sie? Das ist ein bißchen viel, muß ich sagen.**

You   Exactly. What shall I do with them?

M.M.   **Schicken Sie fünfundvierzig zurück, wenn Sie sie nicht brauchen. Und entschuldigen Sie den Fehler. Das kann passieren.**

2.   You wish somebody "to get well". (a speedy recovery)

Gab.   **Hier ist Gabriele, hallo. Wie geht es Ihnen?**

You   I'm fine thanks, and you?

Gab.   **Nicht so gut. Ich muß heute ins Krankenhaus.**

You   What's the matter then?

Gab.   **Meine Schwester hat einen Autounfall gehabt.**

You   Oh dear, how is she then?

Gab.   **Jetzt besser, Gott sei Dank.**

You   I hope she gets well.

Gab.   **Danke schön. Auf Wiederhören.**

You   'Bye. All the best.

3.   You meet someone unexpectedly (At the station).

Andy   **Hallo! Was für eine Überraschung, Sie hier zu treffen! Ich habe Sie ja so lange nicht gesehen.**

You   Yes, isn't it? How are you?

Andy   **Sehr gut, danke. Wohin fahren Sie?**

You   I'm going to visit my uncle in Austria.

Andy   **Oh, wohnt er dort?**

You   Yes, he is living there now; in St. Anton.

Andy   **Ich wünsche Ihnen eine gute Reise!**

You   And so do I. Where are you going to?

Andy   **Ich fahre auch nach Österreich, nach Innsbruck. So ein Zufall!**

4.   You enquire about a bag.

Heike   **Warum schauen Sie mich so an?**

You   Your bag looks very smart. What have you got in it?

Heike   **Keine Ahnung!**

You   You don't know what's in your bag?

Heike   **Das sagte ich doch. Warum möchten Sie das wissen?**

You   I don't like to know it. Don't you want to know it?

Heike   **Wollen schon, aber ich darf es nicht.**

You   Shall I have a look then?

Heike   **Ja, hier bitte. Wenn Sie unbedingt wollen!**

Teil vier: Übungen

Can you fill in the steps, starting with the numbers 2) to 7), i.e. the words across first and then the small letters a) to g) downwards?

2) **Was lernen sie jetzt?** _ _ _ _ _ _

3) **Er ist grün und frisch.** _ _ _ _ _

4) **Zum Frühstück ist** _ _ _ _ _ **besonders gut.**

5) **Torte ohne** _ _ _ _ _ **bitte!**

6) **Das ist eine prima** _ _ _ _ **!**

7) **Sie kommen aus England, Sie sind** _ _ _ _ _ _ _ _

a) **Die Bank hat viel** _ _ _ _

b) **Hildes** _ _ _ _ **ist groß und weiß.**

c) **Sie stellt die Gläser auf den** _ _ _ _

d) **Wir trinken den Wein aus einem** _ _ _ _

e) **Er ißt es zum Frühstück.**

f) **Wo ist das Geschäft? Da, an der** _ _ _ _

g) **Ich kaufe eine Bluse und auch einen** _ _ _ _

1) TaG (a)

2)D̄ _ _ _ _ _ H (b)

3)S̄ – – – T (c)

4)H̄ _ _ _ G (d)

5)S̄ _ _ _ E (e)
6)I _ _ E (f)

7)Ē _ _ _ _ _ _ R (g)

8)KirschE

(The answers are at the back of the book).

182

Kaffeezeit im Café Stöpsil.
Haben Sie Zeit und Lust zu einem Snack?
Do you have time and fancy a snack?

Imagine you have been sightseeing with a friend in Berlin all day. Now you are really exhausted and dying for a cup of iced coffee - **Eiskaffee** - or iced chocolate - **Eisschokolade** - and a snack. Fortunately, you have found a cosy little café just outside Charlottenburg Castle. Look at the menu of Café Stöpsil and read out to your friend what they have on offer.
Then order something for yourself and your friend who is vegetarian and loves ice-cream!
What would you order if you had only 10.-DM left?
Here you go now, start your order with:

Herr Ober, ich möchte ....**bitte.**

oder: Herr Ober/wir möchten ....**bitte.**

Don't forget to ask for the bill as well, and as you have invited your friend, you pay for everything.
(Alles zusammen, bitte.)

Café Stöpsil

Kuchen:

In der Kuchentheke nachschauen!	
Nußschnitte (makro)	2.—
Kuchen	2.50
Torten	2.70
Portion Sahne*	—.60

Eis:

Kleines Eis	2.10
Großes Eis	3.50
Früchteeisbecher	4.80
Sueño d'oro	4.80
(Walnußeis, Amaretto, Sahne)	
Eiskaffee	3.80
Eisschokolade	4.20

*mit Distickstoffoxid

Essen:

Suppe (steht an der Tafel!)	
Vegetarierbrot	2.—
Käsebrot	3.50
Salamibrot	3.50
Schinkenbrot	4.—
Schinkenkäsebrot	4.—
2 Paar Wiener mit Brot	4.—

Sonstige eßbare Sachen stehn an der Tafel!

Teil fünf: Spiele, Rätsel and Reime

**Berühmte Städte -
und Flüsse**
What do you know about:
Hamburg (HH) - Alster, Elbe
Hannover (H) - Leine
Berlin (B) - Spree
Köln (K) - Rhein
Frankfurt a. Main (F)
Stuttgart (S) am Neckar
Wolfsburg (Wo) - Aller

Famous towns and rivers

München (M) - Isar
Salzburg (S) - Salzach
Bayreuth (Bay) - Main
Genf (GE) - Rhone; Genfer See
Dresden (R or Y) - Elbe
Zürich (ZH) - Zürich See
Wien (W) - Donau

Underline these places on the map, take a piece of paper and write out what you know about each town.
If nothing comes to mind, look at the back of the book, where we have given you one or two ideas, i.e. the main features of each of them.
If you know more, prima!
(For your interest we have given you the number plates of each place behind the name of the town.)

REMINDER
Are you still following *all* the steps? It will fully repay you to do so.

Akt 12

Scene 1 The mystery is solved.	**Szene 1** **Das Geheimnis klärt sich auf**

Erzähler

It was exactly 12.58, two minutes to one, when Peter got out of the taxi outside 12 Berner Straße He saw a sign at the door: Mr. H. D. Zuckermann, solicitor and commissioner for oaths, 3rd floor. The lift was out of order, so Peter had to walk up the stairs to the third floor. Still quite out of breath, he knocked at the door. A man of about sixty opened the door.

Es war genau 12.58, zwei Minuten vor eins, als Peter vor der Berner Straße zwölf aus dem Taxi stieg. Er sah ein Schild an der Tür: Herr H. D. Zuckermann, Rechtsanwalt und Notar, dritter Stock. Der Lift funktionierte nicht, also mußte Peter die Treppen nehmen bis zum dritten Stock. Noch ganz außer Atem, klopfte er an die Tür. Ein Mann von ungefähr sechzig Jahren öffnete die Tür.

Rechtsanwalt und Notar

H. Zuckermann
Good afternoon. You are Peter Wilson? Please, do come in.
Guten Tag. Sie sind Peter Wilson? Kommen Sie doch bitte herein.

Peter
Yes, that's right. I'm glad that, at last, I can hand over these two parcels to you. They are from Mr. Holz.
Ja, richtig. Ich bin froh, daß ich Ihnen endlich diese zwei Pakete überreichen kann. Sie sind von Herrn Holz.

Erzähler
Peter opened the briefcase, took the parcels out and put them onto the desk. The solicitor studied the papers very carefully for a couple of minutes. Then he smiled and said to Peter:
Peter öffnete die Aktentasche, nahm die Pakete heraus und legte sie auf den Schreibtisch. Der Anwalt sah sich die Papiere ein paar Minuten lang ganz gründlich an. Dann sagte er lächelnd zu Peter:

H. Zuckermann
May I see your passport please?
Darf ich bitte Ihren Paß sehen?

Erzähler
Peter had not expected this. For a moment he hesitated, but then he gave his passport to Mr. Zuckermann.
Das hatte Peter nicht erwartet. Er zögerte ein bißchen, reichte aber dann Herrn Zuckermann seinen Paß.

H. Zuckermann
My congratulations, Peter! Now I can tell you: from today you are a shareholder in the Bieler import-export company. How come? About three months ago, Mr. Strauman died, suddenly and unexpectedly.
Herzliche Glückwünsche, Peter! Jetzt kann ich es Ihnen ja sagen: Sie sind ab heute Teilhaber in der Import-Export Firma Bieler. Wieso? Vor ungefähr drei Monaten ist ein Herr Straumann gestorben, plötzlich und unerwartet.

187

I know that you did not know him personally, but the fact is that he was a relative of yours. Through his death, you have inherited his fortune. You now own 20% of the import-export company and a little house on the Sarner lake.	**Ich weiß, daß Sie ihn nicht persönlich gekannt haben, aber er war tatsächlich ein Verwandter von Ihnen. Durch seinen Tod haben Sie sein Vermögen geerbt. Sie besitzen jetzt zwanzig Prozent der Import-Export Firma und dazu ein kleines Haus am Sarner See.**

Peter Pardon? I cannot believe all this! Are you sure it's true?

Wie bitte? Das kann ich nicht glauben! Sind sie sicher, daß das wahr ist?

H. Zuckermann Yes, certainly, without any doubt. Surely, we should celebrate this.

Ja, ganz sicher, da gibt es keinen Zweifel. Eigentlich müßten wir das feiern.

Erzähler Mr. Zuckermann took a bottle of champagne out of his fridge. He opened it with a bang: Cheers!

Herr Zuckermann holte eine Flasche Champagner aus dem Kühlschrank. Er öffnete sie und ließ den Korken knallen: Prost!

der Import-Export Firma

Peter This has left me speechless; I don't know what to say. But why all these mysteries? Why didn't Hilde and her uncle just *tell* me?

Mir hat's die Sprache verschlagen; ich weiß nicht, was ich sagen soll. Aber warum alle diese Geheimnisse? Warum haben Hilde und ihr Onkel es mir nicht einfach gesagt?

H. Zuckermann You must not forget, Peter, that this is a family business. They were very anxious to get to know you first, of course. They wanted to find out whether you would accept this position altogether, and if you would cooperate well with the others. I know by now that they all look forward to working with you.

Sie dürfen nicht vergessen, Peter, daß dies ein Familienunternehmen ist. Sie wollten Sie natürlich zuerst einmal kennenlernen. Sie wollten feststellen, ob Sie diese Stellung überhaupt annehmen, und ob Sie gut mit den anderen zusammenarbeiten. Ich weiß inzwischen, daß sie sich alle darauf freuen, mit Ihnen zu arbeiten.

Erzähler Peter had to sit down; he was quite overcome by all this news! Perhaps it was the champagne, or was it the thought of working with Hilde from now on? Or was it simply the fact that he was suddenly very rich? Whatever the reason for it, he felt very, very happy!!

Peter mußte sich erst einmal hinsetzen, so aufgeregt war er über diese Nachricht! Vielleicht war es der Champagner, oder war es der Gedanke, ab jetzt mit Hilde zu arbeiten? Oder war es einfach die Tatsache, daß er plötzlich sehr reich war? Was auch immer der Grund war, er fühlte sich überglücklich!

The End   **Das Ende**

Er
war
plötzlich
sehr
reich

The Name Game

One more read through the Name Game - especially parts 2 and 3 will definitely benefit you now.

Teil zwei Dialoge

1. Turning up late for an appointment. **Freitag, der 13!**

Andreas
It's now twenty past 12. **Es ist jetzt zwanzig nach zwölf.**
I had expected you at 12. **Ich hatte Sie um zwölf erwartet.**
But you are quite out of breath. **Sie sind ja ganz außer Atem!**

Bettina
I'm sorry. I had (really) bad luck. This **Das tut mir leid. Ich hatte wirklich**
is a black day for me. **Pech. Ein schwarzer Tag für mich.**
Everything went wrong. **Alles ging schief!**

Andreas
What do you mean? **Wie meinen Sie das?**

Bettina
Well, the train arrived late. **Nun, der Zug kam spät an.**
Then I couldn't get a taxi; **Dann konnte ich kein Taxi bekommen;**
and besides the lift here **und außerdem funktionert der Lift**
isn't working either. **hier im Haus nicht.**

Andreas
I must say that's really too bad. First **Ja, ich muß sagen, das ist wirklich**
get your breath back. **ärgerlich. Kommen Sie erst**
Do sit down. **mal zu Atem. Setzen Sie sich doch hin!**

Bettina
Thanks. No wonder, today is **Danke. Kein Wunder, heute ist**
Friday the 13th. **Freitag, der dreizehnte!**

2. To express surprise and disbelief **Unerwartetes Glück**

Heike
I have a surprise for you. **Ich habe eine Überraschung für Sie!**

Gabi
What is it, please do tell me! **Was ist es denn, sagen Sie es mir doch!**

Heike
Have a guess. **Raten Sie mal.**

Gabi
What could it be? I have **Was könnte es nur sein? Ich habe**
no idea. **keine Ahnung.**

Heike
Imagine you had won **Stellen Sie sich vor, Sie hätten**
the pools. **das große Los gezogen.**

Gabi
What do you mean? **Was meinen Sie?**

Heike
As I said: You have won a **Wie ich sagte: Sie haben eine**
huge amount of money. **Menge Geld gewonnen.**

Gabi
What, me? Really? How come? **Was ich? Wirklich? Wie denn das?**
I don't know what to say. **Ich bin sprachlos.**

Heike
We should have a **Darauf müßten wir eigentlich einen**
drink on that! **trinken!**

Gabi
Yes, of course. I'll pay for it. **Ja natürlich. Ich lade Sie ein.**

3.

To clarify a confusion (wrong address)

Schmidt ist nicht Schulz; eine Verwechslung

Elvira	Good morning, are you from the express-courier service?	**Guten Morgen, sind Sie vom Express-Kurier-Dienst?**
Axel	Yes, that's right.	**Ja, richtig.**
Elvira	We have been expecting you. Come in.	**Wir haben Sie schon erwartet. Kommen Sie doch herein.**
Axel	Thanks. Did you wait long?	**Danke. Haben Sie lange gewartet?**
Elvira	It's all right. Where are the parcels? Have you got them?	**Es geht. Wo sind die Pakete? Haben Sie sie?**
Axel	Of course. Here you are, both in the name of Schmidt.	**Natürlich. Hier bitte, beide auf den Namen Schmidt.**
Elvira	Schmidt? My name is Schulz, Elvira Schulz.	**Schmidt? Ich heiße Schulz, Elvira Schulz.**
Axel	There must be something wrong. Here it says: Schmidt, Bahnhof Street 12, third floor.	**Da stimmt etwas nicht. Hier steht: Schmidt, Bahnhofstraße zwölf, dritter Stock.**
Elvira	Yes, the address is correct, but we are on the fourth floor. The Schmidts are living on the 3rd floor.	**Ja, die Adresse stimmt, aber wir sind hier im vierten Stock. Schmidts wohnen im dritten Stock.**
Axel	Oh, I'm sorry. Goodbye.	**Ach, das tut mir leid. Auf Wiedersehen.**
Elvira	What on earth did they order? Also with express-courier!	**Was die wohl bestellt haben? Auch beim Express-Kurier.**

4.

Enquiring about a mystery (or good luck?)

Ein Geheimnis?

Gabi	Please tell me inspector, why all these mysteries?	**Jetzt sagen Sie mir bitte, Herr Inspektor, warum alle diese Geheimnisse?**
Andreas	That I will tell you: this man has inherited a fortune and doesn't believe it.	**Das kann ich Ihnen sagen: dieser Mann hat ein Vermögen geerbt und glaubt es nicht.**
Gabi	What do you mean?	**Wie meinen Sie das?**
Andreas	He just can't believe it.	**Er kann es nicht fassen.**
Gabi	Did he really inherit it? Are you sure it's true?	**Hat er es wirklich geerbt? Sind Sie sicher, daß es stimmt?**
Andreas	There are hardly any doubts.	**Da gibt es fast keinen Zweifel.**
Gabi	What do you mean by that?	**Wie meinen Sie das jetzt?**
Andreas	I don't believe it either! It's too good to be true!	**Um ehrlich zu sein, ich glaube es auch nicht. Es ist zu schön um wahr zu sein!**

Teil drei: Dialoge

1.   You have an appointment with the dentist. However, you couldn't quite make it at the arranged time. Things went wrong for you that morning.

Zahnarzt	**Es ist jetzt zwanzig nach elf. Ihr Termin war um elf; Sie kommen sehr spät.**
You	I'm sorry, I was really unfortunate. Everything went wrong.
Zahnarzt	**Wie meinen Sie das? Ist etwas passiert?**
You	Well, the bus arrived late; then I had forgotten my money.
Zahnarzt	**Was haben Sie denn dann gemacht?**
You	I had to walk, it's very far, you know.
Zahnarzt	**Ich weiß. Das ist wirklich ärgerlich. Aber leider müssen Sie einen neuen Termin ausmachen. Jetzt ist es zu spät.**
You	When can I come? Is tomorrow all right?
Zahnarzt	**Ja, in Ordnung. Übrigens, morgen ist Freitag, der dreizehnte. Um wieviel Uhr können Sie kommen?**

2.   You have won the first prize in a competition and can't quite believe it at first.

Heike	**Darf ich Ihnen gratulieren?**
You	Me? Why?
Heike	**Sie haben das große Los gezogen.**
You	What do you mean? I can't understand you.
Heike	**Sie haben den ersten Preis gewonnen. Herzlichen Glückwunsch.**
You	Really? How come? I don't know what to say.
Heike	**Ja wirklich! Sie sollten sich freuen. Möchten Sie nicht wissen, was der Preis ist?**
You	Yes, of course. What is it then? I have no idea.
Heike	**Es ist eine Flugreise nach Berlin, für zwei Personen. Hotel, Vollpension, Stadtbesichtigung, alles inklusive!**

3.   You had ordered something by mail order; but when it eventually arrives, something is not quite in order:

Andreas	**Guten Morgen. Bin ich hier richtig bei H. Meyer?**
You	Yes, that's right. Please come in.
Andreas	**Hier sind Ihre Pakete. Sie hatten doch fünf bestellt, nicht wahr?**
You	Five, did you say? No, I had ordered three only.
Andreas	**Hier steht: Heinrich Meyer, Rathausstraße zwölf, dritter Stock.**
You	The address is correct, but this is the 2nd floor. And it's Hans Meyer, not Heinrich.
Andreas	**Oh, das tut mir leid! Entschuldigen Sie bitte vielmals. Auf Wiedersehen!**
You	Hm, pity! Goodbye.

4.   You want to find out more about an alleged mystery...

Andreas	**Also, Sie möchten mich gern interviewen?**
You	Yes please; tell me, why all these mysteries?
Andreas	**Es ist eine unglaubliche Geschichte.**
You	What do you mean by that?
Andreas	**Ein Kollege von mir hat ein Vermögen geerbt und kann es einfach nicht glauben.**
You	What? He can't believe it? I would believe it at once!
Andreas	**Genau! Ich auch.**
You	But are you sure it's true?
Andreas	**100 prozentig. Da gibt es gar keinen Zweifel.**
You	What did he inherit then?
Andreas	**Eine schöne Summe Geld und dazu ein Chalet in der Schweiz.**
You	Not bad, is it? What do you think?
Andreas	**Ich? Ich finde das prima! Hoffentlich spendiert er uns wenigstens ein Bier!**

Teil vier: Übungen

Would you find your way on the Underground in Berlin?

Die Berliner U-Bahn oder das Berliner U-Bahn-Netz

1.   Do you remember Hilde and Peter go to the ‚Wittenbergplatz' which is on tube line number one (U1). Now let's suppose they would meet there; then you would say:

Sie treffen sich am Wittenbergplatz.

Now you are asked to find these places listed below on the Berlin underground map and to say correspondingly, e.g. **Sie treffen sich an der Kurfürstenstraße** or **Sie treffen sich am Kudamm.** Pay attention to the correct gender.

Start each sentence with the question:

Wo treffen sich Peter und Hilde? or
Wo treffen sie sich?

  Antwort: Sie treffen sich am Kudamm

                Die U-Bahn Stationen:
                a) Kottbusser Tor
                b) Richard-Wagner-Platz
                c) Bismarckstraße
                d) Deutsche Oper
                e) Olympiastadion
                f) Berliner Straße
                g) Heidelberger Platz
                h) Rathaus Schöneberg
                i) Kurt-Schumacher-Platz
                j) Kleist-Park

Variation:
You could also say:

Sie treffen sich an der U-Bahn Station Wittenbergplatz, Kurfürstendamm, Berliner Straße etc. without "**am**" or "**an der**".

Zur Wiederholung: Now put the questions and answers into the past and let's assume that Hilde and Peter had met at all these different places yesterday:

Wo haben sich Hilde und Peter getroffen?

Antwort: Sie trafen sich am Kleist-Park.

oder: Sie haben sich am Kleistpark getroffen.

Viel Spaß!!

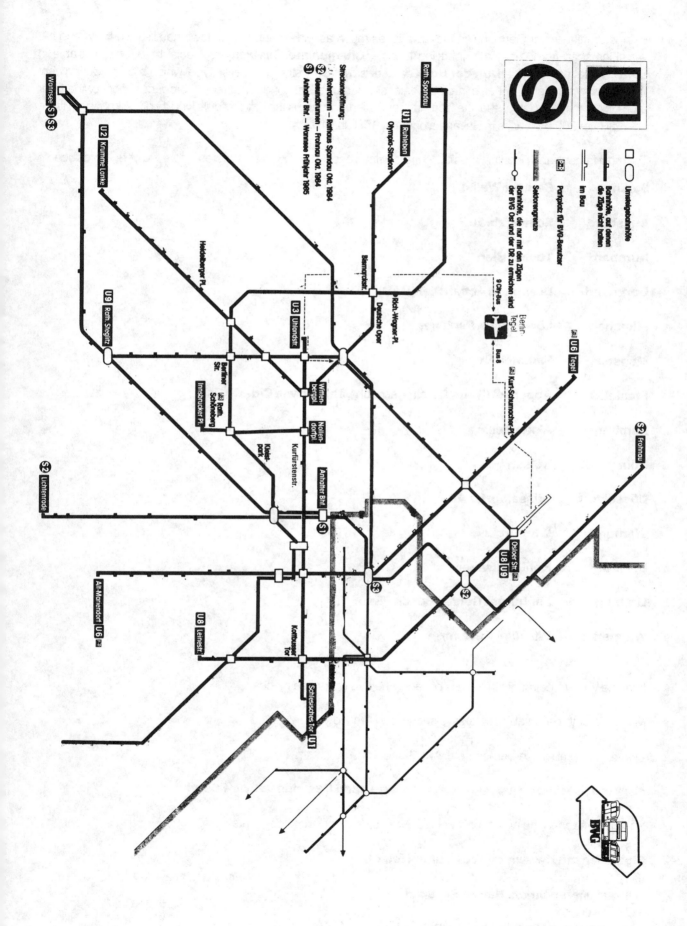

Streckeneröffnung:
S1 S3 Rohrdamm – Rathaus Spandau Okt. 1984
S2 Gesundbrunnen – Frohnau Okt. 1984
S1 Anhalter Bhf. – Wannsee Frühjahr 1985

Wannsee S1 S3
U2 Krumme Lanke
Heidelberger Pl.
U9 Rath. Steglitz
U3 Uhlandstr.
Berliner Str.
Witten- bergpl.
Nollen- dorfpl.
Rath. Schöneberg
Kleist- park
Kurfürstenstr.
Anhalter Bhf.
S1
S2 Lichtenrade
Alt-Mariendorf U6
U8 Leinestr.
Kottbusser Tor
Schlessisches Tor U1

Rath. Spandau
U1 Ruhleben
Olympia-Stadion
Bismarckstr.
Rich.-Wagner-Pl.
Deutsche Oper

U6 Tegel
Kurt-Schumacher-Pl.
S2 Frohnau
Osloer Str.
U8 U9
S3
S2

Berlin-
Tegel
Bus 8
9 City-Bus

☐○ Umsteigebahnhöfe
Bahnhöfe, auf denen die Züge nicht halten
in Bau
Parkplatz für BVG-Benutzer
Sektorengrenze
Bahnhöfe, die nur mit den Zügen der BVG Ost und der DR zu erreichen sind

BVG

Zeit und Grund zum Feiern. It's celebration time!

Beer is drunk all over Germany, in fact at least as much as wine. Each bigger town has its own brew and the variations span from very light, sparkling types - **Champagner Weizen ,** a special brew only available in Bavaria - to almost black - **Dunkler Bock** , a dark brown, very strong sweetish type, which is drunk during Lent in Bavaria in particular, but also in other regions. Dortmund in the industrial region produces most of the beer drunk in Northrhine-Westphalia, the Dortmunder-Actien-Brauerei is the biggest of its kind. Did you know that there are well over 200 breweries in Bavaria alone and 1500 in all?

The most famous and popular types of beer are written beside the towns and places where the beer is produced:

Berlin	**Berliner Weiße**
Augsburg	**Schwarzbräu**
Nürnberg	**Tucher Bier**
Dortmund	**Dortmund Actien Bier (DAB)**
München	**Löwenbräu, Paulaner**
Münster	**Münster Alt**
Frankfurt	**Äppelwoi (!) aus Äpfeln gemacht, ähnlich wie Cider.**
Hamburg	**Alsterweiße**
Köln	**Kölsch**
Düsseldorf	**Düsseldorfer Alt**
Warburg	**Warburger**
Duisburg	**König-Pilsener**
Limburg	**Limburger Golden Busch Pils**
Wuppertal	**Wicküler Pilsener**

Imagine you are being given a glass of each when visiting these places.

Make two or three suitable remarks to show how pleased you are.

Do you remember the games from **Akt 7** and **10.**

Many of these phrases are very appropriate, e.g. **Prost! Das müssen wir feiern!**

You have reached the end of your course. Now it's time for you to celebrate.

Eigentlich müßten wir das zusammen feiern.

Wir gratulieren Ihnen. Hatten Sie Spaß?

Lassen Sie den Korken knallen. Prost!!!

Teil fünf: Spiele, Rätsel und Reime

Spielanleitung für das Konversations-Spiel (40 word cards)

Separate all the cards and divide them into two equal packs. Put them face down in front of you. Pick up the first card of one pack and read aloud what is written on it **Zum Beispiel: Wir sparen Geld.** Now pick the top card of the second pile and read aloud **zum Beispiel: ich gratuliere Ihnen, oder: ich bin überglücklich.**

Is it a match? We would say yes. Put those two cards away. Whenever two cards match, put them aside; if they don't match, put them back into the pile. When you have found or matched ten pairs of cards which you think are good matches, write out the complete statement.

Note: Many combinations are possible. Use your imagination and ideas for various situations and you will find that almost any combination is (almost!) possible, or as the Germans say:
Es gibt nichts, das es nicht gibt.

Sprichwörter zu Glück und Unglück

The following proverbs are typical for expressing luck and/or bad luck; most of them have English counterparts.

Glück braucht der Mensch	You need to be lucky
Glück im Unglück!	Every cloud has a silver lining
Jeder ist seines Glückes Schmied	God helps him who helps himself
Scherben bringen Glück	Breaking a dish is lucky
Ein Unglück kommt selten allein!	Bad luck often comes in threes

As the word **‚Glück'** is quite difficult to pronounce, say it and apply it as often as possible. After all, it conveys an optimistic view and a positive state of mind and attitiude, the key to successful learning!
So that at the end of your course, we can say with you and to you: **Sie haben Glück! Wir gratulieren Ihnen, herzlichen Glückwunsch! Genau wie Peter, erinnern Sie sich?**

FOREWORD TO THE GLOSSARY:

In all cases throughout this glossary we have given you the translation of the words within the context of the story, i.e. as they appear in this course. For additional information and/or different meanings of some of them, please refer to a dictionary.

For example, when you come across the word **springt auf** (opens), you will find it under **S**. Directly beside it, however, we have given you the ground form of the word, i.e. **aufspringen** (to open) in this case, as you would find it listed in a dictionary.

The numbers from 1 - 3000   0 = null

1 = eins	11 = elf	21 = einundzwanzig	90 = neunzig
2 = zwei	12 = zwölf	22 = zweiundzwanzig	100 = (ein)hundert
3 = drei	13 = dreizehn	23 = dreiundzwanzig	200 = zweihundert
4 = vier	14 = vierzehn	24 = vierundzwanzig* etc.	300 = dreihundert
5 = fünf	15 = fünfzehn	30 = dreißig	etc...
6 = sechs	16 = sechzehn	40 = vierzig	
7 = sieben	17 = siebzehn	50 = fünfzig	1000 = (ein)tausend
8 = acht	18 = achtzehn	60 = sechzig	2000 = zweitausend
9 = neun	19 = neunzehn	70 = siebzig	3000 = dreitausend
10 = zehn	20 = zwanzig	80 = achtzig	etc...

* Notice how it is exactly the same as old English when we used to say four and twenty blackbirds.

N.B. 1867 is achtzehnhundertsiebenundsechzig
1956 is neunzehnhundertsechsundfünfzig

Explanation to the plurals shown in brackets:

Plural nouns are abbreviated and shown in brackets thus:

(-)   = no change, same as singular noun, e.g. **das Zimmer - die Zimmer**
(¨)   = umlaut over first **o, a** or **u** in the word, e.g. **Laden - Läden**
(¨-er)   = umlaut over first **o, a** or **u** in the word, e.g. **Haus, Häuser**
(¨e)   = umlaut over second of any of these three vowels **a, o** or **u**, e.g. **Farbton - Farbtöne**

Note: When a noun has the double-vowel **au** in it, the umlaut is *always* on the first vowel, i.e. over the **a**. **(Haus-Häuser,** etc.)

Abbreviations in the Glossary:-

English/German:

s.th.	= something	inf.	= infinitive	
s.b.	= somebody	fem.	= female	
lit.	= literally	temp.	= temporary	

German/English:

etw.	= etwas	jdm.	= jemand (em)
Inf.	= Infinitiv	jdn.	= jemand (en)

GERMAN — ENGLISH

A

ab away, from
ab from (temp.)
abbiegen to turn off
das Abenteuer(-) the adventure(s)
aber but
abliefern to deliver
die Abwechslung(en) von the change(s) from
addieren to add
die Adresse(n) the address(es)
die Ahnung(en) the idea; clue(s)
die Aktentasche(n) the briefcase(s)
alkoholisches s.th. with alcohol in it
alle all
allerdings though; mind you; certainly
alles everything
als as, than
als when (temp.)
also therefore
alt old
die Altstadt(¨e) old part of the town
am on the, at the
die Ampel(n) the traffic light(s)
sich amüsieren to have a good time, have fun
an on, at
der Anfang(¨e) the beginning(s)

angenehm pleasant
die Angst(¨e) the fear, worry (s, ies)
ankommen to arrive
(darauf) ankommen to depend (upon)
die Ankunft(¨e) the arrival(s)
anrufen to telephone
anschauen to look at
ansehen to look at
die Ansichtskarte(n) the picture postcard(s)
antworten to answer
der Anzug(¨e) the suit(s)
apart elegant, striking
der Apfel(¨) the apple(s)
die Apotheke(n) the drug dispensing chemist(s)
appetitlich appetising
die Arbeit(en) the work(s)
arbeiten to work
ärgerlich(sein) (to be) annoyed
der Arm(e) the arm(s)
arm poor
der Ärmel(-) the sleeve(s)
der Arzt(¨e) the doctor(s)
die Ärztin(nen) the lady doctor(s)
das Aspirin the aspirin
die Aspirintablette(n) the aspirin tablet(s)
der Atem the breath
atmen to breathe

die **Atmosphäre**   the atmosphere
auch   also
auf   on
der **Aufenthalt(e)**   the stay(s)
die **Auffahrt(en)**   the approach road(s)
aufgeregt(sein)   (to be) excited
aufmachen   to open
das **Auge(n)**   the eye(s)
der **Augenblick(e)**   the moment(s)
aus   out, from
ausgehen   to go out
auspacken   to unpack
(sich) ausruhen   to rest
aussehen   to look like, have the   appearance
aussteigen   to get off, to get out
sich ausweisen   to prove one's identity
das **Auto(s)**   the car(s)
die **Autobahn(en)**   the motorway(s)
die **Autofahrt(en)**   the car trip(s), journey(s)
die **Autovermietung(en)**   the car hire firm(s)

B

das **Bad(-er)**   the bath(s)
das **Badetuch(--er)**   the bathtowel(s)
das **Badezimmer(-)**   the bathroom(s)
der **Bahnsteig(e)**   the platform(s)
bald   soon
der **Balkon(s)**   the balcony(ies)
das **Ballett**   the ballet
die **Bank(en)**   the bank(s)
das **Bargeld**   the cash
der **Baum(-e)**   the tree(s)
die **Bäckerei(en)**   the baker's shop(s)
der **Beamte(n)**   the official(s)
bedeuten   to mean
die **Bedienung**   the service
sich beeilen   to hurry, rush
beenden   to finish
etwas befürchten   to be afraid of s.th.
begrüßen   to greet
bei   close to
beide   both
beim   at
bekommen   to receive
beobachten   to observe
bequem   comfortable
bereits   already
der **Berg(e)**   the mountain(s)
berühmt   famous
beschäftigt sein   to be busy
beschließen   to decide
besichtigen   to visit (sights)
besitzen   to possess, to own
besonders   especially
besprechen   to discuss
bestätigen   to confirm
das **beste**   the best
bestellen   to order, to book
bestimmt   surely, certainly
der **Besuch(e)**   the visit(s)
besuchen   to visit
betrachten   to view
betreten   to enter
der **Betrüger(-)**   the swindler(s)
das **Bett(en)**   the bed(s)
die **Bettdecke(n)**   the quilt(s)
bezahlen   to pay
das **Bier(e)**   the beer(s)
die **Bierflasche(n)**   the beer bottle(s)
billig   cheap
billiger   cheaper
am billigsten   cheapest
die **Birne(n)**   the pear(s)
bis   till, until
bitte   please
bitten   to request
ein bißchen   a little bit
blau   blue
bleiben   to remain, stay
der **Blitz**   the lightning
blitzsauber   very clean

blond   blond(e)
die **Blume(n)**   the flower(s)
die **Bluse(n)**   the blouse(s)
die **Bordkarte(n)**   the boarding card(s); pass(es)
der **Bote(n)**   the messenger(s)
brauchen   to have to, to need (to)
braun   brown
(sich etwas) brechen, bricht   to break s.th., breaks s.th.
der **Brief(e)**   the letter(s)
der **Briefkasten(-)**   the letter box(es)
die **Briefmarke(n)**   the stamp(s)
die **Brieftasche(n)**   the wallet(s)
die **Brille(n)**   the glasses
das **Brillenetui(s)**   the spectacle case(s)
bringen   to bring
das **Brot(e)**   the bread(s)
das **Brötchen(-)**   the breadroll(s)
der **Bruder(-)**   the brother(s)
das **Buch(-er)**   the book(s)
buchen   to book
das **Büfett(s)**   the counter(s)
bunt   (multi)coloured
der **Bus(se)**   the bus, coach(es)
der **Bürgersteig(e)**   the pavement(s)
das **Büro(s)**   the office(s)
die **Butter**   the butter

C

der **Chef(s)**   the boss(es)
chic   elegant, smart
die **Cousine(n)**   the cousin(s), fem.

D

da   there
da sein   to be there, present
dahin   here; there
die **Dame(n)**   the lady(ies)
danach   after that, afterwards
daneben   next to it
der **Dank**   the thanks (pl.)
danke(n)   thank you, to thank
dann   then, after that
daran   about how (about that)
darauf   after that(temp.)
darüber   about it
dauern   to last
dazu   in addition to
daß   that
die **DDR**   the GDR (German Democratic Republic)
decken   to lay the table, to cover
denken   to think, to have an opinion of something
denn   then, (What's this then?)
deshalb   therefore
deutsch   German
das **Deutsch**   the German language
Deutschland   Germany
dick   fat
diese, -r, -s   this
direkt   direct
dividieren   to divide
doch   yes do
der **Donner (-)**   the thunder
es donnert und blitzt   there is thunder and lightning
das **Dorf(-er)**   the village(s)
dort   (over) there
draußen   outside
drin, drinnen   inside
dritte(n)   third
drücken   to press
du hälst davon   you (familiar) have an opinion of
dunkel   dark
durch   through
durch etwas gehen,   durchgehen   to pass through s.th.
im Durchschnitt   on average
durchwählen   to dial through
durstig sein   to be thirsty
die **Dusche(n)**   the shower(s)
dürfen, darf   may, he, she, it may

E

die Ecke(n) the corner(s)
es ist mir egal I don't mind
ehrlich honest
das Ei(er) the egg(s)
eigentlich really
ein, eine a, an
einbiegen to turn (into)
die Einbildung(en) the imagination(s)
einchecken to check in
einfach simple, simply, single
einkaufen to go shopping
einladen to invite
einlösen to cash(in)
einmal once, once(in a while)
einpacken to pack, wrap in
einschlafen to fall asleep
einstecken to put in, into
der Eintritt the entrance(fee)
einverstanden(sein) to agree
das Einzelkind(er) the single/only child(ren)
elegant elegant, smart
die Eltern the parents
die Empfangsdame(n) the receptionist(s)
zu Ende finished
das Ende the end
endlich at last
eng narrow, tight
der Engländer(-) the Englishman(men)
entgegen towards
entlang along
Entschuldigen Sie! excuse me!
die Entschuldigung(en) the excuse(es)
entsetzlich horrible, shocking
er he
die Erbse(n) the pea(s)
die Erdbeere(n) the strawberry(ies)
die Erdbeertorte(n) the strawberry tart(s)
das Erdgeschoß the ground floor
sich erholen to relax
erklären to explain
erlaubt(sein) (to be) allowed to
ernst serious
das Ersatzteil(e) the spare part(s)
erst einmal lit: first of all
erstaunt sein to be astonished
erste, ersten first
erwarten to expect, to await
erwidern to reply
erzählen to tell, relate
der Erzähler(-) the narrator(s)
der Esel (-) the donkey (s)
das Essen the food
essen to eat
das Etui(s) the case(s)
etwas something
der Euroscheck(s) the Eurocheque(s)
der Export the export
der Expressionismus the expressionism (style in art)
die Expressionisten the expressionists
extra especial(ly)

F

das Fach(-er) the subject(s) of something
die Fahrbahn(en) the carriageway, lane(s)
fahren to drive, go by vehicle
der Fahrer(-) the driver(s)
die Fahrkarte(n) the ticket(s)
der Fahrkartenschalter(-) the ticket office(s)
das Fahrrad(-er) the bicycle(s)
die Fahrt(en) the(car) journey, trip(s)
die Familie(n) the family(ies)
das Familienunternehmen(-) the family business(es)
die Farbe(n) the colour(s)
der Farbton(-e) the shade(s) of colour
fast nearly
faszinierend fascinating
faszinieren to fascinate
fährt heim, heimfahren drives home, to drive home
fährt drives, goes by vehicle

etw. fassen (können) to believe s.th.
die Feier(n) the celebration(s)
feiern to celebrate
das Feld(er) the field(s)
das Fenster(-) the window(s)
der Fensterplatz(-e) the window seat(s)
das Fernsehen(-) the television(s)
fernsehen to watch television
fertig sein to be ready
feststellen to find out, to state
finden to find
die Firma (Firmen) the firm(s), company(ies)
flach flat
die Flasche(n) the bottle(s)
flau queasy
der Flug(-e) the flight(s)
der Flughafen(--) the airport(s)
das Flugzeug(e) the plane(s)
das Flugzeugunglück(e) the plane accident(s)
die Forelle(n) the trout(-)
förmlich formal
das Foyer the lobby
fragen to ask (a question)
das Fräulein(-) the Miss(es)
das Freilichttheater(-) the open-air theatre(s)
das Freizeithemd(en) the casual shirt(s)
sich freuen to be glad
freundlich friendly
frisch fresh
froh(sein) to be pleased
froh sein to be glad
früh early(in the morning)
der Frühling the spring
frühstücken to have breakfast
das Frühstück the breakfast
funktionieren to function
sich(wohl) fühlen to feel (good)
führt; führen guides, to guide
der Führerschein(e) the driving licence(s)
füllen to fill
fünf five
fünfzig fifty
für for
füllt aus, ausfüllen fills in/out, to fill in/out
zu Fuß on foot

G

der Gang(-e) the aisle(s)
ganz completely
die Gastgeberin(nen) the hostess(es)
das Gebäude(-) the building(s)
geben to give
geboren werden to be born
gebraten fried
der Gedanke(n) the thought(s)
das Gedicht(e) the poem(s)
geduldig patient
gefallen, gefällt to please, pleases
das Gefühl(e) the feeling(s)
die Gegend(en) the area(s)
gegenüber opposite
das Geheimnis(se) the mystery(ies)
geheimnisvoll mysterious
gehen to go, walk
die Geige(n) the violin(s)
gelb yellow
das Geld the money
die Gelegenheit(en) the opportunity(ies)
das Gemüse the vegetable(s)
der Gemüsestand(-e) the vegetable stand(s)
genau(so) exact(ly) (as)
der Generaldirektor(en) the managing director(s)
das Gepäck the luggage
gerade just now, straight
geradeaus straight on
die Geranie(n) the geranium(s)
das Gericht(e) the dish(es)
gern gladly, to like
das Geschäft(e) the shop(s)
geschäftlich on business(matters)

die Geschäftsführung(en)   the management(s)
geschwärzt   blackened
die Geschwister   the siblings
das Gesicht(er)   the face(s)
gestern   yesterday
gewinnen   to win
gibt, geben   gives, to give
gießen   to pour
das Glas(¨er)   the glass(es)
die Glatze(n)   the bald head(s)
glauben   to believe, think
gleich   soon, close by (geogr.)
das Glück   the good fortune
glücklich   happy
der Glückwunsche(¨e)   congratulation(s)
golden, goldenes   golden
das Gramm   the gramme
grau   grey
die Grenze(n)   the border(s)
der Grenzübergang(¨e)   the border crossing(s)
die Größe(n)   the size(s)
groß   tall
großartig   great, fantastic, terrific
der Grund(¨e)   the reason, cause(s)
grün   green
gründen   to found, establish
gründlich   thoroughly
gut stehen   to suit well
gut   good

H

das Haar(e)   the hair
haben   to have
der Hagel(-)   the hail(s)
es hagelt   its hailing
halb   half
halten(davon)   to have an opinion of
die Hand(¨e)   the hand(s)
der Haupteingang   the main entrance
das Hauptgericht(e)   the main dish(es)
die Hauptstadt(-¨e)   the capital(s)
das Haus(¨er)   the house(s)
hält an, anhalten   stops s.b., to stop s.b.
hängen   to hang
heiraten   to marry
heiter   fair, bright
heiß   hot
heißen   to be named
helfen   to help
hellblau   light blue
hellbraun   light brown
das Hemd(en)   the shirt(s)
herausnehmen, nimmt heraus   to take out, takes out
der Herbst   the autumn
herein(!)   in, come in!
der Hering(e)   the herring(s)
der Herr(en)   the gentleman(men)
die Herrenbekleidung   the men's clothing
herrlich   marvellous
herunter, heraus   down
herzlich   cordial
heute   today
hier   here
hierbleiben   to stay here
der Himmel(-)   the sky,(ies), the heaven(s)
(sich) hinsetzen   to sit down
das Hobby(ies)   the hobby(ies)
hoch   high, up
das Hochhaus(-¨er)   the multistorey building(s)
die Hochschule(n)   the College(s)
hoffentlich   hopefully
der Honig   the honey
die Hose(n)   the trousers
das Hotel(s)   the hotel(s)
das Hotelzimmer(-)   the hotel room(s)
höchst   very (highly)
höflich   polite
hören   to hear
hundert   hundred
der Hunger   the hunger

hungrig sein   to be hungry
hübsch   pretty

I

ich   I
die Idee(n)   the idea(s)
ihm   him
ihr   her
immer   always
der Import   the import
inklusive   included
ins   into
intelligent   intelligent
interessant   interesting
das Interesse(n)   the interest(s) (in s.th.)
sich interessieren(für etwas)   to have or show an interest in
inzwischen   by now, meanwhile
ist   is
das Italienisch   Italian

J

die Jacke(n)   the jacket(s)
das Jahr(e)   the year(s)
der Jahrgang(-¨e)   the vintage
das Jahrhundert(e)   the century(ies)
jeder   everybody, each one
jemals   ever
jetzt   now
der Junge(n)   the boy(s)
jünger   younger

K

die Kabine(n)   the changing room(s)
das Kalbfleisch   the veal
das Kännchen(-)   the little jug(s)
die Karotte(n)   the carrot(s)
die Karte(n)   the ticket(s), card(s)
die Kartoffel(n)   the potato(es)
das Kartoffelfeld(er)   the potato field(s)
der Käse(-)   the cheese(s)
der Käsestand(¨e)   the cheese stand(s)
die Kasse(n)   the cash desk(s)
Kasseler Rippchen   smoked ribs(German meat dish)
die Katastrophe(n)   the catastrophe(s)
kaufen   to buy
das Kaufhaus(-¨er)   the department store(s)
keine ... mehr   no ... more
der Kellner(-)   the waiter(s)
die Kellnerin(nen)   the waitress(es)
kennen   to know (about)
kennenlernen   to get to know someone
die Kerze(n)   the candle(s)
das Kind(er)   the child(ren)
das Kino(s)   the cinema(s)
der Kiosk(e)   the kiosk(s)
die Kirsche(n)   the cherry(ies)
klärt sich auf, sich aufklären   is solved, to solve(s.th.)
das Kleid(er)   the dress(es)
die Kleidung   the clothing
klein   small
der Klingelknopf(¨e)   the bell button(s)
klingeln   to ring
klopfen   to knock
knapp   scarcely
der Knopf(¨e)   the button(s)
kochen   to cook
der Koffer(-)   the suitcase(s)
der Kohlrabi(s)   kohlrabi(s)
das kommt darauf an, darauf ankommen   that depends, to depend on s.th.
können, kann   can, he, she, it, one can
könnten   could
der Kopf(¨e)   the head(s)
das Kopfkissen(-)   the pillow(s)
der Kopfsalat(e)   the lettuce(s)
der Kopfschmerz(en)   the headache(s)
der Korken(-)   the cork(s)
kosten   to cost

die **Kragenweite(n)** the collar size(s)
das **Krankenhaus(--er)** the hospital(s)
die **Kreditkarte(n)** the credit card(s)
der **Krieg(e)** the war(s)
der **Kuchen(-)** the cake(s)
das **Kuchenbüfett(s)** the cake counter(s)
die **Kuh(-e)** the cow(s)
kühl cool
der **Kühlschrank(-e)** the refrigerator(s)
der **Kunde(n)** the customer(s)
der **Kurierdienst(e)** the courier service(s)
der **Kurs(e)** the rate(s) of exchange
kurz short, brief(ly)

L

lachen to laugh
der **Laden(-)** the shop(s)
das **Laken(-)** the sheet(s)
das **Lammfleisch** the lamb's meat
aufs Land into the country
das **Land(-er)** the country(ies)
die **Landkarte(n)** the map(s)
lang long
langsam slow, slowly
lassen to let, allow
lächeln to smile
lächelnd smiling
der **Lärm** the noise
laß uns let(familiar) us
der **Leberkäs** meat pate
die **Leberwurst(-e)** the liver sausage(s)
das **Leder** the leather
legen to place, lay down
leicht slightly, easy
leicht light(weight)
leider unfortunately
leihen to borrow
die **Lese(n)** the harvest,(wine, corn etc)
lesen to read
leuchten to shine
liegen to lie, repose
liest reads
der **Likör(e)** liqueur(s)
links left
los; was ist los? What's the matter?
sich lösen to fall off
die **Luft(-e)** the air

M

machen to make, do
macht an switches on
die **Mahlzeit(en)** the meal(s)
das **Mal(e)** (e.g.the first) time(s)
mal just once
man one (followed by verb in 3rd P. Sing.)
der **Mann(-er)** the man(men)
der **Mantel(-el)** the coat(s)
die **Mark(stücke)** the mark(s)
der **Markt(-e)** the market(s)
die **Marktfrau(en)** the market woman(women)
der **Marktplatz(--e)** the market place(s)
der **Markttag(e)** the market day(s)
die **Marmelade(n)** the jam(s)
die **Maschine(n)** the plane(s)
das **Mädchen(-)** the girl(s)
mehr more
mein my
der **Meter(-)** the metre(s)
der **Metzger(-)** the butcher(s)
die **Metzgerei(en)** the butcher's shop(s)
mieten to hire
die **Milch** the milk
mild mild
das **Mineralwasser(-)** the mineral water(s)
mir (to) me
mit with
mitkommen to come with
jdm. etwas mitteilen to inform, tell s.b.
die **Möbel** the pieces of furniture

möchten would like
modern modern
mögen, mag to like, be partial to, likes
das **Mohnbrötchen(-)** the poppyseed roll(s)
mollig comfortably warm
der **Moment(e)** the moment(s)
der **Monat(e)** the month(s)
der **Morgen(-)** the morning(s)
morgen tomorrow
morgens in the morning
der **Moselwein(e)** the Mosel wine(s)
das **Motorrad(--er)** the motorbike(s)
multiplizieren to multiply
die **Münze(n)** the coin(s)
müßten should, ought to, would have
ich muß,(müssen) I have to, (to have to)

N

na! well!
die **Nachricht(en)** the message(pl. the news)
nachsehen, sieht nach to take a look, has a look
die **Nacht(-e)** the night(s)
der **Nachtisch** the dessert
nah(e) near
der **Name(n)** the name(s)
die **Nationalgalerie** the National Gallery
natürlich of course
nächst, e, es next
in der Nähe nearby, close to or by
naß wet
der **Nebel(-)** the fog, mist(s)
neben next to
neblig foggy, misty
der **Neffe(n)** the nephew(s)
nehmen, nimmt to take, takes
nein no
nett nice
neu new
nicht wahr? isn't that so? (lit. isn't that true?)
nicht not
die **Nichte(n)** the niece(s)
der **Nichtraucher(-)** the non-smoker(s)
nichts nothing
nicken to nod
niemand nobody
nimmt an, annehmen accepts, to accept
noch nicht not yet
noch yet(more), still
der **Notar(e)** the commissioner(s) for oaths
nötig(sein) to be necessary
0, null zero
die **Nummer(n)** the number(s)
nur only

O

der **Ober(-)** the waiter(s)
das **Obst** the fruit
oft, öfters often
ohne without
der **Onkel(-)** the uncle(s)
der **Ölstand** the oil level
der **Orangensaft(--e)** the orange juice(s)
in Ordnung in order
öffnen to open

P

paar a few
die **Packung(en)** the packet(s)
das **Paket(e)** the parcel(s)
das **Papier(e)** the paper(s)
die **Papiere** the papers(personal, only in plural)
das **Parken** parking
passend fitting, suitable
passieren to happen
der **Paß(-sse)** the passport(s)
die **Paßkontrolle(n)** the passport control(s)
das **Pech** the pitch, bad luck
die **Person(en)** the person(s)

persönlich   personally, in person
die Petersilie   the parsley
der Pfennig(e)   the Pfennig(s)
das Pfund(e)   the pound(s)
der Pfundschein(e)   the pound note(s)
das Picknick   the picnic
der Plan(¨e)   the plan(s)
das Plätzchen(-)   the spots
die Platte(n)   the record(s)
plötzlich   suddenly
die Politesse(n)   the traffic warden (fem.)
die Porzellansammlung(en)   the porcelain collection(s)
mit der Post   by post, mail
die Post   the post office, the mail
praktisch   practical
prima   excellent
pro   per
probieren   to try
das Programm(e)   the programme(s)
Prost!   Cheers!
prüfen   to check
der Pumpernickel   Westphalian dark bread
der Punkt(e)   the dot(s)
pünktlich   punctual(ly)

R

raschelnd   rustling
der Rasierapparat(e)   the shaver(s)
sich rasieren   to shave oneself
raten, geraten   to guess, guessed
der Raucher(-)   the smoker(s)
der Rauchschinken(-)   the smoked ham(s)
der Raum(¨e)   the room(s)
reagieren   to react
rechnen   to calculate, work out
die Rechnung(en)   the bill(s)
rechts   right
der Rechtsanwalt(¨e)   the solicitor(s)
regnen   to rain
reich   rich, wealthy
reif   ripe
der Reifendruck   the tyre pressure
gute Reise!   bon voyage!
der Reisepaß(¨sse)   the passport(s)
der Reisescheck(s)   the travellers' cheque(s)
die Reparatur(en)   the repair(s)
reservieren   to reserve
das Restaurant(s)   the restaurant(s)
richtig   correct
riechen   to smell
das Rindfleisch   the beef
der Rock(¨e)   the skirt(s)
die Rolle(n)   the role(s)
der Rollmops(¨e)   the pickled herring(s)
romantisch   romantic
rosig   rosy
rot, gelb, grün,   red, amber, green
rot   red
rufen   to call
der Ruhestand   the retirement
ruhig   quiet, calm
die Rückfahrkarte(n)   the return ticket(s)
der Rückflug(¨e)   the return flight(s)

S

die Sache(n)   the business, the thing(s)
sagen   to say
die Sahne   the cream
die Salami   the salami
der Salat(e)   the salad(s)
die Sammelkarte(n)   the multiple ticket(s)
sauber   clean
sauer   sour
schade!   pity!
der Schalter(-)   the counter(s), desk(s)
schauen(auf)   to look at
das Schaufenster(-)   the shopwindow(s)

der Scheck(s)   the cheque(s)
die Scheibe(n)   the slice(s)
scheinen   to shine
schenken   to give as a present
schick   stylish, smart
das Schild(er)   the(road) sign(s), notice board(s)
der Schinken(-)   the ham(s)
schlafen   to sleep
schläft ein, einschlafen   falls asleep, to fall asleep
Schlesisches Tor   a tube stop in West Berlin (lit. Silesian Gate)
schließen   to close
schließlich   finally
der Schlips(e)   the tie(s)
der Schloßgarten(¨en)   the palace gardens
der Schloßhof(¨e)   the courtyard(s)
der Schluck(e)   the sip(s)
der Schlüssel(-)   the key(s)
schmecken   to taste
der Schmerz(en)   the pain(s)
schnell   fast, quickly
die Schokolade(n)   the chocolate(s)
schon   already
schön   beautiful
schrecklich   dreadful, terrible
der Schreibtisch(e)   the writing desk, table(s)
der Schuh(e)   the shoe(s)
die Schule(n)   the school(s)
die Schürze(n)   the apron(s)
schütteln   to shake
das Schützenfest(e)   fair featuring shooting competition(s)
schwarz   black
das Schweinekotelett(s)   the pork chop(s)
schwer   heavily, hard
die Schwester(n)   the sister(s)
schwimmen   to swim
der Sektor(en)   the sector(s)
der See(n)   the lake(s)
sehen(auf)   to look at
sehr   very
sei unbesorgt!   don't worry!
die Seife(n)   the soap(s)
sein,-e, -er, -es   his(poss. pronoun)
sein   to be
selbstverständlich   of course
seltsam   strange, weird
servieren   to serve
ich setze auf, aufsetzen   I put on, to put on
sich duschen   to take a shower
sicher(sein)   to be sure, certain
sie, Sie,   her (pronoun), you
sieben   seven
sieht an, ansehen   looks at, to look at
sieht aus, aussehen   looks like, to look like
sieht hoch, auf; aufsehen   looks up, to look up
sieht sich um, sich umsehen   looks around, to look around
die Situation(en)   the situation(s)
der Sitz(e)   the residence(s)
sitzen   to sit
die Socke(n)   the sock(s)
sogar   even
sollen   shall, to be obliged
der Sommer(-)   the summer(s)
die Sommerresidenz   the summer residence
sondern   but
die Sonne(n)   the sun(s)
die Sonnenbrille(n)   the sunglasses
der Sonnenschirm(e)   the sun umbrella(s)
sonnig   sunny
der Sonntag(e)   the Sunday(s)
sonntags   on Sundays
sonst noch etwas?   anything else?
sonst   otherwise
die Sorge(n)   the trouble(s), worry(ies)
sich Sorgen machen   to trouble oneself, to worry
der Sortenschalter(-)   the foreign exchange counter(s)
soviel   so much
sparsam   economical
spät   late
später   later
die Speisekarte(n)   the menu card(s)
der Speisesaal(säle)   the dining room(s)
die Sperre(n)   the channel(s), barrier(s)
die Spesen(pl. only)   the expenses

die Spezialität(en)   the speciality(ies)
der Spiegel(-)   the mirror(s)
spielen   to play
der Sport   sport(s)
die Sprache(n)   the language(s)
sprechen, spricht   to speak, speaks
die Sprechstundenhilfe(n)   the surgery assistant(s), nurse(s)
das Sprichwort(¨er)   the proverb(s)
springen   to jump
springt auf, aufspringen   jumps open, to jump open
spüren   to feel, to sense
die Stadt(¨e)   the town(s)
die Stadtbesichtigung(en)   the sightseeing tour(s)
der Stand(¨e)   the stand(s)
stark   strong, heavy
die Station(en)   the stop, station(s)
stecken   to put; to be inside s.th.
stehen   to stand
steht auf   gets up
die Stellung(en)   the position(s)
sterben, stirbt   to die, dies
die Stimme(n)   the voice(s)
stimmen   to be right, correct
stimmt   right, exact(ly)
das Stockwerk(e)   the floor(s), storey(s)
die Straße(n)   the street(s)
die Straßenbahn(en)   the tram(s)
der Straßenlärm   the street noise
der Straßenrand(¨er)   the curb(s) of the street
die Strumpfhose(n)   the tights
das Stück(e)   the piece(s)
der Student(en)   the student(s)
studieren   to study
das Studium(Studien)   the studies
der Stuhl(¨e)   the chair(s)
subtrahieren   to subtract
suchen   to search

T

der Tag(e)   the day(s)
der Tank(s)   the tank(s)
tanzen   to dance
die Tasche(n)   the (hand)bag(s)
die Tasse(n)   the cup(s)
die Tatsache(n)   the fact(s)
tatsächlich   indeed, really, in fact
das Taxi(s)   the taxi(s)
der Taxifahrer(-)   the taxidriver(s)
der Tee(s)   the tea(s)
der Teilhaber(-)   the partner(s), associate(s)
telefonieren   to make a 'phone call
telefonisch   by telephone
der Teller(-)   the plate(s)
das Tennis   the tennis
der Teppich(e)   the carpet(s)
teuer   expensive
teurer   more expensive
das Theater(-)   the theatre(s)
der Tiergarten   a district or area in West Berlin
der Tilsiter(Käse)   the Tilsit cheese
der Tisch(e)   the table(s)
der Tod   the death
die Toilette(n)   the toilet(s)
die Tomate(n)   the tomato(es)
die Torte(n)   the tart(s)
total   completely
der Tourist(en)   the tourist(s)
tragen, trägt   to wear, wears
treffen, trifft   to meet, he, she, it, one meets
die Treppe(n)   the stairs
das Treppenhaus(¨er)   the well(s) of staircase(s)
trinken   to drink
das Trinkgeld(er)   the tip(s)
trotzdem   in spite of, however
die Tür(en)   the door(s)

U

die U-Bahn(en)   the tube (underground train)(s)
über   above

überall   everywhere
überglücklich   very happy(lit. over-happy)
überhaupt   anyway, anyhow; at all, altogether
überhaupt nicht   not at all
übernachten   to stay overnight
übernimmt, übernehmen   takes over, to take over
überqueren   to cross
überraschen   to surprise
die Überraschung(en)   the surprise(s)
übrigens   by the way
die Uhr(en)   the clock(s), watch(es)
um   at, about
sich umdrehen   to turn round
umkommen   to perish, die, get killed
der Umschlag(¨e)   the envelope(s)
umsonst   for nothing, gratis
umsteigen   to change(trains etc.)
unbesorgt   without trouble(s), worries
und   and
unerwartet   unexpected(ly)
ungefähr   about
unhöflich   impolite
uns   us
unser, -e, -es   our
unten   downstairs
unter   beneath
die Untergrundbahn(en)   the underground(train)(s)
sich unterhalten   to talk, converse
unterschreiben   to sign
die Unterwäsche   the underwear
der Urlaub   the holiday(s)

V

sich verabreden   to make a date, arrange
die Verabredung(en)   the meeting(s)
sich verabschieden   to say goodbye, to depart
verbringen(Zeit)   to spend (time)
vergessen, vergißt   to forget, he, she, it, one forgets
verheiratet sein   to be married
verkaufen   to sell
der Verkaufsdirektor(en)   the sales director(s)
der Verkäufer(-)   the salesman(men)
der Verkehr   the traffic
verlassen, verläßt   to leave, leaves
sich verlaufen, verläuft sich   to lose one's way, loses his way
verletzt   injured
verlieren   to lose
das Vermögen(-)   the fortune(finance)
(jdn/etw.) verpassen   to miss s.b. or s.th.
die Sprache verschlagen   to be struck dumb
etw. versichern   to promise s.th.
verstehen   to understand
versuchen   to try
jdm. vertrauen   to trust s.b.
verwirrt(sein)   to be confused
(etwas) verzollen   to declare s.th.
viel, viele   much, many
vielleicht   perhaps
vier   four
das Vitamin(e)   the vitamin(s)
die Volksbank(en)   the people's bank(s)
voll   full(up)
die Vollkaskoversicherung   the fully comprehensive
   insurance
von mir aus!   I don't mind
von   of
vor   before, in front of, by
vorbei   past, along
vorbeikommen   to pass
vorgestern   the day before yesterday
etwas vorhaben   to have plans
der Vorhang(¨e)   the curtain(s)
vorher   beforehand
vormals   formerly
der Vorschlag(¨e)   the suggestion(s)
vorschlagen, schlägt vor   to propose, proposes
vorsichtig(sein)   (to be) careful
die Vorspeise(n)   the starter(s)
vorstellen   to introduce
(sich etwas) vorstellen   to imagine(s.th.)

die Vorwahlnummer(n)   the area code(s)

W

wacht auf   wakes up
wählen   to choose
wahr   true
während   during
wahrscheinlich   probably
das Wahrzeichen(-)   the landmark(s)
der Wald(¨er)   the wood(s)
warm   warm
warten   to wait
warum   why
wasserlöslich   water soluble
wechseln   to change
der Weg(e)   the way(s)
weg sein   to be away, be gone
weg   away
wegen   because of, about
weich   soft
weil   because
der Wein(e)   the wine(s)
weit   far
weiter   further(on)
weiterfahren   to drive on
weiß   white
welch,(e, er, es)   which(one)
wenigstens   at least
wer   who
werden, wird   will, he, she, it, one will, is going to be
die Werkstatt(¨en)   the workshop(s)
wertvoll   valuable
das Wetter   the weather
der Wetterbericht(e)   the weather forecast
wichtig   important
wie   how
wieder   again
auf Wiederhören   goodbye (on the 'phone)
die Wiederholung(en)   the repetition(s)
auf Wiedersehen   goodbye
die Wiese(n)   the meadow(s)
wieso   why, how come
willkommen   welcome
windig   windy
die Winterjacke(n)   the winter jacket(s)
wir   we
wirft zu, zuwerfen   throws towards, to throw towards
wirft ein, einwerfen (eine Karte usw.)   posts, mails, to post,
wirklich   really
die Wirtschaft   economics
wissen, weiß   to know(a fact), knows
wo   where
die Woche(n)   the week(s)
das Wochenende(n)   the weekend(s)
wohl   possibly, about, perhaps
wohnen   to live, reside
wolkenlos   cloudless
die Wolke(n)   the cloud(s)
wollen, will   to want, he, she, it, one wants
der Wollstoff(e)   the woollen material(s)
woran   about what (do you think)
wunderschön   marvellous, wonderful
die Wurst(¨e)   the sausage(s)
wünschen   to wish
würde   I, he she, it, one would
würden   would

Z

der Zahnarzt(-¨e)   the dentist(s)
die Zahnbürste(n)   the toothbrush(es)
die Zahnpaste   the toothpaste
zehn   ten
der Zehnmarkschein(e)   the ten mark note(s)
zeigen   to show
die Zeit(en)   the time(s)
die Zeitschrift(en)   the magazine(s)
zerbombt   bombed out
zerstört   destroyed

der Zettel(-)   the slip(s) of paper
ziehen, gezogen   to move, moved
zieht auf   pulls open
zieht aus   takes off(garment)
zieht sich an, sich anziehen   gets dressed, to get dressed
ziemlich   fairly, rather
die Zimmernummer(n)   the room number(s)
die Zitrone(n)   the lemon(s)
der Zoll(¨e)   the Customs
zögern   to hesitate
zu Hause   at home
zu   to, too
der Zucker   the sugar
zuerst   first
auf jdn. zugehen   to walk towards s.b.
zuhören   to listen(to)
zündet an   lights (verb 3rd pers.sing.)
zurück   back
zusammen   together
zusammenstoßen   to collide, crash
der Zwanzigmarkschein(e)   the twenty mark note(s)
zwar   (al)though, actually
zwei   two
der Zweifel(-)   the doubt(s)
zweimal   twice
zweite, er, es   second
die Zwetschge(n)   the plum(s)
die Zwiebelsuppe(n)   the onion soup(s)
zwischen   between

ENGLISH — GERMAN

A

a, an **ein, eine**
about **ungefähr**
about how **daran, wie**
about it **darüber**
about what **woran**
above **über**
accepts, to accept **nimmt an, annehmen**
to add **addieren**
the address(es) **die Adresse(n)**
the adventure(s) **das Abenteuer(-)**
to be afraid of s.th. **etwas befürchten**
after that **danach**
after that(temp.) **darauf**
afterwards **danach**
again **wieder**
to agree **einverstanden(sein)**
the air **die Luft**
the airport(s) **der Flughafen(--)**
the aisle(s) **der Gang(-e)**
all **alle**
(to be) allowed to **erlaubt(sein)**
along **entlang**
already **bereits, schon**
also **auch**
although; actually **zwar**
always **immer**
and **und**
(to be) annoyed **ärgerlich(sein)**
to answer **antworten**
anything else? **sonst noch etwas?**
anyway, anyhow; at all **überhaupt**
appetising **appetitlich**
the apple(s) **der Apfel(-)**
the approach road **die Auffahrt(en)**
the apron(s) **die Schürze(n)**
the area(s) **die Gegend(en)**
the arm(s) **der Arm(e)**
the arrival(s) **die Ankunft(--e)**
to arrive **ankommen**
as, than **als**
to ask a question **fragen**
falls asleep, to fall asleep **schläft ein, einschlafen**
the aspirin **das Aspirin**
the aspirin tablet(s) **die Aspirintablette(n)**
to be astonished **erstaunt sein**
at **beim**
at, about **um**
at all, altogether **überhaupt**
at home **zu Hause**
at last **endlich**
at least **wenigstens**
the atmosphere **die Atmosphäre**
the autumn **der Herbst**
on average **im Durchschnitt**
away **weg**
to be away, be gone **weg sein**
away, from **ab**

B

back **zurück**
the baker's shop(s) **die Bäckerei(en)**
the balcony(ies) **der Balkon(s)**
the bald head(s) **die Glatze(n)**
the ballet **das Ballett**
the bank(s) **die Bank(en)**
the people's bank(s) **die Volksbank(en)**
the bath(s) **das Bad(-er)**
the bathroom(s) **das Badezimmer(-)**
the bathtowel(s) **das Badetuch(--er)**
to be **sein**
to be glad **froh sein, sich freuen**
to be there, present **da sein**
beautiful **schön**
because **weil**
because of, about **wegen**
the bed(s) **das Bett(en)**
the beef **das Rindfleisch**
the beer(s) **das Bier(e)**

the beer bottle(s) **die Bierflasche(n)**
before, in front of, by **vor**
beforehand **vorher**
the beginning(s) **der Anfang(--e)**
to believe, think **glauben**
the bell button(s) **der Klingelknopf(-e)**
beneath **unter**
best **das beste**
between **zwischen**
the bicycle(s) **das Fahrrad(--er)**
the bill(s) **die Rechnung(en)**
black **schwarz**
blackened **geschwärzt**
blond(e) **blond**
the blouse(s) **die Bluse(n)**
blue **blau**
the boarding card(s), pass(es) **die Bordkarte(n)**
bombed out **zerbombt**
bon voyage! **gute Reise!**
the book(s) **das Buch(-er)**
to book **buchen**
the border(s) **die Grenze(n)**
the border crossing(s) **der Grenzübergang(-e)**
boring **langweilig**
to be born **geboren werden**
to borrow **leihen**
the boss(es) **der Chef(s)**
both **beide**
the bottle(s) **die Flasche(n)**
the boy(s) **der Junge(n)**
the bread(s) **das Brot(e)**
Westphalian dark bread **der Pumpernickel**
the breadroll(s) **das Brötchen(-)**
to break s.th., breaks s.th. **(sich etwas) brechen, bricht**
the breakfast **das Frühstück**
to have breakfast **frühstücken**
the breath **der Atem**
to breathe **atmen**
the briefcase(s) **die Aktentasche(n)**
to bring **bringen**
the brother(s) **der Bruder(-)**
brown **braun**
the building(s) **das Gebäude(-)**
the bus, coach **der Bus(se)**
on business(matters) **geschäftlich**
the business, the thing(s) **die Sache(n)**
to be busy **beschäftigt sein**
but **aber**
the butcher(s) **der Metzger(-)**
the butcher's shop **die Metzgerei(en)**
the butter **die Butter**
the button(s) **der Knopf(-e)**
to buy **kaufen**
by now, meanwhile **inzwischen**
by post, mail **mit der Post**
by telephone **telefonisch**
by the way **übrigens**

C

the cake(s) **der Kuchen(-)**
the cake counter(s) **das Kuchenbüfett(s)**
to calculate, work out **rechnen**
to call **rufen**
can, he, she, it one can **können, kann**
the candle(s) **die Kerze(n)**
the capital(s) **die Hauptstadt(---e)**
the car(s) **das Auto(s)**
the car hire firm(s) **die Autovermietung(en)**
the car trip(s), journey(s) **die Autofahrt(en)**
(to be) careful **vorsichtig(sein)**
the carpet(s) **der Teppich(e)**
the carriageway(s), lane(s) **die Fahrbahn(en)**
the carrot(s) **die Karotte(n)**
the cash **das Bargeld**
the cash desk(s) **die Kasse(n)**
to cash(in) **einlösen**
the casual shirt(s) **das Freizeithemd(en)**
the catastrophe(s) **die Katastrophe(n)**
to celebrate **feiern**
the celebration(s) **die Feier(n)**

the century(ies) das Jahrhundert(e)
to be certain, sure sicher(sein)
certainly bestimmt
the chair(s) der Stuhl(¨e)
the change(s) from die Abwechslung(en) von
to change wechseln
to change(trains etc.) umsteigen
the changing room(s) die Kabine(n)
the channel(s), barrier(s) die Sperre(n)
cheap billig
cheaper billiger
cheapest am billigsten
to check prüfen
to check in einschecken
Cheers! Prost!
the cheese(s) der Käse(-)
the cheese stand(s) der Käsestand(¨e)
the cheque(s) der Scheck(s)
the cherry(ies) die Kirsche(n)
the child(ren) das Kind(er)
the single/only child(ren) das Einzelkind(er)
the chocolate(s) die Schokolade(n)
to choose wählen
the cinema(s) das Kino(s)
very clean blitzsauber
clean sauber
the clock(s), watch(es) die Uhr(en)
to close schließen
close to bei
the clothing die Kleidung
the cloud(s) die Wolke(n)
cloudless wolkenlos
the coat(s) der Mantel(¨)
the area code(s) die Vorwahlnummer(n)
the coin(s) die Münze(n)
the collar size(s) die Kragenweite(n)
the College(s) die Hochschule(n)
to collide, crash zusammenstoßen
the colour(s) die Farbe(n)
(multi) coloured bunt
to come with mitkommen
comfortable bequem
comfortably warm mollig
the commissioner(s) for oaths der Notar(e)
completely ganz, total
to confirm bestätigen
(to be) confused verwirrt(sein)
congratulation(s) der Glückwunsche(¨e)
to cook kochen
cool kühl
cordial herzlich
the cork(s) der Korken(-)
the corner(s) die Ecke(n)
correct richtig
to cost kosten
could könnte(n)
the counter(s), the bar(s) das Büfett(s)
the counter(s), desk(s) der Schalter(-)
into the country aufs Land
the country das Land
the courier service(s) der Kurierdienst(e)
the courtyard(s) der Schloßhof(¨e)
the cow(s) die Kuh(¨e)
the cream die Sahne
the credit card(s) die Kreditkarte(n)
to cross überqueren
the cup(s) die Tasse(n)
the curb(s) of the street der Straßenrand(¨er)
the curtain(s) der Vorhang(¨e)
the customer(s) der Kunde(n)
the Customs der Zoll(¨e)

D

to dance tanzen
dark dunkel
the day(s) der Tag(e)
the day before yesterday vorgestern
the death der Tod
to decide beschließen
to declare s.th. (etwas) verzollen

to deliver abliefern
the dentist(s) der Zahnarzt(¨e)
the department store(s) das Kaufhaus(¨er)
to depend (upon) (darauf) ankommen
that depends das kommt darauf an
the desk(s) der Schreibtisch(e)
the dessert der Nachtisch
destroyed zerstört
to dial through durchwählen
to die, dies sterben, stirbt
the dining room(s) der Speisesaal(säle)
direct direkt
to discuss besprechen
the dish(es) das Gericht(e)
to divide dividieren
the doctor(s) der Arzt(¨e)
the donkey(s) der Esel(-)
don't worry! sei unbesorgt!
the door(s) die Tür(en)
the dot(s) der Punkt(e)
the doubt(s) der Zweifel(-)
down herunter, heraus
downstairs unten
dreadful, terrible schrecklich
the dress(es) das Kleid(er)
gets dressed, to get dressed zieht sich an, sich anziehen
to drink trinken
to drive, go by vehicle fahren
to drive on weiterfahren
the driver(s) der Fahrer(-)
drives, goes by vehicle fährt
drives home, to drive home fährt heim, heimfahren
the driving licence(s) der Führerschein(e)
the drug dispensing chemist(s) die Apotheke(n)
during während

E

early (in the morning) früh
easy leicht
to eat essen
economical sparsam
economics die Wirtschaft
the egg(s) das Ei(er)
elegant, smart chic, elegant, apart
the end das Ende
the Englishman(men) der Engländer(-)
to enter betreten
the entrance(fee) der Eintritt
the envelope(s) der Umschlag(¨e)
especial(ly) extra, besonders
the Eurocheque(s) der Euroscheck(s)
even sogar
ever jemals
everybody, each one jeder
everything alles
everywhere überall
exact(ly) genau
exactly as genauso
excellent prima
to be excited aufgeregt(sein)
the excuse(es) die Entschuldigung(en)
excuse me! Entschuldigen Sie!
to expect, to await erwarten
the expenses die Spesen(pl. only)
expensive teuer
to explain erklären
the export der Export
the expressionists die Expressionisten
the expressionism(style in art) der Expressionismus
the eye(s) das Auge(n)

F

the face(s) das Gesicht(er)
the fact(s) die Tatsache(n)
fair featuring shooting competition(s) das Schützenfest(e)
fair, bright heiter
fairly, rather ziemlich
to fall asleep einschlafen
to fall off sich lösen, fallen

the family(ies) **die Familie(n)**
the family business(es) **das Familienunternehmen(-)**
famous **berühmt**
far **weit**
to fascinate **faszinieren**
fascinating **faszinierend**
fast, quickly **schnell**
fat **dick**
the fear(s), worry(ies) **die Angst(¨e)**
to feel, to sense **spüren**
to feel good **sich wohl fühlen**
the feeling(s) **das Gefühl(e)**
a few **(ein) paar**
the field(s) **das Feld(er)**
fifty **fünfzig**
to fill **füllen**
fills in/out, to fill in/out **füllt aus, ausfüllen**
finally **schließlich**
to find **finden**
to find out, to state **feststellen**
to finish **beenden**
finished **zu Ende**
the firm(s), company(ies) **die Firma(Firmen)**
first **erste, ersten, zuerst**
lit: first of all **erst einmal**
fitting, suitable **passend**
five **fünf**
flat **flach**
the flight(s) **der Flug(¨e)**
the floor(s), storey(s) **das Stockwerk(e)**
the flower(s) **die Blume(n)**
the fog, mist(s) **der Nebel(-)**
foggy, misty **neblig**
the food **das Essen**
for **für**
formerly **vormals**
for nothing, gratis **umsonst**
the foreign exchange counter(s) **der Sortenschalter(-)**
to forget, he, she, it, one forgets **vergessen, vergißt**
formal **förmlich**
the fortune(finance) **das Vermögen(-)**
to found, establish **gründen**
four **vier**
fresh **frisch**
fried **gebraten**
friendly **freundlich**
from(temp.) **ab**
the fruit **das Obst**
full(up) **voll**
to function **funktionieren**
(the pieces of) furniture **die Möbel**
further(on) **weiter**

G

the GDR (German Democratic Republic) **die DDR**
the gentleman(men) **der Herr(en)**
the geranium(s) **die Geranie(n)**
German **deutsch**
the German language **das Deutsch**
Germany **das Deutschland**
to get off, out **aussteigen**
to get to know someone **jdn. kennenlernen**
gets up **steht auf**
the girl(s) **das Mädchen(-)**
to give **geben**
to give as a present **schenken**
gives **gibt**
gladly, to like **gern**
the glass(es) **das Glas(¨er)**
the glasses **die Brille(n)**
to go out **ausgehen**
to go shopping **einkaufen**
to go, walk **gehen**
golden **golden, goldenes**
good **gut**
the good fortune **das Glück**
goodbye (on the 'phone) **auf Wiederhören**
goodbye **auf Wiedersehen**
the gramme **das Gramm**
great, fantastic, terrific **großartig**

green **grün**
to greet **begrüßen**
grey **grau**
the ground floor **das Erdgeschoß**
to guess, guessed **raten, geraten**
to guide, guides **führen, führt**

H

the hail(s) **der Hagel(-)**
it's hailing **es hagelt**
the hair **das Haar(e)**
half **halb**
the ham(s) **der Schinken(-)**
the hand(s) **die Hand(¨e)**
to hand (over) **(über)reichen**
to hang **hängen**
to happen **passieren**
happy **glücklich**
the harvest(s), (wine, corn etc) **die Lese(n)**
to have **haben**
to have a good time, have fun **sich amüsieren**
to have an opinion of **halten(davon)**
to have or show an interest in s.th. **(sich) interessieren (für)**
to have plans **etwas vorhaben**
I have to (to have to) **ich muß(müssen)**
to have to, to need (to) **brauchen**
he **er**
the head(s) **der Kopf(¨e)**
the headache(s) **der Kopfschmerz(en)**
to hear **hören**
heavily, hard **schwer**
heavy **stark**
to help **helfen**
her **ihr**
her, you **sie, Sie**
here **hier**
here, there **dahin; daher**
the herring(s) **der Hering(e)**
to hesitate **zögern**
high, up **hoch**
him **ihm**
to hire **mieten**
his(poss. pronoun) **sein,-e, -er, -es**
the hobby(ies) **das Hobby(ies)**
the holiday(s) **der Urlaub**
honest **ehrlich**
the honey **der Honig**
hopefully **hoffentlich**
horrible, shocking **entsetzlich**
the hospital(s) **das Krankenhaus(¨-er)**
the hostess(es) **die Gastgeberin(nen)**
hot **heiß**
the hotel(s) **das Hotel(s)**
the hotel room(s) **das Hotelzimmer(-)**
the house(s) **das Haus(¨-er)**
how **wie**
hundred **(ein)hundert**
hunger **der Hunger**
to be hungry **hungrig sein**
to hurry, rush **sich beeilen**

I

I **ich**
I don't mind **von mir aus! es ist mir egal**
the idea(s) **die Idee(n)**
the imagination(s) **die Einbildung(en)**
to imagine(s.th.) **(sich etwas) vorstellen**
impolite **unhöflich**
the import **der Import**
important **wichtig**
in, come in! **herein(!)**
in addition to **dazu**
in spite of, however **trotzdem**
in the morning **morgens**
indeed **tatsächlich**
to inform, tell s.b. **jdm. etwas mitteilen**
injured **verletzt**
inside **drin, drinnen**

insurance, (fully comprehensive) **die Vollkaskoversicherung**
intelligent **intelligent**
the interest(in s.th.) **das Interesse(n)**
interesting **interessant**
into **ins**
to introduce **vorstellen**
to invite **einladen**
is **ist**
isn't that so? (lit. isn't that true?) **nicht wahr?**
Italian **Italienisch**

J

the jacket(s) **die Jacke(n)**
the jam(s) **die Marmelade(n)**
the(car) journey, trip **die Fahrt(en)**
the little jug(s) **das Kännchen(-)**
to jump, jumps open **springen, springt auf**
just now, straight **gerade**
just once **mal**

K

the key(s) **der Schlüssel(-)**
the kilometre(s) **der Kilometer(-)**
the kiosk(s) **der Kiosk(e)**
to knock **klopfen**
to know(a fact), knows **wissen, weiß**
to know(about) **kennen**
the kohlrabi(s) **der Kohlrabi(s)**

L

the lady(ies) **die Dame(n)**
the lady doctor(s) **die Ärztin(nen)**
the lake(s) **der See(n)**
the lamb's meat **das Lammfleisch**
the landmark(s) **das Wahrzeichen(-)**
the language(s) **die Sprache(n)**
to last **dauern**
late **spät**
later **später**
to laugh **lachen**
to lay the table, to cover **decken**
the leather **das Leder**
to leave, leaves **verlassen, verläßt**
left **links**
the lemon(s) **die Zitrone(n)**
let (familiar) us **laß uns**
to let, allow **lassen**
the letter(s) **der Brief(e)**
the letter box(es) **der Briefkasten(-)**
the lettuce(s) **der Kopfsalat(e)**
to lie, repose **liegen**
light(weight) **leicht**
light blue **hellblau**
light brown **hellbraun**
the lightning **der Blitz**
lights(verb 3rd per.sing.) **zündet an**
to like, be partial to, likes **mögen, mag**
liqueur(s) **der Likör(e)**
to listen(to) **zuhören**
a little bit **ein bißchen**
to live, reside **wohnen**
the liver sausage(s) **die Leberwurst(-e)**
the lobby(ies) **das Foyer(s)**
long **lang**
to take, to have, takes, has a look **nachsehen, sieht nach**
to look at **anschauen, ansehen**
looks around, to look around **sieht sich um, sich umsehen**
looks at, to look at **sieht an, ansehen**
looks like, to look like, **sieht aus, aussehen**
looks up, to look up **sieht hoch, auf, aufsehen**
to lose **verlieren**
to be dumbfounded **die Sprache verschlagen**
to lose one's way, loses his way **sich verlaufen, er verläuft sich**
the luggage **das Gepäck**

M

the magazine (s) **die Zeitschrift (en)**
the main dish (es) **das Hauptgericht (e)**
the main entrance **der Haupteingang**
to make, do **machen**
to make a date, arrange **sich verabreden**
to make a phone call **telefonieren**
the man (men) **der Mann (-e)**
the management (s) **die Geschäftsführung (en)**
the managing director (s) **der Generaldirektor (en)**
the map (s) **die Landkarte (n)**
the mark (s) **die Mark (stücke)**
the market (s) **der Markt (-e)**
the market day (s) **der Markttag (e)**
the market place (s) **der Marktplatz (-e)**
the market woman (women) **die Marktfrau (en)**
to be married **verheiratet sein**
to marry **heiraten**
marvellous **herrlich**
wonderful **wunderschön**
may, he, she, it may **dürfen, darf**
(to) me **mir**
the meadow (s) **die Wiese (n)**
the meal (s) **die Mahlzeit (en)**
to mean **bedeuten**
meat pate **der Leberkäs**
to meet, he, she, it, one meets **treffen, trifft**
the meeting (s) **die Verabredung (en)**
the men's clothing **die Herrenbekleidung**
the menu card (s) **die Speisekarte (n)**
the message (pl. the news) **die Nachricht (en)**
the messenger(s) **der Bote(n)**
the metre(s) **der Meter(-)**
mild **mild**
the milk **die Milch**
the mineral water(s) **das Mineralwasser(-)**
the mirror(s) **der Spiegel(-)**
the Miss(es) **das Fräulein(-)**
to miss s.b. or s.th. **(jdn/etw.) verpassen**
modern **modern**
the moment(s) **der Augenblick(e), der Moment(e)**
the money **das Geld**
the month(s) **der Monat(e)**
more **mehr**
more expensive **teurer**
the morning(s) **der Morgen(-)**
the Mosel wine(s) **der Moselwein(e)**
the motorbike(s) **das Motorrad(-er)**
the motorway(s) **die Autobahn(en)**
the mountain(s) **der Berg(e)**
to move, moved **ziehen, gezogen**
much, many **viel, viele**
to multiply **multiplizieren**
the multistorey building(s) **das Hochhaus(-er)**
my **mein**
mysterious **geheimnisvoll**
the mystery(ies) **das Geheimnis(se)**

N

the name(s) **der Name(n)**
to be named **heißen**
narrow, tight **eng**
the National Gallery **die Nationalgalerie**
near **nah(e)**
nearby, close to or by **in der Nähe**
nearly **fast**
to be necessary **nötig(sein)**
to need **brauchen**
the nephew(s) **der Neffe(n)**
new **neu**
next **nächst, e, es**
next to **neben**
next to it **daneben**
nice **nett**
the niece(s) **die Nichte(n)**
the night(s) **die Nacht(-e)**
no **nein**

no ... more **keine ... mehr**
nobody **niemand**
to nod **nicken**
the noise **der Lärm**
the non-smoker(s) **der Nichtraucher(-)**
not **nicht**
not at all **überhaupt nicht**
not yet **noch nicht**
nothing **nichts**
now **jetzt**
the number(s) **die Nummer(n)**

O

to observe **beobachten**
of **von**
of course **natürlich, selbstverständlich**
the office(s) **das Büro(s)**
the official(s) **der Beamte(n)**
often **oft, öfters**
the oil level **der Ölstand**
old **alt**
old part of the town(s) **die Altstadt(-̈e)**
on **auf**
on, at **an**
on foot **zu Fuß**
on the, at the **am**
once, once(in a while) **einmal**
one(followed by verb in 3rd P. Sing.) **man**
the onion soup(s) **die Zwiebelsuppe(n)**
only **nur**
to open **aufmachen**
to open **öffnen**
the opportunity(ies) **die Gelegenheit(en)**
opposite **gegenüber**
the orange juice(s) **der Orangensaft(-̈e)**
in order **in Ordnung**
to order, to book **bestellen**
other(s) (with noun) **andere**
otherwise **sonst**
our **unser, -e, -es**
out, from **aus**
outside **draußen**
(over) there **dort**

P

to pack, wrap in **einpacken**
the packet(s) **die Packung(en)**
the pain(s) **der Schmerz(en)**
the palace gardens **der Schloßgarten(-̈)**
the paper(s) **das Papier(e)**
the papers (personal, only in plural) **die Papiere**
the parcel(s) **das Paket(e)**
the parents **die Eltern**
the parking **das Parken**
the parsley **die Petersilie**
the partner(s), associate(s) **der Teilhaber(-)**
to pass **vorbeikommen**
to pass through **durchgehen**
the passport(s) **der Paß(-̈sse), der Reisepaß(-̈sse)**
the passport control(s) **die Paßkontrolle(n)**
past, along **vorbei**
the pavement(s) **der Bürgersteig(e)**
to pay **bezahlen**
the pea(s) **die Erbse(n)**
the pear(s) **die Birne(n)**
per **pro**
perhaps **vielleicht**
to perish, die, get killed **umkommen**
the person(s) **die Person(en)**
personally, in person **persönlich**
the pfennig(s) **der Pfennig(e)**
the pickled herring(s) **der Rollmops(-̈e)**
the picnic **das Picknick**
the piece(s) **das Stück(e)**
the pillow(s) **das Kopfkissen(-)**
the pitch, bad luck **das Pech**
pity! **schade!**
to place, lay down **legen**

the plan(s) **der Plan(-̈e)**
the plane(s) **das Flugzeug(e), die Maschine(n)**
the plane accident(s) **das Flugzeugunglück(e)**
the plate(s) **der Teller(-)**
the platform(s) **der Bahnsteig(e)**
to play **spielen**
pleasant **angenehm**
please **bitte**
to please **gefallen**
to be pleased **froh(sein)**
pleases **gefällt**
the plum(s) **die Zwetschge(n)**
the poem(s) **das Gedicht(e)**
polite **höflich**
poor **arm**
the poppyseed roll(s) **das Mohnbrötchen(-)**
the porcelain collection(s) **die Porzellansammlung(en)**
the pork chop(s) **das Schweinekotelett(s)**
the position(s) **die Stellung(en)**
to possess, to own **besitzen**
possibly, about, perhaps **wohl**
the post office(s) **die Post, das Postamt(-̈er)**
to post, posts, mails **(eine Karte usw.) einwerfen, wirft ein**
the picture postcard(s) **die Ansichtskarte(n)**
the potato(es) **die Kartoffel(n)**
the potato field(s) **das Kartoffelfeld(er)**
the pound(s) **das Pfund(e)**
the pound note(s) **der Pfundschein(e)**
to pour **gießen**
practical **praktisch**
to press **drücken**
pretty **hübsch**
probably **wahrscheinlich**
the programme(s) **das Programm(e)**
to promise s.th. **etw. versichern, versprechen**
propose(s), suggest(s),**vorschlagen, schlägt vor**
to prove one's identity **sich ausweisen**
pulls open **zieht auf**
punctual(ly) **pünktlich**
to put, to be inside s.th. **stecken**
to put in, into **einstecken**
I put on, to put on **ich setze auf, aufsetzen**

Q

queasy **flau**
quiet, calm **ruhig**
the quilt(s) **die Bettdecke(n)**

R

to rain **regnen**
the rate(s) of exchange **der Kurs(e)**
to react **reagieren**
to read, reads **lesen, liest**
to be ready **fertig sein**
really **eigentlich, wirklich**
really, in fact **tatsächlich**
the reason, cause(s) **der Grund(-̈e)**
to receive **bekommen**
the receptionist(s) **die Empfangsdame(n)**
red **rot**
red, amber, green **rot, gelb, grün,**
the refrigerator(s) **der Kühlschrank(-̈e)**
to relax **sich erholen**
to remain, stay **bleiben**
the repair(s) **die Reparatur(en)**
to reply **erwidern**
to request **bitten**
to reserve **reservieren**
the residence **der Sitz(e)**
to rest **(sich) ausruhen**
the restaurant(s) **das Restaurant(s)**
the retirement **der Ruhestand**
the return flight(s) **der Rückflug(-̈e)**
smoked ribs(German meat dish) **Kasseler Rippchen**
rich, wealthy **reich**
right **rechts**
to be right, correct **stimmen**
right, exact(ly) **stimmt**

to ring   **klingeln**
ripe   **reif**
the role(s)   **die Rolle(n)**
romantic   **romantisch**
the room(s)   **der Raum(-̈e)**
the room number(s)   **die Zimmernummer(n)**
rosy   **rosig**
rustling   **raschelnd**

S

the salad(s)   **der Salat(e)**
the salami   **die Salami**
the sales director(s)   **der Verkaufsdirektor(en)**
the salesman(men)   **der Verkäufer(-)**
the sausage(s)   **die Wurst(-̈e)**
to say   **sagen**
to say goodbye, to depart   **sich verabschieden**
scarcely   **knapp**
the school(s)   **die Schule(n)**
to search   **suchen**
second   **zweite, er, es**
the sector(s)   **der Sektor(en)**
to sell   **verkaufen**
serious   **ernst**
to serve   **servieren**
the service   **die Bedienung**
seven   **sieben**
the shade(s) of colour   **der Farbton(-̈e)**
to shake   **schütteln**
shall, to be obliged   **sollen**
to shave oneself   **sich rasieren**
the shaver(s)   **der Rasierapparat(e)**
the sheet(s)   **das Laken(-)**
to shine   **leuchten, scheinen**
the shirt(s)   **das Hemd(en)**
the shoe(s)   **der Schuh(e)**
the shop(s)   **der Laden(-̈), das Geschäft(e)**
the shopwindow(s)   **das Schaufenster(-)**
short, brief(ly)   **kurz**
should, ought to   **müßten**
to show   **zeigen**
the shower(s)   **die Dusche(n)**
the siblings   **die Geschwister**
the sightseeing tour(s)   **die Stadtbesichtigung(en)**
the(road) sign(s), notice board(s)   **das Schild(er)**
to sign   **unterschreiben**
simple, simply, single   **einfach**
the sip(s)   **der Schluck(e)**
the sister(s)   **die Schwester(n)**
to sit   **sitzen**
to sit down   **(sich) hinsetzen**
the situation(s)   **die Situation(en)**
the size(s)   **die Größe(n)**
the skirt(s)   **der Rock(-̈e)**
the sky(ies), the heaven(s)   **der Himmel(-)**
to sleep   **schlafen**
the sleeve(s)   **der Ärmel(-)**
the slice(s)   **die Scheibe(n)**
slightly   **leicht**
the slip(s) of paper   **der Zettel(-)**
slow, slowly   **langsam**
small   **klein**
to smell   **riechen**
to smile   **lächeln**
smiling   **lächelnd**
the smoked ham(s)   **der Rauchschinken(-)**
the smoker(s)   **der Raucher(-)**
so much   **soviel**
the soap(s)   **die Seife(n)**
the sock(s)   **die Socke(n)**
soft   **weich**
the solicitor(s)   **der Rechtsanwalt(-̈e)**
is solved, to solve(s.th.)   **klärt sich auf, sich aufklären**
something   **etwas**
soon   **bald**
soon, close by   **gleich**
(I'm) sorry!   **(es) tut mir leid!**
sour   **sauer**
the spare part(s)   **das Ersatzteil(e)**
to speak, speaks   **sprechen, spricht**

the speciality(ies)   **die Spezialität(en)**
the spectacle case(s)   **das Brillenetui(s)**
the speed limit(s)   **die Geschwindigkeitsbegrenzung(en)**
to spend (time)   **verbringen(Zeit)**
the sport(s)   **der Sport**
the spot(s)   **das Plätzchen(-)**
the spring   **der Frühling**
the stairs   **die Treppe(n)**
the stamp(s)   **die Briefmarke(n)**
the stand(s)   **der Stand(-̈e)**
to stand   **stehen**
the starter(s)   **die Vorspeise(n)**
the stay(s)   **der Aufenthalt(e)**
to stay here   **hierbleiben**
to stay overnight   **übernachten**
the stop, station(s)   **die Station(en)**
stops s.b., to stop s.b.   **hält an, anhalten**
straight on   **geradeaus**
strange, weird   **seltsam**
the strawberry(ies)   **die Erdbeere(n)**
the strawberry tart(s)   **die Erdbeertorte(n)**
the street(s)   **die Straße(n)**
the street noise   **der Straßenlärm**
strong, heavy   **stark**
the student(s)   **der Student(en)**
the studies   **das Studium(Studien)**
to study   **studieren**
stylish, smart   **schick**
the subject(s) of something   **das Fach(-̈er)**
to subtract   **subtrahieren**
suddenly   **plötzlich**
the sugar   **der Zucker**
the suggestion(s)   **der Vorschlage(-̈e)**
the suit(s)   **der Anzug(-̈e)**
to suit well   **gut stehen**
the suitcase(s)   **der Koffer(-)**
the summer(s)   **der Sommer(-)**
the summer residence   **die Sommerresidenz**
the sun(s)   **die Sonne(n)**
the sun umbrella(s)   **der Sonnenschirm(e)**
the Sunday(s)   **der Sonntag(e)**
on Sundays   **sonntags**
the sunglasses   **die Sonnenbrille(n)**
sunny   **sonnig**
to be sure, certain   **sicher(sein)**
surely, certainly   **bestimmt**
the surgery assistant(s), nurse(s)   **die Sprechstundenhilfe(n)**
the surprise(s)   **die Überraschung(en)**
to surprise   **überraschen**
to swim   **schwimmen**
the swindler(s)   **der Betrüger(-)**
switches on   **macht an**

T

the table(s)   **der Tisch(e)**
to take, takes   **nehmen, nimmt**
to take a shower   **sich duschen**
to take out, takes out   **herausnehmen, nimmt heraus**
takes off(garment)   **zieht aus**
takes over, to take over   **übernimmt, übernehmen**
to talk, converse   **sich unterhalten**
tall   **groß**
the tank(s)   **der Tank(s)**
the tart(s)   **die Torte(n)**
to taste   **schmecken**
the taxi(s)   **das Taxi(s)**
the taxi driver(s)   **der Taxifahrer(-)**
the tea(s)   **der Tee(s)**
to telephone   **anrufen**
the television(s)   **das Fernsehen(-)**
to tell, relate   **erzählen**
ten   **zehn**
the ten mark note(s)   **der Zehnmarkschein(e)**
the tennis   **das Tennis**
thank you, to thank   **danke(n)**
the thanks(pl.)   **der Dank**
that   **daß**
the theatre(s)   **das Theater(-)**
then (What's this then?)   **denn**
then, after that   **dann**

there **da**
therefore **deshalb, also**
to think, to have an opinion of something **denken**
third **dritte(n)**
to be thirsty **durstig sein**
this **diese, -r, -s**
thoroughly **gründlich**
though, mind you; certainly **allerdings**
the thought(s) **der Gedanke(n)**
through **durch**
throws towards, to throw towards **wirft zu, zuwerfen**
the ticket(s) **die Fahrkarte(n)**
the ticket(s), card(s) **die Karte(n)**
the multiple ticket(s) **die Sammelkarte(n)**
the ticket office(s) **der Fahrkartenschalter(-)**
the return ticket(s) **die Rückfahrkarte(n)**
the tie(s) **der Schlips(e)**
the tights **die Strumpfhose(n)**
till, until **bis**
the Tilsit cheese **der Tilsiter(Käse)**
(e.g.the first) time(s) **das Mal(e)**
the time(s) **die Zeit(en)**
the tip(s) **das Trinkgeld(er)**
the thunder(s) **der Donner(-)**
there is thunder and lightning **es donnert und blitzt**
to, too **zu**
today **heute**
together **zusammen**
the toilet(s) **die Toilette(n)**
the tomato(es) **die Tomate(n)**
tomorrow **morgen**
the toothbrush(es) **die Zahnbürste(n)**
the toothpaste **die Zahnpaste**
the tourist(s) **der Tourist(en)**
towards **entgegen**
the town(s) **die Stadt(¨e)**
the traffic **der Verkehr**
the traffic light(s) **die Ampel(n)**
the traffic warden(fem.) **die Politesse(n)**
the tram(s) **die Straßenbahn(en)**
the travellers' cheque(s) **der Reisescheck(s)**
the tree(s) **der Baum(¨-e)**
the trip(s) **die Fahrt(en)**
the trouble(s), worry(ies) **die Sorge(n)**
to trouble oneself, to worry **sich Sorgen machen**
the trousers **die Hose(n)**
the trout **die Forelle(n)**
true **wahr**
to trust s.b. **jdm. vertrauen**
to try **probieren, versuchen**
the tube **die U-Bahn(en)**
to turn (off) **einbiegen, abbiegen**
to turn round **sich umdrehen**
the twenty mark note(s) **der Zwanzigmarkschein(e)**
twice **zweimal**
two **zwei**
the tyre pressure **der Reifendruck**

U

the uncle(s) **der Onkel(-)**
the underground (train(s)) **die Untergrundbahn(en)**
to understand **verstehen**
the underwear **die Unterwäsche**
unexpected(ly) **unerwartet**
unfortunately **leider**
to unpack **auspacken**
until **bis**
us **uns**

V

valuable **wertvoll**
the veal **das Kalbfleisch**
the vegetable(s) **das Gemüse**
the vegetable stand(s) **der Gemüsestand(¨e)**
very(highly) **höchst**
very **sehr**
very happy(lit. over-happy) **überglücklich**
to view **betrachten**
the village(s) **das Dorf(¨er)**

the vintage(s) **der Jahrgang(¨-e)**
the visit(s) **der Besuch(e)**
to visit(sights) **besichtigen**
to visit **besuchen**
the vitamin(s) **das Vitamin(e)**
the voice(s) **die Stimme(n)**

W

to wait **warten**
the waiter(s) **der Kellner(-), der Ober(-)**
the waitress(es) **die Kellnerin(nen)**
wakes up **wacht auf**
to walk towards s.b. **auf jdn. zugehen**
the wallet(s) **die Brieftasche(n)**
to want, he she, it, one wants **wollen, will**
the war(s) **der Krieg(e)**
warm **warm**
to watch television **fernsehen**
water soluble **wasserlöslich**
the way(s) **der Weg(e)**
we **wir**
to wear, wears **tragen, trägt**
the weather **das Wetter**
the weather forecast(s) **der Wetterbericht(e)**
the week(s) **die Woche(n)**
the weekend(s) **das Wochenende(n)**
welcome! **willkommen!**
the well(s) of staircase(s) **das Treppenhaus(¨-er)**
well! **na!**
Westphalian dark bread **der Pumpernickel**
wet **naß**
what **was**
What's the matter? **los; was ist los?**
when **als**
where **wo**
which(one) **welch,(e, er, es)**
white **weiß**
who **wer**
why **warum**
why; how come **wieso**
will, he, she, it, one will **werden, wird (Futur)**
to win **gewinnen**
the window(s) **das Fenster(-)**
the window seat(s) **der Fensterplatz(¨-e)**
windy **windig**
the wine(s) **der Wein(e)**
the winter jacket(s) **die Winterjacke(n)**
to wish **wünschen**
with **mit**
without **ohne**
without trouble(s), worries **unbesorgt**
the wood(s) **der Wald(¨-er)**
the woollen material(s) **der Wollstoff(e)**
to work **arbeiten**
the work(s) **die Arbeit(en)**
the workshop(s) **die Werkstatt(¨-en)**
would **würden**
would have (to) **müßten**
would like **möchten**
the writing desk(s), table(s) **der Schreibtisch(e)**

Y

the year(s) **das Jahr(e)**
yellow **gelb**
yes do **doch**
yesterday **gestern**
yet(more), still **noch**
you(familiar) have an opinion of **du hälst davon**
younger **jünger**

Z

zero **0, null**

Akt 1

Part three
Teil drei

Dialog 1
Ich heiße ...
Ich wohne in ...
Sie wohnt Blütenweg Nummer acht.
Sie wohnt in Hannover.
Er wohnt in London.

Dialog 2
Ja, ich wohne hier.
Nein, ich wohne nicht hier.
Ja, ich bin aus England.
Nein, ich bin nicht aus England.
Hier ist das Paket.
Ja, das ist alles.

Dialog 3
Ja, es ist in der Königsstraße.
Nein, das ist nicht weit.
Es ist rechts, hundert Meter rechts.

Dialog 4
Ja, er hat ein Zimmer reserviert.
Ja, er hat einen Reisepaß.
Nein, er hat Zimmer Nummer sieben.

Part four
Teil vier

Übung 2-Exercise 2

Correct answer: b) Ja, Fräulein Hilde.

Übung 4 - Exercise 4
1) Hilde Holz.
2) Erika Becker.
3) Walter Vogelsang.
4) Hans Büttner.
5) Heinrich Wunderlich.

Part five
Teil fünf

2. Correct answer: **Guten Tag.**

4. **Haustür**
    aus
    Empfangsdame
    Geranien
    Klingelknopf
    Bett
    Balkon
    Gesicht
    Stockwerke
    Paket

    [Augenblick]

Akt 2

Teil drei: Dialoge

1. Guten Morgen
   Ich heiße X . . . und ich komme aus . . .
   Ich kenne Hamburg auch nicht.
   Das Zimmer gefällt mir nicht.
   Nein, ich habe nicht gut geschlafen.
   Ich höre den Straßenlärm.
   Mein Zimmer ist im ersten Stock.

2. Ich ziehe die Vorhänge auf. Es regnet nicht.
   Es ist warm.
   Ich ziehe mein kurzes, rotes Kleid an.
   Das hellbraune Kleid gefällt mir gut.
   Es ist im Badezimmer. Es ist naß.

3. Die Brötchen schmecken gut.
   Ja bitte.
   Nein danke.

4. Guten Morgen. Ja, das ist Zimmer Nummer sieben.
   Augenblick bitte.
   Er ist im Badezimmer. Er duscht sich.

5. Ja, er ist da. Er rasiert sich.
   Bitte warten Sie.
   Bitte schön.

Teil vier
Übung 1

wacht auf - sieht . . . um -. steht auf - zieht - auf.
macht - an. - zieht - an.

Übung 3

a) Guten Tag (guten Morgen). Ich heiße X.
   (Ich bin X). Wie heißen Sie? Ich habe
   Glück. Ich bin in Liechtenstein. Bis
   morgen.
b) Luxemburg ist klein. Es ist wichtig. Ich
   habe Glück! Bis morgen. Auf
   Wiedersehen.
c) Ich heiße X. Ich bin in Zürich. Das Wetter
   ist schön. Morgen bin ich in Berlin. Bis
   morgen! Auf Wiedersehen!
Did you get - **Morgen bin ich in Berlin** -
right? Then give yourself „**Prima! Prima!**"

Übung 4

Mohnbrötchen

Teil fünf
Answers for the dice game:

   1. Ich dusche mich.
   4. Wo ist die Seife?
   7. Ich ziehe mich an.
10. Nein danke.
12. Wieviel Uhr ist es? or: Wie spät ist es?
14. Bitte, wo ist der Blütenweg?
16. **Only one hundred metres on your right.**

Akt 3

Teil drei: Dialoge

1. Nein, ich bin zum ersten Mal hier.
   Prima!
   Ja bitte. Ich habe heute morgen nichts vor.
   Ja, das geht.
2. Was ist das?
   Ich will es gern probieren.
   Ja, Erdbeeren mag ich besonders gern.
3. Haben Sie Geranien?
   Ich möchte rote Geranien.
   Wie schade! Wiedersehen.
4. Ein Kilo Tomaten, bitte.
   Einen Kopfsalat und eine Gurke, bitte.
   Nein danke.
   Hier ist ein Zehnmarkschein.
   Fünf Mark achtzig.
5. Tut mir leid.
   Ich wohne nicht hier. Sprechen Sie Englisch?
   Bitte sprechen Sie langsam.
   Was möchten Sie wissen?
   100 (hundert) Meter geradeaus.
   Bitte schön.

Teil vier
Übung 1
1. gehen 2. riecht 3. schmeckt 4. ist 5. hängen
Übung 2
1h, 2i, 3b, 4i, 5a, 6c 7d, 8e, 9f, 10g.
While other answers are possible, each conclusion should only be used once.

Teil fünf

Richtig: Prost

Guests are coming: „Würfelspiel"
  6. Leberkäs, Schinken, Wurst, Salami
12. Kopfsalat, Gurke, Tomaten
18. Erdbeeren, Birnen, Äpfel
24. Sechs Teller und sechs Gläser
30. Ich lege den Käse und den Aufschnitt/Leberkäs auf einen Teller/eine Platte
36. Eine Flasche Weißwein

Akt 4

Teil drei: Dialoge

1. Augenblick. Ja, das geht. Hier sind eins, zwei, drei. vier, fünf Markstücke. Oh, Sie brauchen Kleingeld? (Alternative: Ach so. . .) Augenblick bitte. Ja, ich habe fünf Zehnpfennigstücke und ein Fünfzigpfennigstück.

2. Entschuldigen Sie bitte. Können Sie ein Fünfmarkstück wechseln? Danke. Ich möchte telefonieren. Haben sie zwei Zehnpfennigstücke? Wunderbar! Hier ist eine Mark. Vielen Dank.

3. Ich möchte nach Berlin telefonieren. Wissen Sie die Vorwahlnummer für Berlin? Vielen Dank.

4. Ich möchte Reiseschecks einlösen. Für zweihundert Pfund bitte. Bitte schön. Wo bekomme ich das Geld?

5. Dieser Herr braucht Hosen. Haben sie auch Hemden, Jacken und Schuhe? Na gut. Ein Unterhemd und eine Unterhose bitte. Größe 40. Er möchte ein Freizeithemd, ein weißes bitte. Dieses (hier). Was kostet das bitte? Vielen Dank.

Teil vier: Übungen

1. a - Mark und Pfennig. b - Mark und Pfennig. c - Franken und Rappen. d - Schilling und Groschen.

2. a - falsch, b - falsch, c - richtig, d - falsch, e - richtig, f - falsch.

3. Dear Peter! I was in Austria and have still a few Groschen. You want to go to Austria soon, don't you? The bank takes no coins, only notes. Therefore the Groschen are for you. Only 200 Groschen. Not a lot, only for a glass of Wein. Fritz

4. Answer: Stimmt! Ich will nach Österreich. Vielen Dank für das Geld. Das ist eine prima Idee. Prost!

5. 1. Er möchte Obst und Gemüse auf dem Markt einkaufen.
   2. Ich kann heute Obst und Gemüse einkaufen.
   3. Wir wollen auf dem Markt einkaufen.

6. 1 - Er sieht sich im Zimmer um.
   2 - Sie zieht die Vorhänge auf.
   3 - Ich mache die Fenster auf.
   4 - Er macht das Licht an.
   5 - Um fünf Uhr ruft Frau Meyer an.
   6 - Er wählt direkt durch.
   7 - Der alte Herr löst seine Reiseschecks ein.
   8 - Peter sieht Hilde an.
   9 - Feter sieht sich die Hemden an.
   10 - Ich schlage jetzt etwas vor.

Akt 5

Teil drei: Dialoge

1. Guten Abend. Wie geht es Ihnen? - Möchten Sie drinnen oder draußen sitzen? - Nein, nein, die Bar drinnen ist nett. - Die Bedienung ist freundlich. - Es gefällt mir. Ich frühstücke auch hier. - Nein, aber es gibt einen Speisesaal. - Neben dem Hotel ist ein Restaurant. Ich esse immer da.

2. Vielen Dank. Das ist sehr nett von Ihnen. - Um sieben Uhr vielleicht? Ja, sieben Uhr geht. Bis 7 dann.

3. Vielen Dank. - Wo ist ein Telefon bitte? - Danke. -

4. Ich habe starke Kopfschmerzen. Haben Sie Aspirintabletten?
   Wie viele Tabletten sind in der kleinen Packung? - Ich nehme die kleine Packung. - Vielen Dank.
   Ja, bitte.

5. Die Zeitung? Ja, in der Bar liegt eine.- Vielleicht ist / liegt die Zeitung an / bei der Rezeption? - Bitte schön.

6. Herr Ober! - Ich möchte noch eine Tasse Tee. Tee mit Milch bitte. - Entschuldigen Sie bitte. Können Sie mir bitte den Zucker geben? - Vielen Dank.

Teil vier: Spiel Vier

Here are some of the sentences which you were asked to pick out of the scenes from Acts 1-5:
(Act 1) Peter geht langsam zur Haustür. Peter geht zum Hotel.Er geht zu Bett.
(Act 2) Er geht zu den großen Fenstern. Peter geht zum Bett zurück. Was gibt's zum Frühstück? Sind Sie zum ersten Mal in Hannover?
(Act 3) Wir gehen jetzt zur Bäckerei, zur Metzgerei und dann zum Markt. Wir können zu Fuß gehen.
(Act 4) Dieser Schlips paßt gut zu dem neuen Hemd.
(Act 5) Sie gehen zu dem langen Kuchenbüffet. Hilde geht zu einem Kaufhaus. Sie geht zu einer Kabine.

Akt 6

Teil drei: Dialoge

1. - Was für Suppen? - Nein danke. Was für Eier gibt es? - Was für Fisch? - Ich möchte russische Eier / gefüllte Eier. - Ja, bitte. Ich esse gern Schweinefleisch. - Weißwein trinke ich gern / Ich trinke gern Weißwein. Danke schön.

2. - Ich wohne in ———. Ich bin in ——— geboren. - Ich habe einen Bruder und eine Schwester. - Ich bin verheiratet / Ich bin nicht verheiratet. - Ich habe Kinder / Ich habe keine Kinder.

3. Guten Morgen Frau Doktor. Ich habe starke Zahnschmerzen. Wann kann ich kommen? - Mein Name ist ———. Ich bin hier zu Besuch. Ich wohne im Hotel Sonne. - Ja, sehr stark. Entsetzlich! - Ja,natürlich. Ich komme gleich. Auf Wiedersehen. Vielen Dank.

4. Ja. Ich sehe sie und zwei Herren in Braun. Wer ist der Herr mit der Glatze neben ihr? - Sie sieht sehr freundlich aus. - Oh! Hat sie Kinder? - Ich möchte Frau Becker gern kennenlernen.

Teil vier: Übungen

3. 1) Onkel Wilhelm hat angerufen.
   2) Das hat prima geschmeckt.
   3) Ich habe es von meiner Mutter gelernt.
   4) Ich habe das blaue Hemd gekauft.
   5) Hilde hat ihm einen Schlips geschenkt.
   6) Sie hat ein Kleid gesehen.
   7) Er hat sich verlaufen.
   8) Die Eltern haben in Hannover geheiratet.
   9) Sie haben eine Firma gegründet.

4. 1) Ich sitze im Cafe.
   2) Dann spreche ich mit dem Kellner.
   3) Der Kellner bringt den Wein.
   4) Er gießt den Wein in mein Glas.
   5) Ich trinke den Wein.
   6) Ich leihe mir die Zeitung von dem Mann am nächsten Tisch.

5. 1) Ich bin ins Cafe gegangen.
   2) Die Tür ist aufgesprungen.
   3) Er ist im Hotel geblieben.
   4) Peter ist aufgewacht.
   5) Hilde ist ausgegangen.
   6) Wir sind in die Altstadt gefahren.
   7) Sie sind nach Berlin gezogen.
   8) Wir sind ausgegangen.

6. Liebe Erika! Heute hat unsere Helga wirklich Pech. Im Kaufhaus sieht sie ein schönes, weißes Kleid. Sie probiert es an und es paßt. Leider ist es teuer. Es gefällt ihr gut und sie kauft es. Sie zieht es gleich an. Um sieben Uhr ist sie mit Ralf verabredet und sie geht in das Restaurant. Er ist noch nicht da und sie setzt sich an einen Tisch und wartet auf ihn. Das Restaurant ist ziemlich voll. Neben ihr hängt ein Spiegel und da sieht sie ihr hübsches, neues Kleid. Sie freut sich. Dann kommt der Kellner. Der sieht sie leider nicht. Er trägt zwölf, ja 12 Gläser Rotwein. Plötzlich steht eine Dame auf. Der Kellner gießt den Rotwein über das schöne, weiße Kleid! So ein Pech!Helga fährt gleich mit dem Taxi nach Hause. Ralf ruft an. Er hat Zahnschmerzen und ist beim Zahnarzt. Viele Grüße und ein Küßchen von Deiner Schwester L.

Teil fünf: Übung 2

a = 5 - Lisa,	g = 9 - Mia,	
b = 6 - Bernd Kunz	h = 11 - Hans,	
c = 8 - Claudia Moll,	i = 1 - Meta Böll,	
d = 7 - Jürgan,	j = 2 - Fritz Müller,	
e = 2 - Emma,	k = 3 - Ingrid,	
f = 10 - Ralf,	l = 4 - Georg Braun.	

Akt 7

Teil drei: Dialoge

1. Sonntags spiele ich Golf. Ja, aber ich schwimme auch gern. Ja, aber nur wenn ich gewinne.

2. Zur Zeit lerne ich Italienisch. Ich finde, es ist leicht zu lesen, aber nicht so leicht zu schreiben. Ja, ich kann es / sie lesen, aber nicht alles verstehen.

3. Ja, morgen habe ich Zeit. Nein, ich kenne Berlin nicht. / Berlin kenne ich nicht. Das ist eine prima Idee! Könnten / Können wir dort ein Auto mieten? Mit dem Auto können / könnten wir mehr sehen.

4. Ja, aber ich darf nicht zu langsam fahren. Dürfen wir hier rechts abbiegen? Und wir müssen rechts abbiegen!

Teil vier: Übungen

1. 1. Vollkaskoversicherung.
   2. Autovermietung.
   3. Geschwindigkeitsbegrenzung.
   4. Ersatzteil.
   5. Reifendruck.
   6. Verkehrsampel.
   7. Krankenhaus.
   8. Straßenrand.
   9. Grenzübergang.

3. 3. Wir könnten in die Stadt fahren.
   4. Wir könnten ein Taxi nehmen.
   5. Wir könnten essen gehen.
   6. Wir können kein Taxi nehmen.
   7. Dann können wir auch nicht essen gehen.
   8. Also, was können wir (dann) machen?
   9. Wir können Radio hören / Fernsehen schauen / ins Theater gehen / ins Kino gehen / faulenzen / tanzen gehen / eine Reise machen / Ferien machen / in der Sonne liegen / schwimmen gehen, usw.

Teil fünf:

1. Dort darf ich nach rechts und / oder nach links fahren. Nein, dort darf ich nicht geradeaus fahren.

2. Ja, das geht. / Ja, das kann ich. Ja, das geht auch. / Ja, das kann ich auch.

3. Nein, das kann ich nicht / das darf ich nicht. Ich kann nach rechts fahren / abbiegen; Ich kann (auch) geradeaus fahren.

4. a) Ich kann am Bahnhofsplatz über die Straße gehen.
   b) Ich kann in der Seidlstraße die Straße überqueren.
   c) In der Dachauerstraße kann ich die Straße überqueren.

5. Man darf dort nicht nach links fahren. Man kann geradeaus und nach rechts fahren.
   Other possible answers:
   Man darf dort parken / halten; Man darf / kann dort nicht parken / halten; Man / Ich kann / darf / muß dort (nicht) am Samstag und / oder abends nach 19.00 parken.

Akt 8

Teil drei: Dialoge

1. Ja bitte. Ich möchte gern ein Zimmer reservieren, ein Einzelzimmer — Mit Dusche bitte — Für morgen — (Für) eine Nacht bitte. Für . . .

2. Ich kann das Hotel nicht finden. — Ja, mit dem Auto; ich bin am Kennedy-Platz, (am) Rathaus Schöneberg. — Wie komme ich dorthin/dahin? Ich hoffe es. Vielen Dank, bis bald/bis gleich.

3. Ich habe Mein Studium gerade beendet. Und Sie? — Was studieren Sie? — Oh, das ist sehr interessant. — Und wo studieren Sie?

4. Ich möchte (gern) die Porzellan-Sammlung sehen./Ich möchte mir gern die Porzellan-Sammlung anschauen. — Wie schade. Warum? — Ach so. Hoffentlich machen sie nichts kaputt!/Ich hoffe, sie machen nichts kaputt. — Ja bitte. Einmal bitte/Eine Karte bitte. Wo ist sie?

5. Natürlich, jeder hat ein Hobby. — Ich höre gern Musik und ich treibe/mag gern Sport. Und was ist Ihr Hobby? — Ich höre/mag lieber Jazz. — Nein, ich kenne Berlin nicht so gut./Berlin kenne ich nicht (so) gut. Können Sie mir ein Jazzlokal/eins empfehlen? — Vielen Dank für den Rat/Tip!

Teil vier: Übungen

1. Wir sind hier in der Bismarckstraße. Wie kommen wir zum Schloß bitte? Da gehen Sie (am besten) geradeaus, die Schloßstraße entlang, bis zum Spandauer Damm. Schloß Charlottenburg liegt direkt gegenüber.

2. Wir sind hier in der Zillestraße. Wie kommen wir zum Schloß bitte? Da gehen Sie (am besten) hier geradeaus, bis zur Schloßstraße. Dann gehen Sie rechts die Schloßstraße entlang, bis zum Spandauer Damm; das Schloß liegt direkt gegenüber.

3. Wir sind hier in der Schloßstraße. Wie geht's zum Schloß bitte? Da gehen Sie immer geradeaus, bis zum Spandauer Damm und das Schloß liegt direkt gegenüber.

4. Wir sind hier am Stadtring. Wie kommen wir zum Schloß bitte? Da gehen Sie (am besten) hier immer geradeaus. Die zweite Straße rechts ist der Spandauer Damm; da/den gehen Sie entlang; ungefähr 200 Meter links ist das Schloß.

5. Wir sind (hier) am Luisenplatz. Wie kommen wir zum Schloß bitte? Da gehen Sie (hier) den Spandauer Damm entlang. Etwa 200 Meter auf der rechten Seite ist das Schloß.

6. Wir sind (hier) in der Otto-Suhr-Allee. Wie geht's zum Schloß bitte? Da gehen Sir hier (am besten) geradeaus, bis zum Luisenplatz. Dort gehen Sie links in den Spandauer Damm. Etwa 200 Meter rechts liegt das Schloß Charlottenburg.

1. Ich bin (hier) in der Bismarckstraße. Wie komme ich zum Schloß bitte?

2. Ich bin hier in der Zillestraße. Wie komme ich zum Schloß bitte?

3. Ich bin (hier) in der Schloßstraße. Wie geht's zum Schloß bitte?

4. Ich bin (hier) am Stadtring. Wie komme ich zum Schloß bitte?

5. Ich bin hier am Luisenplatz. Bitte, wie komme ich (am besten) zum Schloß?

6. Ich bin hier in der Otto-Suhr-Allee. Wie komme ich zum Schloß bitte?

Teil fünf: Spiele

Berühmte Leute — Famous people
Mögliche Antworten:
Er hat Don Juan in Salzburg komponiert. (Mozart)

Er hat Die Blechtrommel in Danzig geschrieben. (Grass)

Er hat Die blaue Donau in Wien komponiert. (Strauss)

Er ist vor drei Jahren in München gestorben. (1982; Faßbinder)

Berühmte Schlösser und Burgen

Mögliche Antworten auf die Frage:
Wofür ist (name of place or castle) berühmt?

1. Schloß Herrenhausen ist berühmt für die Schloßgärten.
2. Das Schloß Sigmaringen ist berühmt, weil es der Sitz der Hohenzollern war. (Note the different way of answering the question.)
4. Schloß Charlottenburg ist berühmt für seinen reinen Barock-Stil. Dieses Schloß haben Hilde und Peter besichtigt, erinnern Sie sich?
8. Schloß Heidelberg ist berühmt, weil es eine herrliche Aussicht über den Neckar bietet.
10, 11. Schloß Linderhof und Schloß Neuschwanstein sind berühmt, weil sie wie Schlösser aus einem Märchen aussehen. Weil sie in einer sehr romantischen Lage mit einer herrlichen Umgebung sind. Weil König Ludwig II von Bayern sie gebaut hat und weil er damit berühmt geworden ist. (unter anderem).

Akt 9

Teil drei: Dialoge

Dialog 1

Ja, ich bin zum ersten Mal hier. — Ich interessiere mich für Kunst und Gemälde. Die Expressionisten vom/aus dem zwanzigsten Jahrhundert. — Ja, mein deutscher Lieblingsmaler ist Kandinsky. — Ich mag auch Turner und Constable sehr gern./Turner und Constable gefallen mir auch sehr gut. — In der Tate Gallery und in der Nationalgalerie in London. — Vielen Dank. Bitte schön.

Dialog 2

Guten Morgen. Es geht mir gut, danke./Mir geht's gut, danke — Wissen Sie, wie heute das Wetter wird? — Haben Sie eine Zeitung? Ich möchte gern nachsehen/nachschauen. — In Berlin wird es sonnig und warm, ungefähr 30 Grad. — In London natürlich. — Ja, laut Wetterbericht bleibt es (dort) kühl, windig und naß.

Dialog 3

Es hat mir sehr gut geschmeckt. Aber ich hätte lieber Tee gehabt/getrunken. Das habe ich nicht gewußt. — Sehr gern. Ich hätte gern einen. — Dann nehme ich nur eine Tasse Tee bitte.

Dialog 4

Ja, ich habe ihn zufällig gesehen. — Das blaue Auto ist bei rot über die Ampel gefahren. — Nur eine Person ist verletzt. — Er ist zum Glück nur leicht verletzt./ Zum Glück ist er nur leicht verletzt. Da/hier kommt der Krankenwagen.

Dialog 5

Das/Dies ist alles sehr seltsam! — Die Sache mit deinem Onkel. — Werde ich ihn jemals treffen? — Bist du sicher? — Das hast du gestern schon gesagt.

Teil vier: Übungen
1. wird 2. wird 3. werden 4. wird 5. wirst 6. wird 7. wird

Die Wettervorhersage: Die Vorhersage für morgen. In Lübeck wird es bedeckt.
Zwölf Grad. In Hannover wird es (auch) bedeckt, 15 (fünfzehn) Grad. In Düsseldorf wird es wolkig, 12 (zwölf) Grad. In Leipzig wird es heiter, 12 Grad. In Prag wird es wolkenlos, elf Grad. In Wien wird es heiter, 11 Grad. In Warschau wird es (auch) heiter, zehn Grad. In Istanbul wird es bedeckt, acht Grad. In Tokio wird es heiter, sechzehn Grad. In *Kairo* wird es auch heiter, zwanzig Grad. In *Moskau* wird es heiter, aber nur sieben Grad.
(The cities in italics are the ones with the warmest and coldest temperature).

The 'Zugspitze' is in South Germany, near Garmisch-Partenkirchen, in the Bavarian Alps, and it is West Germany's highest mountain.

Am Flughafen Berlin-Tegel.
3.   Richtig oder falsch?
1. Richtig. 2. Falsch, das Flugzeug aus München kommt fünf Minuten später an. 3. Richtig. 4. Falsch, die Maschine aus Amsterdam landet fünf Minuten früher. 5. Richtig. 6. Falsch; das Flugzeug landet zehn Minuten früher. 7. Falsch, die Maschine aus Luton kommt fünf Minuten später an.

Akt 10

Teil drei: Dialoge

1. Nein, ich habe kein Gepäck, nur Handgepäck. — Ja, ich komme/fliege heute abend schon zurück. — Am Fenster, wenn es geht. — Oh, das mag ich nicht. Ich bin Nichtraucher./Ich rauche nicht. — Das macht nichts. Ich sitze lieber am Gang als hinten. — Vielen Dank.

2. Ich habe einen Flug gebucht und möchte (gern) mein Ticket abholen. — Nach Zürich, einen Rückflug am Samstag/Sonnabend. — Ja, gestern nachmittag; auf den Namen . . . Ich habe mit Frau Luthi gesprochen, glaube ich. — In bar. Können Sie mir eine Rechnung geben bitte? Vielen Dank.

3. Lieber aus Silber /Ich mag Silber lieber. Können/Könnten Sie mir welche zeigen? — Ja, für mich (selbst). — Hm; der kleine hier gefällt mir. Wieviel kostet der/er? — Ja gut. Ich glaube, den nehme ich .

4. Er ist sehr groß und ziemlich/sehr dick. — Nein, er trägt keine Brille. — Er hat kurzes dunkles Haar. — Er ist immer sehr elegant gekleidet. Meistens im dunklen Anzug. — Er heißt Heinrich Zille. Er ist ein echter Berliner!

Teil vier: Übungen

Sind Sie ein Kulturgeier? Are you a culture vulture?
Wie gut kennen Sie Berlin? How well do you know Berlin?
The correct words:

1. Brandenburger Tor. 2. Berliner Weiße. 3. Gedächtniskirche. 4. Porzellansammlung. 5. Schloßgarten. 6. Belvedere. 7. Kudamm. 8. Tiergarten. 9. Potsdamer Brücke. 10. Nationalgalerie. 11. Schloß Charlottenburg. 12. Spandauer Damm. 13. Spreemetropole. 14. Nofretete.

Aus welchem Material?
Einige Möglichkeiten. Some possibilities.
Das Hemd ist aus Baumwolle. Es/das gefällt mir. Das Kleid ist aus Wollstoff. Das gefällt mir (auch). Die Handtasche ist aus Leder und Synthetik. Die gefällt mir nicht.
Das Geld ist aus Papier (oder aus Kupfer). Die Strumpfhose ist aus Synthetik (oder aus Seide). Die gefällt mir.
Die Zeitung ist aus Papier.
Der Ring ist aus Gold. Der gefällt mir (sehr).
Die Schuhe sind aus Leder. Die gefallen mir.
Die Hose ist aus Wollstoff. Die gefällt mir.

Akt 11

Teil drei — Dialoge

1. Ja bitte. Ich habe Ihr Paket heute morgen erhalten/bekommen. — Das Paket mit den Krawatten. — Nein leider nicht; da ist/es gibt ein Problem. — Ich habe 5 Krawatten bestellt. Im Paket sind 50./Da sind fünfzig im Paket. — Genau./Richtig. Was soll ich (damit) machen/tun?

2. Mir geht's gut./Es geht mir gut, danke, und Ihnen? Was ist denn los? — Oh je, wie geht es ihr denn? Ich wünsche ihr gute Besserung. — Auf Wiederhören. Alles Gute.

3. Ja, nicht wahr?/ das kann man wohl sagen. Wie geht es Ihnen? — Ich will meinen Onkel besuchen, in Österreich. — Ja, er wohnt jetzt dort/da, in St. Anton. — Und ich Ihnen auch. Wohin fahren Sie (denn)?

4. Ihre Tasche sieht sehr schick/elegant aus. Was haben Sie (denn) in der/da drin? — Sie wissen nicht, was in Ihrer Tasche ist? — Ich möchte es nicht wissen. Wollen Sie es/das nicht wissen? — Soll ich mal nachschauen/nachsehen?

Teil vier — Übungen Stufenrätsel

2. Deutsch. 3. Salat. 4. Honig. 5. Sahne. 6. Idee. 7. Engländer
a. Geld. b. Haus. c. Tisch. d. Glas. e. Ei. f. Ecke. g. Rock.

Teil fünf — Berühmte Städte und Flüsse
1. Hamburg (HH) größter deutscher Hafen, 'Tor zur Welt', Pressestadt.
2. Hannover (H) größte deutsche Messestadt.
3. Berlin (B) ehemalige deutsche Hauptstadt; die Mauer trennt West — und Ostberlin; Ostberlin ist die Hauptstadt der DDR.
4. Köln (K) berühmter gotischer Dom; Geburtsstadt Bölls; Stadt und Zentrum des Karnevals.
5. Frankfurt a.M. (F) Stadt der Banken, größter europäischer Transit-Flughafen, Goethe-Haus, Paulskirche.
6. Stuttgart (S) das reichste Dorf Europas; Sitz von Mercedes-Benz.
7. Wolfsburg (Wo) Volkswagenwerk (VW)
8. München (M) Hauptstadt Bayerns, 'Weltstadt mit Herz', Alte und Neue Pinakothek, Oktoberfest, Hofbräuhaus.
9. Bayreuth (Bay) Bayreuther Festspiele (Wagner).
10. Genf (GE) Zentrale des Roten Kreuzes; Kirchenreformator Calvin.
11. Dresden (R or Y) Kulturzentrum; Der Zwinger; besonders berühmt für Porzellan aus dem 18. Jahrhundert und Dresdner Stollen.
12. Zürich (ZH) Stadt der Banken; Zürich See.
13. Salzburg (S) Mozart-Festspiele, Mozarthaus, berühmte Festung.
14. Wien (W) Hauptstadt Österreichs, Schloß Belvedere und Schönbrunn, Stephansdom, Spanische Hofreitschule, Fiaker.

Akt 12

Teil drei — Dialoge

1. Das tut mir leid, ich hatte (wirklich) Pech. Alles ging schief. — Nun, der Bus kam spät (an); dann hatte ich mein Geld vergessen. — Ich mußte zu Fuß gehen/laufen, es ist sehr weit, wissen Sie. — Wann kann ich kommen? Geht es morgen?

2. Mir? Warum? — Was meinen Sie? Ich verstehe Sie nicht. — Wirklich? Wie denn das? Ich bin sprachlos./Ich weiß nicht, was ich sagen soll. Ja, natürlich. Was ist es denn? Ich habe keine Ahnung.

3. Ja, das ist richtig/(das) stimmt. Bitte kommen Sie (doch) herein. — Fünf sagten Sie?/haben Sie gesagt? Nein, ich hatte nur drei bestellt. Die Adresse stimmt, aber das hier ist der zweite Stock. Und es ist Hans Meyer, nicht Heinrich. — Hm. Schade! Auf Wiedersehen.

4. Ja, bitte; sagen/erzählen Sie mir, warum alle diese Geheimnisse? Wie meinen Sie das?/Was meinen Sie damit? — Was? Er kann es nicht glauben? Ich würde es sofort glauben. — Aber sind Sie sicher, daß es stimmt/daß es wahr ist? — Was hat er denn geerbt? — Nicht schlecht, nicht wahr?Was finden Sie?/Was sagen Sie dazu?